D1486263

PARSON'S PITCH

PARSON'S PITCH

BY

DAVID SHEPPARD

HODDER AND STOUGHTON

First printed 1964
Second impression 1964

PRINTED AND BOUND IN GREAT BRITAIN FOR
HODDER AND STOUGHTON LIMITED, ST. PAUL'S
HOUSE, WARWICK LANE, LONDON, E.C.4
BY C. TINLING AND CO. LIMITED, LIVERPOOL
LONDON AND PRESCOT

To my wife Grace
the best partner in my life

CONTENTS

ILLUSTRATIONS

BOYS ON THE PITCH

I was the umpire standing at square-leg when I noticed a large pair of shoes, unoccupied, standing in the gully. Their owner stood beside them in his socks. He was bowling at the other end, and had obviously taken his shoes off to give his feet a rest. England's great fast bowler Brian Statham often has a conversation with his feet when they complain of too much hard work, but he can't rest them on the field like this in a Test match.

The game in which I was umpire was in West Ham Park and it was between our team of older boys from the Mayflower Family Centre and another nearby club in the East End of London. The shoes that were standing in the gully were of the pointed variety. Our team's clothing is usually in the up-to-date fashion, but I find it very difficult to persuade them to wear white flannels—particularly at home where such unusual dress might attract some colourful comment from their mates. But pointed shoes, drainpipe trousers, braces, cloth caps and all, our team enjoy themselves, bowl pretty well and usually field magnificently. Batting presents more difficult problems as most of our matches are played on a pitch with enough bumps in it to mean that after one ball has hit you on the boot the next may fly past your ear. This means that most of our matches are finished in an afternoon with each side totalling no more than 60–100 runs.

In Australia boys who play their cricket in the parks play on concrete pitches, where at least the ball comes through at a regular height. This means that the batsman can learn to play shots with confidence. English cricketers are inclined to say that even a bad grass wicket is better than a concrete wicket; we have a lot of fun in this sort of cricket but it is almost impossible for a boy playing in such conditions to get very far in the game, while a number of Australian park cricketers have climbed to the first-class game.

We live in a pleasant flat in the Mayflower Family Centre where I am the warden. Our activities range from a Nursery School to a Grandfathers' club and they take me into many homes. Some of these are in the crowded old streets of terraced houses which were built a hundred years ago to house men who worked in the nearby Royal Docks and in the great factories which sprang up beside them. For years we have walked across the debris of the bombed sites which Hitler caused. They made a great playground for children. Here we might pass a group experimenting with fire; here some would be building a ramshackle house; there others would be finishing off the wreck of an old car dumped there a night or two before. Now the debris and the old streets are fast disappearing and often my visits take me into fine new flats or maisonettes which have been built since the war.

Our district is not particularly keen about cricket, though I know a number of great enthusiasts. But of course there is street cricket as there is in every country where the game is played. I joined in a game recently in the street in Sydney where we lived for some months after the 1962–63 tour of Australia. Some of the local rules were different. Instead of three stumps we had a schoolboy's case, and I had to learn to say 'Strike' if I did not want to risk a second run. In Sussex we always said 'Walking' in that situation, when there was only one batsman at a time. During a game in our Sydney street, a small boy came over to me and asked, "Do you have to say 'strike' when you're playing in a Test match?" But some parts of these games are the same anywhere in the world. I overheard this conversation when I was sitting at home in Sydney preparing a talk:

"You're not going to bat at all."

"Well I don't want to bat."

"Well anyway you're not going to."

Often the games we played as boys involved taking over the

personality of some first-class cricketer or even of a whole Test XI—this would include wearing a cap at the correct angle and all the mannerisms of the hero. First-class cricket has an important place in providing the inspiration for boys. R. C. Robertson Glasgow, whose whimsical writings spring out of a real knowledge and love of the game and of people, caught the atmosphere of small boys' cricket in a preparatory school setting in a pre-1939 book.

"I see Copson's got his hundred wickets. I've got 19 so far."

"Counting nets?"

"Yes, counting nets."

"Oh, I never count nets."

"And it wouldn't do much good if you did, as the ball usually goes into the next net when you bowl."

My father died in 1937, when I was eight years old. He had already planted a great enthusiasm for the game in me. We lived in London where he was a solicitor, and my first games were watched at Lord's or, when we were on holiday, at Hove. The first county matches I saw included some very slow batting, but this never affected my loyalty to cricket. There was an atmosphere about the ground, perhaps sitting on the grass at the sea end at Hove or in the public stands at the Nursery End at Lord's. I would always set myself to identify every fielder as soon as I could, for there were no flashing lights telling his number on the score-card then. There was the discussion going on among the knowing ones, who would tell you all the personal histories of the players and why some batsman wasn't very strong in his shots on the leg-side. And the players became real characters, even from a distance.

It was a wonderful game for a boy to follow, for every day in the summer there were the English county scores to read about in the newspaper. There were books to read—particularly *Wisden* which possessed a goldmine of facts and figures. Sometimes in the winter there was the most romantic of cricket moments, when we would switch the wireless on early in the morning, and hear an Australian voice through the crackles telling us about the ups and downs of the day's play in a Test match. I have a vivid memory of going down the King's Road in Chelsea one dark winter afternoon in 1936 and seeing the newspaper placard saying BRADMAN FAILS AGAIN. So much was expected of him, for when we read the story, we found that he had made 82.

When I was eight years old my father organised a team called Slinfold Colts in the Sussex village where we had a week-end cottage. For years I remembered with pride my 23 against the Veterans' XI, and because I batted that day at No. 5, I decided that this was my favourite place to bat. We were less successful when we played Storrington Colts who were well trained and brought over by Hugh de Selincourt, who managed to make village cricket live on paper in some of his books like *The Cricket Match*.

One of the healthiest things I know about post-war cricket is how village cricket has grown again. It had almost stopped by 1945 but there are many villages where it has become youthful and strong once more. I have quite often taken our Mayflower team (some of us adults making up the team with our older boys) to Slinfold and we have had some exciting days. In one match the scores were level and two balls remained before stumps were to be drawn, when our last man went to the wicket. His experience of cricket was not large. He had spent more of the afternoon making the acquaintance of a young lady from Slinfold than in seeing how his team was getting on. Now all our fortunes rested on his shoulders. He wandered out to the wicket, throwing replies over his shoulder to the comments which came from his mates. When he reached the wicket there were some cheerful remarks for the umpires and the opposition. First ball he swung at and missed. The Slinfold fast bowler delivered the last ball of the day. It bowled him middle stump, but the umpire (the Slinfold umpire!) called 'No Ball' and we had won by one wicket. We took a suitcase of white flannels with us one of those Saturdays. The flannels eventually appeared on the field, but were being worn by the girls who had come to support us.

After my father died we moved down to Slinfold and my

school holidays included many days at Hove. We would also
go and visit my grandparents in Gloucestershire—most con-
veniently when the Cheltenham cricket week was on—so that
we could watch two or three matches there. If I was lucky
there would be a day or two at Lord's or the Oval to see a Test
match, and I saw one day of Len Hutton's record-breaking
364 in 1938.

Hedley Verity, the Yorkshire and England slow left arm
bowler, was my hero in those days. He was to die of wounds in
Italy in the war. I used to collect autographs in a small way,
only because other boys did. Verity's was the only one I really
wanted, and I never did get it. I asked him for it one day as he
was walking round to the practice nets at Lord's and my disappointment that I didn't get it remained for a long time. But
my loyalty stayed firmly fixed to him and my indigation was
great if he was ever left out of the England team.

I followed Verity because my main cricket ambition then
was to be a slow left arm bowler. When I was ten years old I
won a place in the 1st XI at my preparatory school: I batted
last and got quite a few wickets. I had picked up the ball one
day with the seam across, bowled a huge off-break and decided
that this must be the 'grip for the off-break'. So I trotted up
and bowled what cricketers call the 'Chinaman' without
having any notion of the technique of how to do it. A little
later I started reading books and learning how to spin the ball
properly, and I have never been able to spin the ball, off breaks
or leg breaks, from that day to this. Well, that's not quite
true. I remember that I turned a ball quite sharply from the
leg when I was playing for the Chelmsford Clergy one day in
1958! My bowling has always been something of a joke, and I
wish that I had kept my preparatory school headmaster's
comments in 1939. Of course I have always remembered what
he said: "Young Sheppard, if I am not very much mistaken,
will one day cause a great many batsmen a great deal of
trouble with his left arm slows." Sadly, he was very much
mistaken.

Verity was my hero, but there were others who had their

places in my firmament. 'Tich' Cornford, the tiny and extremely skilful Sussex wicket-keeper, probably had a special place for many small boys. Someone so small did not seem too far removed from us. Then there were others whom I had not necessarily ever seen, but who had a melodious ring to their names and initials. I met Les Townsend, who used to play for Derbyshire, in New Zealand in 1963. I told him I had followed him as a boy, but was too embarrassed to tell him that I used to have a song I would sing to myself which went to one of the tunes from the *Three Little Pigs*.

Oh Townsend (L.F.)
Oh Townsend (L.F.)
Oh Townsend Townsend Tiddle Iddle Townsend
Oh Townsend (L.F.)

Towering above all the others to me was Wally Hammond. He was more than a hero: he was like one of the Greek gods from Mount Olympus. I was lucky. What with the Cheltenham matches, and several games I watched at Lord's I saw him make a great many runs. I can almost recapture now the thrill I used to feel as I waited for him to come in to bat at Lord's. None of your 'incoming batsman must pass the outgoing batsman on the field of play'. There was always a pause, and then from my seat in the stand facing the pavilion I would see through the windows a white shirt moving through the Long Room; then out through the doors, down the steps and on to the field. We have sharply etched memories from boyhood and I can picture many of his strokes now—mostly his forcing back shots and drives into the covers, or a thunderous straight drive back over the bowler's head.

The war came when I was ten years old. For six years I learned about our warships and aircraft with the striking amount of details which lodge in a boy's memory. I listened to the News bulletins with intensity and heard the grim scorecards of wartime; "81 enemy aircraft are claimed to have been shot down. 35 of our planes are missing."

Towards the end of the war my sister had a job in London at the B.B.C. Sometimes the holidays were spent in London, sometimes in Sussex. Petrol rationing meant that it was difficult to see anyone else if you lived out in the country, and one way or another my mother and I were on our own at home for most of the school holidays. I learned to read a good deal, from the lightest school stories to *War and Peace*, Churchill's *Marlborough*, Galsworthy, Thackeray, and Jane Austen. I developed a passion for classical music, with Beethoven at the head of the list. My mother and I often used to go to concerts, opera, and particularly the ballet. Margot Fonteyn danced almost every night then, and we often saw her with Robert Helpman in *Swan Lake* or *Giselle*. Her technique was superb, but as with any great performer the skill was not paraded as she entered completely into the character she was playing. She never seemed to be in a hurry. Sometimes an air-raid would be announced during a performance and if we weren't feeling too brave, we would hurry off to the underground. One evening, after waiting a long time in an underground station while nothing happened, we emerged and walked home. We had hardly left the station when we heard the broken-down car noise of a V1 flying bomb and saw the red glow of its exhaust only a few hundred feet above our heads.

London had the lake in Regent's Park where I often went rowing, and courts for squash which was the only other game I ever played well. In Sussex the war, which was followed so closely on the maps indoors, was fought out in imaginary battles at battalion level in the fields and woods around us.

But cricket went on in the garden: my mother was a faithful steady underarm bowler, but my sister would never stoop to bowling underarm. She would bowl fast round arm and about every other delivery meant a prolonged search in a prickly hedge for the ball. She was probably cleverer than she knew, as I organised my cricket on my own without demanding her services. I met the sister of a great friend of mine in New Zealand. It appears that she and her brother played five day Test matches which would start promptly at 11 a.m. each day: halfway through the morning their mother would bring out the drinks on a tray—for the batsman and all eleven fielders.

B

He always chose to be England and she had to be Australia. She got ten innings for her team and he one innings for his: but she said that trees which were the fielders had a disconcerting habit of diving full length to take a wonderful catch when she was batting, while they remained very still when he was at the wicket. Anyway that was her story.

One day three or four of us in the England dressing-room were discussing the kind of games we played as boys, and we discovered that each of us had invented some kind of homemade cricket which we played alone or with a friend. I was alone and my pitch used to be the coal-shed door. I would throw a tennis ball at the door, and then bat as it rebounded. I still have a notebook with the matches I played this way: I started a full English County Championship season—seventeen counties playing each other, and I had to be each player in turn on either side. I got through the whole month of May and well into June. I have never dared to reckon up how many hours must have been spent in this way. But I believe that I learned more about batting then than in any other way. I tried to stand in the way the great players did, to play the same strokes they did, and I had to concentrate especially hard if Hammond, Compton or Hutton were batting.

I went to boarding school when I was nine years old— Northcliffe House School at Bognor on the Sussex coast. When the threat of air-raids and invasion came in 1940 the school took a large house near Truro in Cornwall. We still played plenty of cricket and I think I must have been a very correct little player though I was not outstanding. The same was true when I went on to Sherborne School in Dorset. I was very small until I was past 16, and was not strong enough to be a dominant batsman. But I played each year in the right team for my age and I remained a great enthusiast for cricket.

There were other enthusiasms too: particularly I gave a lot of time to music. I learnt to play the piano, without ever really 'breaking through' to play with real enjoyment. But it helped to give me a great delight in music: singing took a large part of my time as my voice did not break until I was sixteen and I was one of the two leaders of the choir trebles for two years at Sherborne. For four or five years I was involved in singing a wide range of music, and whether it was singing solo or leading the choir it meant a responsibility which was very good for a small boy.

I learnt much through singing which was to stand me in good stead when I wanted to speak in public later on. And I had my first experience of stage fright: I had quite often sung solos in a church before, but this was the first time at a large school concert at Sherborne. The whole audience was in darkness and I was alone in light on the dais there. I remember catching hold of a brass knob which was on a little rail at the front and holding on to it for all I was worth while I got through *Who is Sylvia?* and *Where'er you walk*. It is not obvious that there is anything in common between singing, public speaking and batting; but in fact there is a sense of ordeal about each of them which has to be overcome.

My music master who remained a very good friend, was very angry with me when at 16, under pressure of a lot of work for examinations and increasing calls of cricket, I gave up my singing and piano playing. "When you're old, you'll not have your cricket," he said, "but you can always have music." As it has turned out I don't think he was necessarily right in my case as cricket has given so much to me. And, though I cannot be a performer, I have kept a keen appreciation of music, now widened to take in a liking for jazz and pop records. Perhaps the highlights of my singing days were the many times when we sang in Sherborne Abbey. It was ideal for a Byrd motet, and at every pause the rich chord would ring round the Abbey. We sang much of the great Church music, and years later, when my Christian faith came alive, I realised what wonderful words I had been singing. But at the time I am afraid I was only interested in the words to make them audible, and to give the right expression to them. It is all too easy to handle holy things without consciously coming close to God at all.

My great friend for three or four years at school was Bill Anstice-Brown. He was an artist of considerable skill and the different studies we occupied were usually littered with oil paints and palate knives. He has gone back to Sherborne to teach art. Cricket was not one of the interests we held in common. In those days the whole school had to watch for at least two hours when the 1st XI played another school. We were playing Downside and Bill was sketching the scene. He called the drawing 'School v. Downside with Westcott House in the background'. I said it was more like 'Westcott House with cricket in the foreground'. It was unlucky that a master chose to ask him who was the fielder nearest to him. It was unlucky that the Downside fielder who had been standing there had been one Hussey who had happened to be at prep. school with Bill. It was still more unlucky that when he answered "Hussey" without looking up, our own team had been fielding for the previous hour or more.

Neither Bill nor I was any good at Rugby football which was the game which raised the greatest enthusiasm at Sherborne. We would have given a lot to be able to bask peacefully on the edge of the third-grade house matches we played in. But he was very tall, so that the ball was always thrown to him in the line out. I was very short and played scrum-half, so he always threw it to me at about the same moment that the opposing forward landed on top of me. My school memories of Rugby were that it was generally wet and greasy. Our side always appeared to try to 'get the ball back', the other side decided to 'take it on', and I had to try to fall on the ball. When I was larger and able to look after myself better, in Army days, Rugby seemed a different game and I enjoyed it in a way which I failed to do at school when I was neither large, nor tough, nor quick.

As I grew older I seemed naturally to make a number of good friends rather than have one very close friend. One of the reasons why I most thank God for cricket is that it has helped me to have real friendships with a wide circle. My education was in many ways an old-fashioned one. I studied the Classics, and am glad that I did, though at the time I had not wanted to. We all had to fit in to the regular activities of a close-knit community in the school and especially in the house. Sherborne had a very strong house system and the seventy boys who lived in Lyon House had a very fierce loyalty to it. Alick Trelawny-Ross was housemaster for most of my years. He had been a schoolboy at Sherborne and was housemaster for thirty-two years. I suppose that if he and I now sat down to discuss theories of education we should disagree about a good deal. But Alick was a great man, completely dedicated to his job. He had endless time for his boys, and he has been a very good friend to me.

I feel that some boys who did not fit in naturally to the pattern of life in the House might have found themselves more fully in a freer atmosphere. I was successful at work and in sport: I was given responsibility and became head of the House. I enjoyed life very much and learned a great deal about leadership and getting on with others in addition to what I gleaned in the class-room. But some of the less successful enjoyed it all much less, and I cannot now escape from the feeling that we were all stamped rather too decisively with the mould of our public school.

All those years that I had been a cricket 'fanatic' I had never even dreamed that I might play in big cricket myself. I was given every encouragement by schoolmasters at prep. school and at public school, but I was never an infant prodigy. Peter May, who is my exact contemporary, was an outstanding player in the Charterhouse side when he was fourteen, and I remember watching a chubby little thirteen-year-old called Colin Cowdrey make all the runs and take all the wickets with cleverly spun leg breaks for Tonbridge against Clifton at Lord's.

I was seventeen years old when I played my first match for the 1st XI at Sherborne, and I started at rock bottom. First match I was out for 0, second match 0 again. But they continued to give me a chance and the runs began to come. Micky Walford, who played a lot of good cricket for Somerset, as well as Rugby football for Oxford University before the war, and later hockey for Great Britain, came back from the war that year as a schoolmaster. One day that summer he said to me, "You ought to be a first-class cricketer." The idea had never been in my head before, but once he had said that to me I determined that I would play first-class cricket.

Holiday cricket for schoolboys was not very well organised in the years immediately after the war. When I was sixteen the holidays produced only two matches for me. We were living in a flat in London and for one I travelled down to Sussex to play for Horsham. We declared with two wickets down, so that I did not have an innings. The other game was against the Sussex Martlets for the Junior Martlets. This was my first game on the Sussex County Ground at Hove, and a good many youthful hopes were dashed as well as mine. We had fifteen players against their eleven and I batted number 13. We were all out for 57 (Sheppard 1). The next year in the same match we could only manage 33 (all fifteen of us). The following year our morale was much better. We each played eleven a side; we made 270 and won the match.

In case it sounds as though I think I was being heroic in making the effort to travel for my cricket, let me mention what Johnny Martin, the New South Wales slow left arm bowler does. Every Friday night he gets on a train for 250 miles to Sydney where he plays for his grade club every Saturday. then 250 miles back again. That is apart from Sheffield Shield matches which would involve flying 2,000 miles from Sydney when they play Western Australia in Perth. When M.C.C. plays country matches in Australia, we often find that some players have come up to 500 miles for the game.

I was born in Surrey and made one attempt to play some cricket there. When I was in the Colts team at school, I imagined that the Surrey Colts was made up of sixteen-year-olds like me. I wrote, asking if they would give me a trial, not realising that Surrey Colts were really the county 2nd XI and were mainly professional cricketers. I did not receive a very encouraging reply and the next year I was given the chance of good cricket in Sussex which was really our home.

Twice in 1946 Young Sussex played against Young Yorkshire.

Ken Suttle was captain in the first match at Chichester, as he has been reminding me for seventeen years; he also reminds me that I ran him out that day. He made a hundred in the second match at Hastings when Alan Oakman also played for us. I made fifty in each match and received a letter that September from Billy Griffith who was then Sussex captain and secretary, congratulating me and asking me to come and practise at the nets with the county players the next April.

That letter was treasured through the winter and the first icy-cold practice day found me at the nets, with players I had watched and whose exploits I had read about for years. George Cox lived in Warnham, the next village to Slinfold, and every day he would give me a lift in an ancient open Morris 8; we would pick Charlie Oakes up in Horsham and the 'Horsham contingent' would go bumping across the Downs to Hove. No one fell out, though the door was kept shut by a combination of a part of a mowing machine and a simple bolt. On the colder days I would lie on the back seat under a tarpaulin.

I owe a great deal to many different men who encouraged me and taught me. But I learned at least as much from the other Sussex players as from anyone. George Cox and Jim and John Langridge particularly would always point out things that I was doing and have suggestions to make. Even when playing for England I found this a great help, because it is easy to fall into habits without knowing.

One Monday at Sherborne I was in the practice nets when I heard two small boys arguing about me. They were standing on the wall behind me. One said, "That's Sheppard. He made 80 on Saturday." "No it can't be," replied the other, "they're learning in here." The second boy held the opinion that if you could score 80 in a match you had no more to learn. But the longer I have played the more I have realised that there is much to learn all the time.

The Sussex county coach at this time was Patsy Hendren: he told us that Frank Woolley had said it took fifteen years to make a batsman. Some said Patsy did not make the youngsters work hard enough. He was certainly easy-going, but he taught

us a tremendous amount of the 'lore' of cricket. We would try
to get him talking about the great matches he had played in
and apart from the fun of listening to one of the greatest of all
story-tellers, we learned a great deal about the game. Many of
his stories were about the West Indies where he became a tremendously popular figure.

One story conjured up a fascinating scene in the middle of a
Test match in 1930. The West Indies fast bowler Griffith is
waiting to run up to bowl (I suppose a twenty yard run or so);
then twenty-two yards of pitch; then Patsy, batting; then
another twenty yards or so to the wicket-keeper, and, a little
further back, one slip fieldsman, Joe Small. Across this distance
of sixty yards or so Griffith calls, "Hey Joe Small, you go wider".
"No I'm not going wider," says Joe Small. "Joe Small you go
wider." "No I'm not going wider. Hey Mister Patsy Hendren,
would you go wider if you was me?" "No, I wouldn't go wider,"
says Patsy. "Mister Patsy Hendren says he wouldn't go wider
so I'm staying here."

Then Patsy would tell us about the desperate finish to the
Adelaide Test Match in 1928–29, when Jack White took
thirteen wickets for 256 in the match. Australia's ninth wicket
fell with twelve runs still to win: last man in was Don Blackie,
who played his first Test match at the age of forty-six. At
Adelaide the players have a long way to come down from the
dressing-room in full view of the fielders. Coming down the
stairs Don Blackie dropped his bat three times and as he came
on to the field he tripped and fell. Patsy turned to his neighbour
on the field and said, "We've won!" When Blackie, a left-
hand batsman, arrived at the wicket, he was so nervous that
he couldn't hold his bat still for the umpire to give him his
guard. Jack White was bowling and Patsy, close up at short
leg, said to Blackie, "Hit him out of the ground." "I will, I
will," said Blackie. He swung at the first ball and as it went
sailing over his head Patsy thought, "I've done it now!" but
Harold Larwood caught it on the boundary.

Back from the world of first-class cricketers to a last term at
school, it was a pleasantly free time as the previous December

I had won an Exhibition to Trinity Hall at Cambridge University. Those last two terms at school were not entirely wasted: they helped me to learn that education is not only for the purpose of passing examinations. I began to read more widely and to pursue ideas which interested me. But I have to admit that it was pleasant to have plenty of time for cricket.

We had a good school side that year: our captain, as the previous year's, was John Lush, who teaches at Eastbourne College now. He had taken a lot of wickets as a natural slow left arm bowler who made the ball drift on in a deceptive way. That last year at school we had a new professional coach, Len Creese, who had played many years for Hampshire. He was a good and thoughtful left arm spin bowler. Here was the dilemma for the cricket coach: should he leave John Lush bowling as he was, so that he would be a good club bowler but never more? Or should he make him alter his action so that he would spin the ball more, and so that he might possibly become a much higher class bowler? In fact John did alter his action and I do not think he ever bowled quite so well as he did when he was seventeen. It is the kind of problem which often faces a coach: personally I feel that a coach should be very cautious about changing the natural style of a boy, but there are times, and I feel that this was one of them, when it is right to take a risk. But the coach is always likely to be blamed for having 'ruined' a promising cricketer by 'over-coaching'.

We had a good bowling side at Sherborne that year, but the batting depended too much on two of us. I made 786 runs in ten completed innings, and Bob Tozer made 357 runs but there wasn't quite enough depth to the batting to make us a thoroughly reliable side.

Bob played a brilliant innings against Blundells who had beaten us by 15 runs the previous year. We had something like 200 to win in a hurry and scrambled home by one wicket. Their opening bowler was tremendously fast for a schoolboy. He was Clem Thomas, who was to be a great Rugby wing forward for Wales, and he was superbly built. I don't know whether he

ever played cricket after his school days. But one day he strolled
over when we were practising in the nets at Cambridge. John
Warr was batting. "Come over and have a bowl, Clem," he
called. I remembered how quick he had been at school and
encouraged him to bowl one which would give John a surprise.
He took his coat off and sent the ball flying past the Cambridge
captain's nose before he had time to play a stroke.

Most teams come unstuck at least once in a season and we
did when we went over to play Marlborough. They bowled us
out for 57 before lunch. Our bowlers made them struggle and
they won by only three wickets, but it spoiled what would have
been an outstanding season for us.

When term finished I played at Lord's for the first time: it
was in a two-day game, Southern Schools v. the Rest. Our
captain was Peter May who made a very good hundred both
in this match and the next when the Public Schools played the
Combined Army Services. For the Southern Schools we also
had Ian Bedford, who had been bowling out several county
sides for Middlesex in the previous month. For two or three
years I believe Ian was the best prospect of a really good leg-
spin and googly bowler that England has had since the war.
But perhaps he grew a further inch or two which affected the
flight of the ball, and I am not sure that he ever wanted to play
big cricket all that much.

To break into Test cricket a player needs to have a tremendous determination to succeed. Sir Leonard Hutton gave
a very good piece of advice on selecting a Test team in Australia.
He said, "Pick the people who really want to play." I know
what he meant. In one sense of course everyone wants to play
for England; but it can become very tough and the thought
goes through your mind, "It would be easier if I weren't
selected." At that sort of moment the determination to win
through separates players who in technical skill are equal. I
was talking one day about Peter May to a contemporary of
ours, a very skilled batsman who was good enough technically
to play for England for years. I said, "Peter May's hungry for
runs. He likes making runs." The other said, "Yes—that's

what I think I ought to be." And the approach made all the difference between a great Test match player and one who hardly made his mark in Test cricket at all.

CHAPTER 2

SUSSEX BY THE SEA

MY first county match was against Leicestershire at Hastings. "They're not a very strong bowling side," I was told. "The only bowler you really want to worry about is Jack Walsh. He bowls one googly you can see, and one googly you can't see." I said I would look out for Walsh. "Then be careful with Watson in the field, because he can throw with either hand." I said I would keep my eyes open for Watson. Unfortunately the only ball I had in the first innings was from Jackson, and they hadn't told me about him. It was a little in-swinger which nipped in and trapped me leg-before wicket—out first ball.

In the second innings I did a little better and at the tea interval on the third day I was o not out. As we went on the field after tea, Les Berry, the Leicestershire captain, said, "There'll be a run for you on the off-side if you want it." I said, "Thank you very much." All the fielders went back a few yards so that I could push an easy single. I did this—and I got one more run without any help. I then was caught at the wicket off Lester for two. And I still hadn't had a ball from Walsh, or recognised which one was Watson.

That evening we set off by coach from Hastings, with its boarding houses sending their smell of fried fish across the pleasant, enclosed, ground, making the fieldsman long for his lunch long before the interval comes at 1.30 p.m. We arrived in Birmingham at 3 a.m. with our match against Warwickshire due to start that morning. The constant travelling adds to the strain of six-days-a-week cricket and when I first played a full season I was very stale after two months of it. But it is possible to grow accustomed to this and to be really keen about your cricket: whether you play first-class cricket for a living or not, it is really your job of work for the time being. And a very pleasant job it is, when playing in a good team which pulls together.

At Birmingham my scores were 15 and 0—the second innings being finished by a ball from Tom Pritchard which knocked my off stump a long way out of the ground. He was then about the fastest bowler in England and was quite a lot quicker than anyone I had batted against before. Then back to Eastbourne where we played Essex and Trevor Bailey made a very good 205. I had been brought up in the school which says that you should move your feet up the wicket to a slow bowler. Peter Smith was bowling leg-spinners for Essex and flighting them quite slowly up in the air. "Why don't you go up the wicket to him?" I asked one of our senior players. "You can if you like," he said. When I went in to bat Peter Smith was bowling, and after a little I skipped up the wicket and hit him for four through the covers. Next ball was invitingly up in the air again. Off I went again. Only this time it was a little wider. I missed it, and was stumped by a long way.

I still believe that it is good to move your feet up the wicket to a slow bowler—though you have got to pick out the right ball. The difficulty for the English first-class batsman is that there are very few slow bowlers who toss it up in the old way. Wilfred Rhodes and Jack White would encourage the batsman to try to drive them, hoping that they would get him out in the process. Patsy Hendren was very quick on his feet, and he told me that he much preferred batting against Rhodes to playing Verity who was much more the modern type of slow bowler. On the whole the great English post-war slow bowlers, Laker, Lock, Wardle, Appleyard and Titmus have pushed the ball through quicker in order to keep a batsman from coming up the wicket. On a true wicket, where the ball is not turning, they say in effect to the batsman, "I'm going to stop you scoring, so that you will do something silly in order to make some runs." The older type of slow bowler said, "Come and hit me—if you can."

Three first-class matches had produced no success in terms of runs, but they had set me a standard which I never forgot while I was playing club cricket and for Sussex 2nd XI during the next two years. These two years were spent in the Army doing my National Service and I believe they were good years for me in many ways. They broke the life of class-room, lectures and books which would otherwise have gone straight on at Cambridge, and reminded me that the majority of men earn their living with their hands. In an Army barrack room I lived close beside men whom I would never have met otherwise.

On the good military principle that you can train young soldiers best by sending them as far from their homes as possible, and putting a stretch of water in between, so that they won't be tempted to go home, we were sent to Palace Barracks near Belfast. We had four months of 'square bashing' which forced us like a mould into a group which thought together and acted together. Little appeal was made to our reason at any point: we must be toughened and not show our feelings or question the orders which came. If you were training men to act like a machine under fire when fear would prompt them to lie down or run away, this was the way to do it. And I think it did us very little harm for a period of time.

It resulted in the kind of situation which I later found myself in as a junior officer. My adjutant was 'tearing me off a strip' for something which I knew wasn't my fault. I stood silently to attention, boiling inside, while he gave me so many extra orderly officer's duties. When he had finished I stepped back, said, "Thank you, sir!" saluted and marched out. It was all quite good for me. There is danger though, when we make this 'stiff upper lip' hiding of the feelings our ideal for the whole of life. One of the features about life in the East End of London is that we say what we think to one another. Therefore we don't hide ourselves from one another, and though it means more embarrassments, I believe it leads to more real relationships between people.

The barrack room at Palace Barracks produced some strong friendships. Four of us in particular went around together; we put on an act at the Christmas concert, when we had perhaps the easiest audience to entertain, as they were in the mood to laugh at everything. Mostly life was rugged and unreasoning: it was meant to be. One day we were playing Rugby football against another company. At half-time our company commander came on to the field, pointed at the wing three-quarter and said, "There's a man there who's not trying. He hasn't got his knees dirty." In fact on a muddy day the ball had never been passed to him, so that he could hardly have been involved in the game so far. But the lesson was not wasted on us, and we all saw to it that our knees were covered in mud before we had been five minutes on the field.

Michael Charlesworth slept in the next bed to me, talented as an entertainer, now a very good schoolmaster, but never a great soldier. Kit inspection would from time to time dominate our lives, when by 8 a.m. we had to have everything we possessed on our beds, squared off, pressed or polished. My memory of Michael in the barrack room was when he spent the whole evening laying out his kit on his bed, and then slept the night on the floor himself.

I have never been very brave physically, and when 'volunteers' for boxing were called for I usually managed to be standing behind someone else. But I am too tall to go unnoticed, and one day I found that I had become one of the 'volunteers'. Five or six of us had to fight for the honour of our platoon against two other platoons. This meant two fights. The contest was not dignified by the name of boxing: it was called 'milling' and you were meant to go into the ring for three rounds of one minute each, and hit the other man as often as you could. My first fight was with someone who was as frightened as I was. We both employed our schoolboy technique of punching with the left hand while turning the face away, shutting the eyes and protecting the head with the right hand. My astonishment was great when, after three rounds of this, I was declared the winner. It was the first fight I had ever won in my life.

But a greater victory was to come: my other opponent was a little man who let it be known to all that he hadn't been beaten in ten years of London boys' club boxing. He ducked and weaved and snorted in the best professional manner. I did have one advantage. I was approximately two and a half stones heavier than he was. After a round I came to the surprising conclusion that he could not hurt me, and that if I looked at him I might hit him. So after a little I swung a right at him as hard as I could. I missed with my fist, but hit him right on the point of the jaw with my elbow. I swung round in a complete circle, and saw him standing glassy-eyed in the middle of the ring. My platoon were screaming to me to "go in and kill him". If I had wanted to, I wouldn't have known how, so that it was a mercy that the bell rang at that moment. But I had won again, and decided to retire from the ring with my unbeaten adult record. Or perhaps I should say that I succeeded in standing behind someone big enough every time 'volunteers' were called for again.

There was one touch of warmth and friendship which we found in Palace Barracks which I think had a lasting influence on me. This was Sandes Soldiers' Home. We said that we went there because egg and chips was cheaper there than at the NAAFI. But the women who ran it offered friendliness and did their best to make it genuinely a home. On Christmas Day an extraordinary thing happened to me. I was watching a rag game of football, and saw a thunderflash explode quite twenty feet away from me. Normally it would not hurt anyone unless he was right on top of it. But the cap flew up and hit me in the mouth, cutting my lip open. I was shaken up a bit, and Miss Walton who was in charge of Sandes Home asked me to go and have Christmas lunch with them. It was a simple act of friendship which meant a great deal to me. Much later on I discovered that some of them had set themselves to pray for me, and after some years I believe that their prayers were answered.

Eaton Hall Officer Cadet School was my next training ground. The army had taken over the Duke of Westminster's huge home near Chester. The atmosphere was altogether different here: it is true that we were chased around the barrack square by sergeant-majors from the Brigade of Guards. But even they would finish whatever pungent remarks they had to make by adding "Sir!" at the end. On our first day at Eaton

Loyal supporters. My mother and my sister followed my cricket through thick and thin.

Young hopefuls. With Peter May before our first match for Cambridge, 1950.

Cambridge had six Test cricketers in 1952. *Back row:* F. C. M. Alexander, R. Subba Row, C. N. McCarthy, G. G. Tordoff, C. J. Kenny, M. H. Bushby. *Front row:* P. B. H. May, R. G. Marlar, D. S. Sheppard (captain).

Hall I was brought out in front of the platoon as an example of how not to dress. But I must have 'got with' the Army's ideas there as I finished up as Senior Under-Officer.

I nearly finished up back as a private as I almost committed the most awful crime in a soldier's experience by losing my rifle. As a Senior Under-Officer I did not carry my rifle on parade and one Sunday, returning on the train from a week-end's leave, I suddenly realised that I hadn't seen it anywhere for about a fortnight, when I should have been lovingly cleaning it as a soldier's best friend every day. A day's frantic search only proved that it was gone. I was on the point of going to tell my Company Commander when a sergeant friend of mine came and told me there was a rifle in the projection room of the theatre. It was mine. Someone had 'borrowed' it for a 'Method of Instruction' playlet and had forgotten to return it. I breathed again. Method of Instruction was first introduced to us by what I still applaud as the most original beginning to a lecture that I have met. A dapper little major walked on to the stage: "You will have seen from your programme," he said, "that this lecture is to be given by Major S. R. Newman . . . I am he."

There wasn't so much time for cricket that summer and I played my one and only game for the Army when I hadn't been playing at all regularly. I made 0 and 1, each innings being l.b.w. I 'shouldered arms' each time, letting the ball hit me on the pads, hoping that I had moved outside the off stump. I wasn't asked to play for the Army again, which was a disappointment at the time. But it worked out very well for me, as I found a sympathetic Commanding Officer who let me have a good deal of leave to play for Sussex 2nd XI and, later, for Sussex.

I also played local cricket at all levels, from an evening league in Chester to Company matches at Shorncliffe in Kent. I was posted there from Eaton Hall and after two or three months at Shorncliffe I joined the 1st Battalion of the Royal Sussex Regiment at Dover. My first day at Shorncliffe I went to report my arrival to my Company Commander. "Oh all right," was

C

his immediate reply. "Do you play cricket? We've got a Company match this afternoon." I learned a good deal about playing on rough wickets in this sort of cricket. Shorncliffe Garrison played a match every week, and their wicket was somewhat fiery that year. A score of 30 there was something to be pleased with.

When I joined the Royal Sussex Regiment I was put in charge of the Battalion cricket. We had the last word in 'gamesmanship' played on us when we went to play the Royal Marine Depot at Deal. As we arrived, the King's Squad of the Royal Marines was going on parade on the square immediately next to the cricket ground. One word of command and they would move for what seemed like two minutes without any further order and with the precision of a well-oiled machine. This was drill of an order we had never known. Half an hour of it and then the cricket began. Stephen Potter, the master of gamesmanship and one-upmanship, would have been proud of it.

Memory photographs certain events in the place where you heard about them, and in August 1948 I was playing for Shorn-cliffe Garrison at Betteshanger Colliery on the day when Lindwall bowled England out for 52 at the Oval. It was the final humbling in a year when Australia beat us by four matches to none. Part of my cricket education was to watch Lindwall and Miller bowl that year, for we had no bowlers to compare with their pace then.

In June, I went and watched them play Sussex. First we saw the Sussex bowler Paul Carey come tearing up from the sea end. There was tremendous effort but very little pace. When Sussex batted, Lindwall bowled from the same end. Slowly his perfectly rhythmic run got under way, accelerating all the way up until with a loose, slingy action he let the ball go. The pace was tremendous compared with anything I had seen before. Add to the pace his control, his change of pace, and his ability to make the ball swing away. Put at the other end Keith Miller, bringing the ball down from much higher, in certain moods the most hostile fast bowler I've ever seen. Add also

Bill Johnston, tall, left arm over the wicket, sometimes bowling fast with a great control of swing, sometimes bowling medium pace with constant accuracy of length and direction—and you realise what England was up against in 1948. Then remember that Australia failed to select the two best wrist spinners of their day for that tour. Bruce Dooland and George Tribe were both left at home and instead of playing for Australia for the next ten years they brought their skills to Nottinghamshire and Northamptonshire. Lindwall, Miller, Johnston, Dooland, Tribe would have made perhaps the best balanced attacking bowling side Australia has ever had. As it was Toshack and Ian Johnson played the part perfectly for Bradman's plan: they would keep the batsmen quiet until the fast bowlers were ready for another onslaught.

I saw the whole of the Lord's Test that year and, watching Hutton and Washbrook go out to bat, I realised that there was something very tough about opening the innings for England. To complete the picture of strength of that Australian team, their batting line up was Morris, Barnes, Bradman, Hassett, Miller, Brown, Harvey—with perhaps their greatest ever wicket-keeper, Don Tallon. Of course cricketers play as well as they are allowed to and it is a great pity that the 1948 Australians were not matched with the great England teams of 1953-1957 when we were choosing our bowling sides from Bedser, Trueman, Statham, Tyson, Bailey, Laker, Lock, Appleyard, Wardle.

From the toughest to some of the most relaxed cricket. While I was stationed at Shorncliffe and Dover I played on most of the lovely Kent grounds; there was good, keen cricket at Dover, Folkestone and Maidstone, but I have some wonderfully happy memories of playing for Highland Court. The ground was Walter Wingham's private one, set between the trees and the cornfields. We were a very strong club side, but the game wasn't taken too seriously. George Stickles, farmer and captain, put his bowlers on strictly in rotation, teas were on a vast scale, and I would go out to field after tea with pockets bulging with cherries.

It was all wonderful fun, but for me there was always the challenge to succeed in the first-class game. Nothing else would do. Good club cricket for Horsham, Sussex Martlets, Dover and Highland Court all helped, but in county cricket there was another skill in field placing, and accuracy in bowling as well as the atmosphere of the big occasion to overcome. Sussex 2nd XI provided a good apprenticeship and also meant that strong friendships grew up with the young professionals who were hoping to make their career out of cricket. Sussex, like most counties, has usually taken on a handful of boys at fifteen or sixteen years old. They help with the work at the County Ground and play for the Club and Ground against the different club sides around the county. In 2nd XI cricket we played against some of the older professionals who couldn't quite hold a place in the first team, and other 'young hopefuls' like ourselves.

I began to find my feet in this cricket and in our last match in 1948 against Kent 2nd XI I really got going. The match was at Aylesford Paper Mills and there was then no scoreboard to show how many runs each batsman had scored. As a boy I would count my runs up to about 20, but if I went on past that I forgot all about it. I was not out at the tea interval and our captain asked me if I knew how many runs I'd made. I thought it must be about 70. "Shall we tell him?" he asked the others, and then went on, "You've made 99". I like to think the 'nervous nineties' have never worried me over much. I have got out in the nineties on several occasions, but I don't really think that the score caused this. I feel the danger is to play any differently because you've made 90—either by saying to yourself, "I must be extra careful" or "I must get there as quickly as I can". If you have played well enough to pass 90, you should reach 100 by playing in exactly the same way. Anyway, that day at Aylesford I went on to 157 not out.

It was my first hundred for the 2nd XI and I'm sure I at once became a better player. I've seen this in others; once a man has made a century, he knows he can do it, his confidence grows and he expects to do it again. So much of success in batting comes not from the technical skill of playing the strokes, but from confidence and concentration. I have seen gifted players who look magnificent in the practice nets and yet never make more than 20 or 30 in a match. And I can think of less talented players who have played for England because they have the right mixture of calmness and determination to 'build an innings'.

Each landmark helps and in June 1949 I made my first fifty for Sussex 1st XI. It was against Oxford University who had a good side that year. Divecha, Philip Whitcombe, Chesterton, Kardar and Van Ryneveld made a strong bowling side, and on an unusually lively wicket for the Oxford Parks they bowled us out cheaply twice and beat us by an innings. I batted through and produced top score in each innings— 32 and 52. Kardar, left arm slow, spun the ball sharply from leg and had 7 for 33 in our first innings. In the second innings George Chesterton took 5 for 40.

We hadn't seen him before, and when Billy Griffith came in to bat he asked me what he was bowling. "He's bowled mostly in-swingers," I said. "But then, he's bowled a good away-swinger as well. And he's made the ball move off the seam as well. And he's bowled a good leg-cutter. And . . ." "Can you tell me why he isn't playing for England then?" interrupted Billy. On the whole it's better to find out for yourself what a bowler bowls rather than look for too much trouble, though it certainly helps to have an idea of what is coming. Even the greatest bowlers often bowl a plain straight ball, though you wouldn't believe that if you heard some of them talking!

I'd now reached the stage where I could quite often survive at the wicket in county cricket, but would find scoring terribly difficult. I would not have been very popular with the crowd just then. But we had one wonderful win which taught me something of the risks you can rightly take at times. Somerset left us 258 to win and not very long in which to make them. John Langridge and I went in first, and he started off straight away with runs all round the wicket. I tried, but the ball kept going straight to the fieldsmen. After thirty precious minutes had gone we had made 36, Langridge 30, Sheppard 6. Our captain Hugh Bartlett walked round to the sight screen and signalled to me to have a hit. Suddenly things seemed to go right and after fifty more minutes I was out for 71. We had made 148 in eighty minutes. In came Jack Oakes who was a great hitter and in another fifty-three minutes our score was 258 for one wicket. Langridge 108 not out and Oakes 55 not out.

I had had a lot to say to the others about that match being played at Frome, because my family once came from Frome. Somerset only played one match a year there, and the cricket ground was a pleasant field with a small pavilion in the corner and benches and chairs making up the ring. After all my talk about the Sheppards of Frome, the laugh was on me on the first morning of the match. Right in the middle of play an old lady walked very slowly with her shopping basket straight across the field of play from one end to the other. Obviously she went that way every day, and a cricket match wasn't going to change her course. Everything stopped and Harold Gimblett who was batting for Somerset said, "Don't worry—that's old Mrs. Sheppard. She always comes across here."

Sussex were an in-and-out kind of team, occasionally playing brilliant cricket as that day against Somerset. But the bowling wasn't really strong enough to lift us out of the bottom half of the county championship and tenth out of seventeen was quite a good season for us in the five years after the war.

Sussex cricket has always had a strong family ring about it. The brothers Jim and John Langridge provided the backbone of our batting for years, each making over 30,000 runs in first-class cricket. In addition Jim took a little matter of 1,500 wickets as a slow left hander, and, if my boyhood hero Verity had not ruled the kingdom of slow left handers in the 1930's, Jim would have probably played a great deal for England. Jim's son Richard goes in first for Sussex now. Then there were two brothers, Jim and Harry Parks, until the war when Jim retired. His son Jim Parks was to play a big part in Sussex cricket and, like his father, play for England. George Cox was for long known as "young George", as his father, also George

Cox, had played for many years for us. Then there were the brothers Charlie and Jack Oakes whose father was our grounds-man at Horsham. Quite by chance Tich Cornford and Jim Cornford who were not relations played in the same side and added to the impression that the whole thing was a 'closed shop' for a few families. Going back a few years, our greatest bowler Maurice Tate was following his father Fred Tate into the side. Arthur Gilligan and Harold Gilligan were brothers, while the great Duleepsinjhi, always wanted to play for Sussex because his perhaps even greater uncle Ranjitsinjhi had done so.

I think it was my first match for Sussex at Hastings when some boys were playing with a tennis ball on the field during the lunch interval. (Perhaps I can be allowed to say that it annoys me greatly when these games are forbidden, because the ball occasionally lands in a member's lunch.) One or two of us were looking out of the dressing-room window and giving a commentary on this game to the rest of the team. Richard Langridge, then I suppose eight years old, and Alan Parks (Harry's son) were the only two who were allowed to bat, and for some time they were the only bowlers too, while other boys were allowed to join in the fielding. Then another small boy joined in the bowling, but he was never given a knock with the bat. He bowled fast and well. We commentators called him the Nipper. After a while Jim Cornford, who was our opening bowler but a not very successful number eleven batsman, came over to the window. "Bless me," he said, "that's my nipper." All strictly within the family.

Jim Cornford had a beautiful rhythm as he bowled: we were told his action was very like Maurice Tate's. But he never had the physique that Tate had—or the feet which were the cartoonists' delight before Freddie Trueman's mop of black hair and Colin Cowdrey's back view took over. We had other fast-medium bowlers, Jack Nye, Paul Carey, Jim Wood and Ted James in the first years after the war: they had their days of triumph, especially Jim Wood, left arm over the wicket, who twice wrecked the great Middlesex batting side on a good wicket in the August Bank Holiday match at Hove—once with 7 wickets for 31, once with 7 for 24. But none got a hundred wickets in a season until Ian Thomson came along in 1953, and made a habit of this every year.

Billy Griffith was Sussex's wicket-keeper when I first played, and he was a very good one. Godfrey Evans was such a great wicket-keeper that Billy's chances of playing for England were limited, but his first Test match produced one of the most remarkable centuries ever made. England were to play West Indies at Trinidad in 1948. Half the team was injured and Billy who usually batted about number 9, was brought into the side as an opening batsman. After about half an hour he ran out Jack Robertson who was the only batsman in the team who was doing well at the time. But after this disastrous start Billy settled down to a determined innings, and it wasn't until well into the second day that they finally dismissed him for 140—the first century he had ever made in a first-class match.

Billy played cricket with great skill and keenness, and also with a friendliness towards all. There have been wicket-keepers who made you feel that cricket was war to the death, with no words to be spoken between the warring armies except those comments muttered just loud enough to unnerve you. But Billy Griffith made the batsman feel welcome—not to stay all day—but welcome to join in a hard contest between friends. Cricket should be that way and it was a good day for the game when he was made secretary of M.C.C., the top administrative post in English cricket, in 1962.

Hugh Bartlett was my first county captain. He had been with Billy Griffith as a boy at Dulwich College; each had played one match for Surrey before coming to Sussex; together they had served in the Glider Pilot Regiment in the war, including the landing at Arnhem; together they played for Sussex for some years after the war. Before the war Hugh was a tremendous hitter, and as a small boy I saw him bat for Sussex against the Australians in 1938. For fifteen minutes he scratched about scoring 1. Then the ball started disappearing to all corners of the ground, mostly full straight drives and on drives, and he

reached his hundred in 57 minutes, the fastest century of the
season. But he never hit like that after the war and struggled to
make the runs which had previously come flowing from the bat.
He was the most obviously nervous batsman I've known; if he
was batting at number 6, when one wicket was down, he would
be all ready to go in and be chain-smoking with his batting
gloves on. In 1949 we won a most exciting game with Middlesex
by five wickets. While Hubert Doggart and Jim Langridge
were making the partnership which really won us the game,
Hugh would not let anyone who came into the little captain's
dressing-room leave the room. By the time we had won the
match the room was so crowded you could hardly see out of
the window.

Jim Langridge, our senior professional, took over as captain
and during his three years the team gradually changed as
younger players arrived. Jim was a kindly, thoughtful cricketer,
as he is a kindly, thoughtful man. He would pretend a sim-
plicity about the game which masked a deep knowledge of it.
Lecturing to some schoolmaster coaches once on 'Captaincy
—tactics in the field', he illustrated a point—"Sometimes I'll
say to Cornie (Jim Cornford) 'Would you like your second slip
over to leg slip' and he'll say to me, 'I don't care. Put 'em
where you like!' "

There is some very complicated jargon at times in cricket.
One day Gubby Allen was talking about the theory of bowling,
and he used terms I had never heard of before. All bowlers, he
said, were either 'front footers', 'back footers' or 'clickers'. These
words refer to the last stride before the ball is delivered. With
a right arm bowler the right foot either comes in front of the
left foot ('front footer'), or behind it, or 'clicks' up to it. The
point that was being made was that it is almost impossible to
bowl really fast if you are a 'back footer'. I thought I would
tease Jim Langridge, guessing that he would not know this
piece of theory. "Jim," I asked, "are you a front footer, or a
back footer or a clicker?" "I'm a comer-up-to-'er" was his
immediate reply. He knew all about it, and he had a good
Sussex translation for 'clicker'.

I was tall, gangly and awkward, when I first played for Sussex and I had a dreadful run of dropped catches in 1949. Confidence means so much in fielding, and of course the more nervous I was the worse I became. I was dropped into the 2nd XI, and spent a long time each day with Jack Oakes hitting me catch after catch. I worked for hours at my fielding in the next few years, as I've always felt that any young man ought to be able to make himself into a competent fielder. I specialised in fielding close to the wicket, particularly in the gully or at one of the short legs. By 1953 I reckoned to catch anything that came within reach, and I think I had as much enjoyment from fielding as from any part of the game. And if a really difficult diving catch 'stuck' it was the most exciting moment in cricket. But it needs constant practice to keep the reactions quick and when in 1962 I came back into the Test side after some years away from it all I was to have another of those horrible runs of dropped catches.

Being dropped from the Sussex team seemed to spark off something new. I made 100 that match against Essex 2nd XI and was brought straight back into the team for the next match against Glamorgan. We fielded first and had half an hour's batting overnight. On the Monday I got hopelessly 'stuck' against some tight, defensive bowling. After three hours in all, I had made 43. George Cox, who knew me well, was batting the other end. At this point he came up the wicket, and said rather aggressively, "You say you can hit the ball through the covers. Well, put your leg up the wicket and hit the ball." The next over I did exactly that; I suppose my feet started moving properly; certainly my confidence flooded in. I went on and on hitting them, and passed my first hundred for Sussex. George made a splendid century at the other end.

The last over of the day started with me at 198. Jim Langridge, who had just come in, came up to me and said, "Don't run a single. You can get a two easily." First ball I played for an easy single and said, "No." Wilf Wooller, Glamorgan's captain said, "That's the game, is it?" and put all his fielders back to give me one but to save two. The next four balls were all hit hard and straight at a fieldsman. Last ball of the day Alan Watkins bowled me a slow long hop; I hit it very hard straight at Phil Clift, an excellent fieldsman. But he dropped it, we ran one, and I finished that day 199 not out. I reached 204 next morning and I was awarded my Sussex cap. Confidence grew and I was a different player after this. Next match I made 147 against Leicestershire, who looked quite different from the giants against whom I had played my first match two years before. And the following match I made 130 against Surrey—and 0, to keep me in my place.

Sussex had helped me to love cricket in a new dimension. First-class cricket offers a different kind of enjoyment from club or village cricket, just as Test cricket is different again. In big cricket there are many occasions when the going is tough when you cannot truthfully say, "I'm enjoying myself". I think the enjoyment is of the whole experience of facing a challenge of skill and nerve in the fellowship of a good team which pulls together. While I can hardly say that I enjoy myself at the moment when I'm going in to bat against Davidson at the start of an Australian Test match, I wouldn't have missed the whole experience for anything.

CHAPTER 3

NEW HORIZONS AT CAMBRIDGE

FIFTY-EIGHT stone steps, frequently with a puddle on each from the damp that streamed down the walls, led to the two rooms I shared with a friend I had known at school and in the Army. Trinity Hall has been part of Cambridge University since 1350. It isn't one of the showpiece colleges which visitors never miss, like Trinity on one side of us or King's two away on the other side. But it stands there by the sleepy little river in the heart of the University, its stone buildings handsome and intimate, if damp, a small college for Cambridge, having three hundred men. It was founded for the study of the Law, and as I had ambitions to be a Barrister-at-Law, to Trinity Hall I went. The plan was to read History for two years and Law for my Third year.

Every week two or three of us would go to a 'supervisor' and read him an essay. The shock of my first supervision still remains with me. At school I had studied Latin and Greek and Ancient History, and I had been told that my answers had been right or wrong. When I had finished reading my first History essay at Cambridge, I waited nervously for my supervisor to tell me the mistakes I had made. Instead he merely said "Yes," and went on to talk about the subject and the ideas I had written about.

I was beginning to discover that education is not simply memorising dates and places, but dealing with the world of people. People cannot be classed simply on one side or the other as 'good ones' and 'bad ones' as they often are in Western films on Television. And I had to learn to argue a case, matching idea with idea and weighing them up.

There is danger in the University approach. A friend of mine, brilliant at his subject, said to me at the end of his University years, "I don't see how you can be sure about anything." He understood every opinion but had none of his own. Education should not leave us at this point, uncommitted to any position. It warns us not to take sides without duly sifting the evidence, but it should not hold us back from committing ourselves to definite beliefs and ideals. The tension of true education is to hold decisive beliefs and at the same time to listen to others who think in another way, and to respect them.

It isn't only the ancient buildings and the calm beauty of 'the Backs' which make up the traditions of a place like Cambridge so that every place in the University is sought by ten. With most undergraduates living in colleges there is time for a common life in a way which a University cannot offer where all live in lodgings some distance away and simply meet over lectures and a hurried lunch. In that common life there is time for sport and music, theatre and politics, for coffee and talk. We would try out our half-believed theories on one another and talk far into the night as men have done at Cambridge for hundreds of years.

It was natural that religion should be one of the topics we discussed. Whether we had strong convictions or not, this was a subject about which most of us would have something to say. Usually we went round and round in circles, pouring scorn on beliefs we disliked, but rarely speaking positively of what we did hold. We usually avoided talking about Jesus Christ Himself. This was too personal and embarrassing by far.

It had always been like that in my life. We could discuss good neighbourliness, or the needs of the poor; we could talk about the new rector's habits, about criticisms of the Bible, or about religious fanatics. But somehow it seemed almost indecent to speak about God and Christ, and I doubt if I had heard anyone speak simply of trust in God since my mother had talked to me as a child.

I do not want to be misunderstood: I am very grateful for the upbringing which I had. My home was one where I always felt wanted and trusted. My mother went to tremendous lengths to take an interest in the things which mattered to me. My mother, my sister and I would have long family conferences, and I think I learned much of how to behave *naturally*, without striving to impress others, from the security of my home. At school I was taught much in the way of being reliable and of being a man of my word. Most of all I was taught the tradition of service, of doing things for others, which I regard as the greatest part of what is good in public school education.

My father had helped to found the Chelsea Boys' Club and had made many friends in that sort of circle. Looking back it seems strange that I never then thought very hard about serving others in this kind of way. I knew little about the needs of those who lived in our great cities, and there was no strong urge inside me to find out or to do anything about them. Perhaps the greatest reason for this was that I was too unsure of myself and my own faith to think that I could help anyone else. Only it was true that I wanted to find a job which had to do with people. I went around sometimes in those days with Tubby Clayton (founder padre of Toc H) who was my father's cousin. Tubby is a man with a happy gift of friendship which produces easy relationships whether he is with a docker or with the Queen. These experiences certainly strengthened my interest in others, but going round to meetings with the great man did not produce more than surface relationships for me. It was to be much later before I ventured deeply into the different relationships and challenges which the East End of London offers, and began to learn for myself.

Christian ideas of worship and morality were impressed strongly on me as a boy. I was confirmed young and tried to have a regular discipline of church-going. I held strong ideals as a teenager; when I was sixteen I remember having a sharp argument with an older man who said that there was no point in having ideals. I believed strongly that I should try to follow Christ's example. But as I grew older and moved out of the well-marked grooves of life at home and at school, I became more and more dissatisfied. It was not that I questioned the ideals. But faced with life among men of all beliefs and none in the Army, the ideals seemed impossible. I knew what I ought to do, and at least half of me wanted to do it, but something always seemed to drag me away from it. St. Paul's words about his own life are a good description of how I felt: "The good which I want to do, I fail to do; but what I do is the wrong which is against my will."*

Strong in me as well was the feeling that God was away in the distance. Prayer seemed like looking up to a cloudy sky. Occasionally the sun would break through, but mostly there was a heavy, overhanging cloud. God did not seem near and real in everyday living, and I found myself praying sincerely mostly when I was up against some crisis or personal failure.

When I reached University I was not consciously 'searching for God'. I would not have felt that I needed to look for Him. The way things seemed to me was that I was already on the road, and must struggle on, becoming a little more religious until one day perhaps I might arrive. The idea that I might not be on the road at all had never occurred to me.

It needed a blunt and aggressive preacher from the United States to jolt me into thinking. Dr. Barnhouse aroused strong feelings during the week of his Mission to the University. He set out to provoke and stab our consciences into thinking. Constantly he attacked the view that being a faithful church member made a man right with God.

Neither at the time nor since then did I agree with everything he said, but one great truth got through my defences and has stuck in my mind ever since. I could persuade myself when I compared my life with others that I was as good as most and better than some. But on the first night that I listened to Barnhouse I realised that I was facing God Himself, was judged by His standards, and that I desperately needed to be forgiven. I saw that sin could not be limited to three or four outward actions; "We have left undone those things that we ought to have done"—that mattered just as much as the other part "We have done those things that we ought not to have done." I needed to be forgiven most because I had turned my

* This quotation from the Letter to the Romans is from *The New English Bible* as are all my quotations from the New Testament.

back on God, gone my own way. And whether I thought I was better or worse than the next man was neither here nor there once I really became aware of God. Again and again Barnhouse returned to his great theme that no man can climb up to God by his own efforts to be kind, neighbourly or religious. Only by the totally unreserved love and grace of Jesus Christ can anyone be accepted. I believe this was also the great theme of the Apostles: "For it is by His grace you are saved, through trusting Him; it is not your own doing. It is God's gift, not a reward for work done. There is nothing for anyone to boast of."

I only went to hear Dr. Barnhouse preach because John Collins asked me to go with him. We had met a week or two before on the squash court. After a very close match which finished 10–8 in the fifth game we had gone off for a cup of tea together. Cricket meant nothing to John, but I remember that when we met a second time he had found out enough about University cricket to take an intelligent interest in what he realised had a foremost place in my life. Clearly he was interested in me as a person. He asked me if I would go along to the Mission with him. My reply must have been a very encouraging one. "I can't come every night," I said. But I went with him to Great St. Mary's Church on the first evening, and after the service I walked back to his room. We sat round the fire and over a cup of coffee we talked until late. Somehow I sensed that John "had something that I hadn't got", and he was ready to explain simply what his faith meant to him.

Ever since then I have vowed to try to be as simple and direct as I can in explaining the Christian faith. I had felt that preachers had often been assuming far too much knowledge and Christian experience and had therefore left me lost and unmoved. I went down to my old school to preach some years ago and the chaplain said to me, "Of course, you don't assume faith in the boys." And I cannot assume, because a boy has gone to a school with a Christian foundation and is a regular church-goer, that he understands the simple truths of how God can meet his needs. I know how long it was for me before the mists were penetrated.

Four! A cover drive off Sobers at Leeds 1957. Alexander the wicket-keeper for West Indies.

Opening with Hutton against India at Manchester 1952.

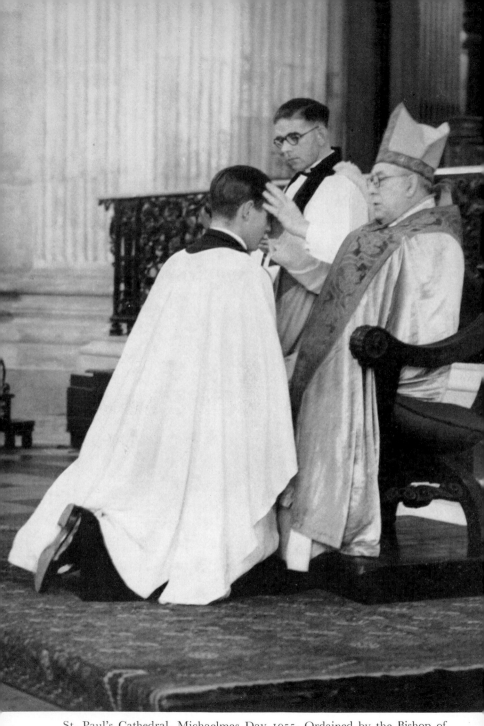

St. Paul's Cathedral, Michaelmas Day 1955. Ordained by the Bishop of London, the Rt. Rev. J. W. C. Wand.

This began with something negative. I saw how much I needed to be forgiven. I saw too that by trying my hardest to follow Christ's example I could never climb through the mists and the cloud to God. Forgiveness had to come from His side. Once I had come this far I listened with quite new urgency to what John Collins told me about Jesus. Numbering Himself with us sinners, deliberately walking to a criminal's death, going out as far as the furthest sinner is from God, He tasted the blackest moment of the sinner's experience as He cried, "My God, My God, why hast Thou forsaken Me?"

I understood the force of words I had heard many times in the Holy Communion service: "He made there . . . a full, perfect and sufficient sacrifice . . . for the sins of the whole world." If Jesus Christ has taken our place on the cross, He has made it possible for us to be forgiven, and to be sure of it. I need no longer mutter about "doing my best" and "never doing anyone any harm". I can stand with the Church of all the years and say, "I believe in the forgiveness of sins"—and mean it. The Christian claim that we can be sure that God has forgiven us is not boastful, because it is a matter of accepting something which He has done for us. He gives something which we can never deserve. We accept it—or better, we accept Him.

I said to John Collins, "This would be wonderful. But it wouldn't be any good. I should be just the same person, and I should never be able to keep it up." The same thing has been said to me over and over again by others who are thinking seriously about the claims of Christ. John helped me to see that there are two answers to this fear which holds so many back from becoming truly committed Christians. First it is quite true that we let Him down—all of us. The Christian Church never claims to be a company of those who have achieved righteousness: it is a band of those who know they are sinful and accept His undeserved forgiveness over and over again.

But the second answer is in a sense the greater; if you sincerely ask Jesus Christ to come into your life as your Friend and Master, you will never be quite the same. A new force will have been let loose in your life. Trust in Christ means putting your

D

hand into the hand of a living Friend whose promise is, "I am with you always." That evening in Cambridge I heard a verse from the Bible for the first time, which in picture language seemed to make this all so clear. "Here I stand knocking at the door; if anyone hears My voice and opens the door, I will come in and sit down to supper with him and he with Me." It made it very plain to me. Either He was outside the door of my life or He was inside. Though I had, so to speak, talked to Him through the keyhole or on the doorstep, I knew very well that I had never sincerely asked Him to enter my life and take charge of it.

I walked back to my rooms in Trinity Hall late that night. I knew that it was more important than anything else in the world that I should become right with God. I knelt in my bedroom and, praying in my own words, I asked Christ to come into my life to forgive me and to be my Friend and Master. Then I prayed something like this, "Lord I don't know where this is going to take me, but I'm willing to go with You. Please make me willing." I knew that this was what I wanted to do today. But I was afraid of myself. Perhaps tomorrow I would not feel like following Christ. "Please make me willing" was an honest prayer, telling Jesus of my own fears.

This all happened to me very suddenly in one sense. But there had been years of Christian background which helped me to understand what it was all about. It was as though a jumble of loose threads fitted into place. Our response to Christ may be sudden or gradual and it has long seemed to me one of the more futile of religious arguments to say that it must *always* be sudden or *always* gradual. What needs saying is that God treats us as reasoning people and calls from us a conscious response to His love. We shall not drift into the Kingdom of God without thought or decision.

It has often been thrown at us that if we are sure of Christ's forgiveness, we shall simply go on sinning as much as we please. This leaves out the power of love. If I do something that hurts my wife and she forgives me, I do not say to myself, "I can go on being beastly to her because I know she'll go on forgiving me." Love doesn't work like that and in fact there is nothing which will so much make me want to be different as her continuing love. The motive for serving Christ is not a stern sense of duty or a desire to be worthy of God's goodness. We can never be that. Gratitude is our motive—gratitude for something we could never deserve. And this is the motive which changes men's lives.

There are those who dislike this kind of language. It smacks too much of enthusiasm and emotion for them. But our Lord said, "Love the Lord your God with all your heart, with all your soul, with all your mind and with all your strength." *Emotionalism* is an enemy of true religion, appealing to our feelings without touching our minds. But if we are to obey this command we must not be afraid of allowing our *emotion* to come into play alongside the mind and the will.

There was no magic change of feelings or of my actions after I prayed that prayer to Christ. Perhaps the first difference was to think rather worse of myself than I had before. Some weeks later I joined a Christian house-party for a week. I said to myself, "I didn't know there were people like this." I did not mean that they were perfect: they were ordinary young men of my own age who were sincerely trying to work out the friendship of Christ every day. Discussing problems of Christian living and simply sharing a common life with them, and with other Christians in Cambridge, particularly in the Christian Union, made the idea of the Church as the family of God come alive. I know that I would never have begun to grow up in the faith if I had not seen a great deal of other Christians.

I questioned, as an enthusiastic young Christian was bound to do, whether it was right for me to spend so much time playing cricket. Perhaps the whole of life must be given to sterner things. As I prayed and thought, I tried to understand what Jesus Christ's attitude would be. He worked with his hands until He was thirty years old; He made time in the middle of His work of teaching and healing to be at the wedding party of a young couple; He said that He came "that men might have life, and have it in all its fullness". He constantly shocked

the religious men of His day by having meals with the ir-
religious. He came to do His Father's will, not on the sidewalks
of life, but in the middle of the world of men. I believe that
today He wants His followers in the middle of every walk of
life, and I am persuaded that it was His will for me to give
some years to playing cricket.

I have often been asked if religion and cricket can mix.
Brian Booth, one of Australia's great batsmen, was taken to
task by a newspaper for saying that God wielded his bat for
him. I believe that by leaving out other things he said at the
same time they made this appear to mean something he did not
intend. Brian is a great friend of mine and we have discussed
this at length. Certainly as a Christian he believes, and I
believe, that health, strength, quickness of eye, all come from
God. Success comes from God—and so too can failure. If I say
my prayers faithfully this is no guarantee that I shall make a
hundred next time I go in to bat. I may make a duck. But I
can make duck or hundred to the glory of God—by the way I
accept success or failure.

This is not fatalism, which says, "It is the will of God.
Whatever will be, will be. There is nothing I can do to change
things." No member of the Australian team would accuse
Brian Booth of tamely accepting failure with a shrug which
feels there is nothing he can do about it. He is deeply respected
by his team-mates as a thoughtful, calm and hard-working
player who pulls his weight in the team 100% of the time. And
such success as I have known has come because I have worked
hard and refused to accept failure without a fight.

There is a mystery about God's part and our part in all
Christian living. "You must work out your own salvation in
fear and trembling; for it is God who works in you, inspiring
both the will and the deed, for His own chosen purpose." A
Christian is called to make time to try to learn God's will in his
everyday affairs; he should commit every part of life to Him in
prayer; then, conscious of his need of God's help in it all, he
will strain every nerve to do the very best he can.

If I am asked what difference my Christian faith has made to the way I have played cricket, I think first about the pressures of the game and getting on with other cricketers. There are times, especially in big cricket, when it feels more like an ordeal by fire than a game. To believe that I am in the place where God wants me to be, and that He is beside me in it has helped me greatly to be relaxed and properly alive.

Batting for Sussex one day I found myself growing very angry with the other side. It was a difficult wicket to score on and the field-placing seemed to me to be ultra-defensive. For a fast-medium bowler long-off and long-on were both right on the boundary and every other fielder was defensively placed. I am afraid some heated words were exchanged between me and the bowler. Anger has never improved my batting and, instead of making a hundred as I should have done, I got out at 92. One member of our side was all ready to 'stir it up'. "You were quite right," he said, to me, "I think they were disgraceful tactics." But as I sat and thought of my behaviour as a Christian, I knew that I couldn't leave it at that. When the other team came off the field I went into their dressing-room and apologised to the bowler in front of them all. He shook my hand, and we have been good friends ever since. No doubt it would have been far better if I had never been angry in the beginning, but had it not been for my Christian faith I believe the row would have been left to simmer and friendships broken.

The year's work had to be done by mid-April if you were going to play cricket for the University. There were some who, with great self-discipline, put in a hard stint of work before a day's cricket. But playing from 11.30 a.m. to 6.30 p.m. six days a week made it very difficult to do any significant amount of work because first-class cricket is a tiring game mentally and physically. Exams came round at the end of May, and I would try to take a week away from cricket to revise immediately before they began. Most of us passed our exams but it has always been rare for a cricket blue to do very well in Honours lists.

Every April 120 hopeful cricketers would be invited to come up early for the Summer term. Some came from two years of

National Service, some straight from school, some from countries overseas: divided into groups of twenty they would be at the practice nets at Fenners every day. After a week there would be the Freshmen's Trial, a two-day match between two teams of Freshmen. Then there would be a two-day Seniors' Trial, followed by some other match to give the probable University team practice before the first county side came up. There would be about nine matches at Cambridge against first-class counties, about six county matches on a tour round the counties ending up with the Varsity match against Oxford at Lord's early in July. We always hoped we would discover some quite unheard of player from all these trials, and I think both Doug Insole and John Warr won their way into the side without anyone's knowing about them before they came to Cambridge. But usually the 'bush telegraph' would have told of likely cricketers coming up.

A delightful Australian, Bill Hayward, played in our Freshmen's Trial. He had played his cricket in the sun at Adelaide, and the only form of cricket head-gear he had brought to England was a floppy, white, sun-hat. He wore this on the field in the Freshmen's Trial, his first game of cricket in England. It just happened that it was the only day I ever played when it was actually snowing.

Bill was a useful medium pace bowler, a cheerful batsman and as good a fieldsman as I have ever seen. One incident is printed clearly in my memory. Cambridge were playing the South Africans in 1951. Jackie McGlew edged a ball from Warr very fast along the ground wide of second slip where Bill Hayward was fielding. McGlew, very nimble, was setting off for a run but turned back quickly as Bill dived full length to his right to stop it. Before the batsman could get his bat back in the crease Bill had jerked himself up and flung the wicket down to run him out. He teaches in Sydney now, as well as ruling his own family tribe, named Tom, Sam, Dan and Kate—the last of whom he delivered in the car as he was driving his wife Alison to hospital.

I was given a chance straightaway and made 130 in my first

match (against Sussex!). For a while everything went right for me. The greatest day was against the West Indies. I had a heavy cold and might have said that I wasn't fit to play if it had not been my first chance of playing against a touring side. Wearing two or three sweaters I went out to bat with John Dewes. I took first ball from Hines Johnson, 6 feet 5 inches tall, who had taken 10 wickets for 96 in the last Test match against England in the West Indies in 1948. The wicket-keeper went and stood well over twenty yards back and the slips even deeper. I wondered what terrifying pace was coming. In fact it was a gentle medium pace ball which bounced three times before it reached the wicket-keeper. Hines Johnson was also feeling the cold, and the Fenners wicket was very easy-paced.

We got away to a good start, and, when the young slow bowlers Ramadhin and Valentine came on, we hit them all round the field. We had never heard their names before as they had been selected for the tour after only three first-class matches between the two of them. John Dewes and I put on 343 for the first wicket before he was out for 183. Hubert Doggart our captain, came in and we added another 150 in ninety minutes before I was out, exhausted more than anything, for 227. We eventually made 594 for 4, and naturally were very pleased with ourselves. We might have got an early breakthrough, but we dropped some easy catches and Stollmeyer and Christiani gave them a good start. Then we dropped Worrell early on and he made 160. But the real lesson we received was from Everton Weekes: cutting and hooking anything short with tremendous power, very quick to skip up the wicket to drive the slow bowlers, and driving in all directions off the back foot, which I had never really seen done before, he massacred our bowlers. Eventually West Indies made 730 for 3, Weekes 304 not out.

Soon after this batting started to seem as difficult as it had seemed easy before. One small score followed another, 4, 3, 0, 0, 9, 0, until I felt I should never get any runs again. One of these games was against Hampshire and Vic Ransom was bowling for them. I had played against him before and remembered that he had bowled big in-swingers. After a little a ball appeared to me to swing in and I let it hit my pad, thinking it would pass wide of the leg stump. Just as it hit me on the pad I realised that the ball in fact was swinging the *other* way. In despair I thought I must be plumb out l.b.w. But there was no appeal from the bowler. A little later I asked the umpire whether it hadn't been a little close to being out. "Oh no," he said, "It was missing the off stump easily." When my judgment was telling me that a ball outside the off stump was outside the leg stump, you may imagine that my confidence took some time to return.

This run of low scores started in a very remarkable match. Four of us, Doggart, Dewes, May and I, were selected to play in the Test Trial match at Bradford, Dewes on the England side, the other three for the Rest. For the three of us it was our first representative match. We arrived at the ground to find a large crowd, and the sun shining down on a wet wicket which no one had bothered to cover. Yardley won the toss for England and put us in to bat. At a quarter past one we were all out—for 27. Jim Laker had taken 8 wickets for 2 runs. It would have been 9 for 2 if Evans hadn't stumped 18-year-old Freddie Trueman with the quickest piece of work I've seen. Trueman swung at a ball from Alec Bedser which lifted sharply, and went between bat, pads, gloves and all. Evans, jumping a foot off the ground, took the ball outside the leg stump and somehow flashed the bails off before Trueman swung his bat round.

The match was a farce as a Test trial and we were beaten by lunch on the second day. Some said it was more bad batting than good bowling and we heard the commentator on the radio say, "The ball has turned, but it's turned slowly." At just that moment Roly Jenkins tried to drive a ball from Laker that was pitched well up to him. The ball bit, turned sharply and hit Jenkins on the shoulder. It was as bad a 'sticky' wicket as I have ever seen. I can speak up for the batsmen, because, you see, I was the other one that Laker didn't get out. I was out before he came on to bowl. It was a superb piece of bowling and our spin bowlers had neither the control nor the power of spin to equal his. This was the first time I had played against Sir Leonard Hutton who was the greatest player on a turning wicket that I played with. He made a beautiful 85 to the Yorkshire crowd's delight, which grew when young Freddie bowled him out. Since Jim Laker came from Bradford, even though he played for Surrey, the crowd thought it was a wonderful Test Trial.

Eventually I got into the runs in another big partnership with John Dewes, 349 this time. I was lucky and was missed three times—by Sussex. Often it seems that a batsman needs a lucky break to climb out of a run of low scores. But, even though I was a Sussex boy, they didn't drop the catches on purpose! Knowing my own side's bowling was an advantage, of course, though not all the time. Charlie Oakes, who was a brilliant natural cricketer, without ever quite translating ability into runs and wickets, was our leg-spin bowler. At least he looked like a leg-spinner: he would come up with arm, wrist and fingers whirring as though the ball must fizz away in a leg break. But in fact it would drift in a little from off to leg and he often trapped a batsman l.b.w. who expected the ball to turn. Whenever a batsman came in against us, who hadn't seen Charlie before, his partner would go over to him, and whisper. We all knew that he was saying, "He doesn't turn the ball from leg." I had, of course, warned my partner of this before Charlie came on to bowl. First ball he bowled me I played for it to come in a little from the off. Only this one *did* turn. But my luck held, and it turned too much, and missed both bat and stumps. For the next five years Charlie kept saying to me, "I wish you'd got a little edge on that one."

Hubert Doggart was a wonderful all-round games player. He captained Cambridge at Cricket, Soccer, Rackets and Squash Rackets and won a half-blue for Rugby Fives for full measure. At his best for Sussex and Cambridge he was a dashing stroke-maker with a strong pinch of the daring. He loved to sweep the ball behind square on the leg side. In 1950 he made 159 not out on a slowly-turning wicket against Tom Goddard and Sam Cook. He kept sweeping Sam against the spin off the middle stump for four. Sam had never seen anyone get away with this for long and kept on thinking that he must get him out: so he wouldn't put a man back to stop the four.

Hubert was given a very tough baptism of fire for his only two matches for England. They were the first two Tests against the West Indies in 1950 and Ramadhin and Valentine that year made the most dominant pair of slow bowlers between O'Reilly and Grimmett and Laker and Lock. The sweep which helped him make 159 against Gloucestershire let him down against Ramadhin at Lord's and he was l.b.w. for 0.

We went to Lord's in 1950 as red-hot favourites to beat Oxford, as we did all three years that I played for Cambridge. It is never a pleasant thing to be over-fancied, and, in the event, in the three matches we drew two and lost one. The Varsity match is unique in its way. In Test cricket there are five matches in a series in which to 'come good'; but the whole University cricket season is made or marred by one match. It is often a 'nervy' sort of game with both sides too conscious of winning—or of not losing. Sometimes good cricketers do not do themselves justice in it.

When I captained Cambridge in 1952 I told the team that I thought you could easily work yourself up into too nervous a state about the University match. I said that we should try to play the match as a normal game of cricket; and I suggested that it might be a sensible thing not to arrive too early at the ground on the first morning, as sitting around waiting for 11.30 to come can increase the tension. One of the team, who had played before said, "I don't agree at all," so I said, "You go to the ground whenever you like." He set off from the hotel, about a mile from the ground, at 9.15 a.m. saying, "I shall never be ready." And he wasn't. As we were going out to field he called, "Wait, I haven't got my boots done up."

We won the toss in 1950 and went out into the electric atmosphere of the first morning of the big match. So much always hangs on the start and the opening batsmen have two responsibilities. First they must try to 'see off' the fast bowlers so that they don't take a quick wicket while the ball is stil shiny and new. Secondly they must get the score moving along at a reasonable pace, for, if they go too slowly, they may do the team more harm than good as later batsmen have to take great risks to speed things up. Often running short singles is the best way to keep the score clicking along at the start.

As I walked out with John Dewes for my first University match, I naturally felt rather nervous. But I was encouraged in an unexpected way. We passed the Oxford fast bowler, Australian Tony Jose, on the way to the wicket. As I looked at him I realised that he was far more nervous than I: it had never occurred to me before that moment that a bowler might be as much on edge as a batsman. I think most of my nervousness vanished at that point.

Oxford's best bowlers that year were Divecha, bowling fast-medium and Van Ryneveld who bowled his leg breaks very well. Every time we looked like getting thoroughly on top someone was out. Peter May was very unlucky to be run out, and Hubert Doggart was caught by the wicket-keeper on the leg side: he tried to tuck away a short ball from Van Ryneveld and only just touched it. I made 93 before Donald Carr bowled me with a short ball which turned a lot. I was trying to hit it for four past cover point and the amount of turn beat me. We were all out for 200.

John Warr was our only really hostile bowler: he was never genuinely fast, but he was lively and a tremendous trier. He could make the ball swing away from the bat and he kept the batsman guessing with a good change of pace. He took 4 for 44 and Oxford were out for 169. For a while in our second innings we were in trouble but Peter May played an excellent little innings of 39 and Mike Stevenson made 64 not out. Rain delayed the innings too long for the match to be finished.

May came into his own the following year. Previously he had always been a brilliant stroke-maker. Now he tightened up his defence and added a great determination to his flowing range of strokes. He was very strong off the back foot and from the first time I played with him he was able to force a ball just short of a length wide of mid-on with a straight bat, a shot which few learn until they have played first-class cricket for years. I rarely saw him hook or square-cut, but he played all the straight bat shots. Some Australian critics said that his driving of the fast bowlers along the ground back past the stumps was the fiercest they had seen. In 1951 he was in wonderful form. He needed to be for us at Cambridge. Dewes and Doggart had gone and the batting was very weak apart from Peter and myself. I had been in Australia in the winter and was working desperately to cram a year's work into six weeks before exams. Somehow I managed to do this and passed in the II 2 class. Cambridge honours degrees are classified as I, II 1, II 2, and III. One supervisor entered into the spirit of the thing; he was a Yorkshireman and very keen on cricket. I went to him to study American history. At the end of the M.C.C. Tour of Australia and New Zealand I had bought the large two-volume History by Morison and Commager, and in a feeble kind of way tried to read it on the aeroplane coming home. I mentioned to my supervisor that I had bought this. "You don't want to read Morison and Commager," he said. "It's all in Nevins and Commager" and produced a 200-page book. "Go away and read that."

So I only came into the side after exams were over and played rather badly. I had found the going tough on the tour in Australia and was struggling to take in to my game some of the lessons I had learned. For weeks Peter May carried the side alone. Just before the Varsity match he made a superb 178 not out against Hampshire. Then came two inexplicable failures against Oxford: it was a low scoring game. Divecha changed that year to bowling off-spinners and bowled them extremely well, supported by magnificent fielding. Boobbyer played a stubborn and brave innings of 80 for Oxford, and finally we were left 219 to win. May made 33, Sheppard 42, and we were beaten in a thrilling finish by 21 runs.

For some strange reason Peter May never made more than 39 in the Varsity match. No one could say that he had not got the 'big match temperament' for he was one of the calmest of

cricketers. His next match after Oxford v. Cambridge was his
first appearance in Gentlemen v. Players. He made an excellent
119 not out and was selected for England against South Africa
the following week. In this, his first Test, he made 138. Soon he
became our greatest batsman.

When I was brought back into the England team against
Australia I found him toughened as a player. He had come
through the fire of great Test matches and he was even hungrier
for runs than he had been before. There was an intensity of
concentration that I have only seen matched by Hutton and
Barrington among English players. This was obviously the
quality which Sir Donald Bradman had above anyone and I
feel only Bobby Simpson has had it in quite the same way
among more recent Australians.

Many things in Peter May did not change. It was always
delightful to bat with him, as I was lucky enough to do a great
deal. There have been great players who wanted all the strike
when they were batting, so that you had to be ready to run like
mad for a single on the last ball of the over. But Peter remained
an absolutely unselfish player, as he has remained an utterly
modest man.

I do not think he took very easily to captaincy. His personality
is not an assertive one, and there were many moments when
he wanted to withdraw from the centre of things. He is a
sensitive person and found it difficult to take in his stride some
of the more wounding, personal things that were written.
When he was captain in Australia in 1958–9 his fiancée,
Virginia, went out for part of the tour. England were doing
badly, and any scapegoat must be found. So some newspapers
proclaimed that he was giving no time to the team because he
was so wrapped up with his fiancée. Others on the tour have
told me that this was quite untrue, and that it was doubly
hard as he had always gone out of his way to find points of
interest about the team to give the journalists at their weekly
Press conference. He felt very bitter towards the Press after
this, and there is no doubt in my mind that the fierceness of
this pressure had a big part in speeding the day when his

business commitments in London and his happy home in Surrey pulled him out of big cricket.

He struggled through the West Indies tour of 1959–60 suffering from ill health and had to come home before the Fifth Test for a second operation. But David Allen, who was a new boy on that tour, told me how Peter made each player who wasn't in the Test team feel that as captain he was relying on them to play the big part for him in the non-Test matches. He made each man believe that he was truly wanted.

Peter May was unlucky that his team in Australia contained a number of great players who were a little 'over the hill'. And in 1961 in England illness prevented him from playing regularly. So he went out of Test cricket with the music playing rather softly in the background. Perhaps a stronger lead would have brought better results. I don't know. He certainly had a hard job. He was a most conscientious captain, and a tough competitor who yet brought a certain gentleness into the Test arena.

One change for the good has certainly come to Test cricket in the last few years. When I first played against Australia in 1951, most of their side would not look at us on the field and there was a minimum of contact off the field except by friendly individuals. "Do you think you can learn to hate these Australians for the next six months?" did not represent the whole atmosphere in which the game was played, but those words were actually said to me by a senior player on the ship going out to Australia in 1950. In 1956 it was quite different. The two teams talked on the field, were in and out of each others' dressing-rooms: the game was played just as hard, but in a new atmosphere of friendliness. This atmosphere has stayed, thanks to the attitude of recent Test cricketers, and I hope it always stays. But the captains in 1956 were May and Ian Johnson and much of the credit must go to them.

CHAPTER 4

TEST MATCH APPRENTICE

A TELEGRAM sat on my locker in our dressing-room at Hastings in 1950 when we came in for the tea interval: I nearly missed it, and it was only just before we went out to field that I saw it. Cyril Washbrook was injured, and I had been selected to take his place for England. As we went on the field the evening newspapers being sold round the ground were saying the same thing. The next day the *Daily Mail* had a banner headline, SHEPPARD'S HAPPY DAY. I had made 129 against Surrey and had been selected for England. But in fact I felt far from happy about it: partly this was probably sheer nervousness, but it had been a struggling innings against Surrey. I didn't feel that I was playing very well, and I didn't believe that I was ready for this. It was typical: you long for something, dream of it, and when it comes, you want to run away.

The West Indies had marched in triumph all over England and when we m et for the last Test match they were leading by two matches to one. The 'Three W's' had murdered our bowling and in their different style had delighted English crowds. At one time or another each of them could have claimed to be the greatest. Frank Worrell most naturally attracted the English eye: a classical, graceful stroke player, he played all the shots that our coaches taught us to play. He stayed in the game longer than the others, batting lower down the order, and not making so many runs, but bringing a mature knowledge of the game to his captaincy. Like a skilled jockey giving a frisky colt his head, he encouraged his players to go out after their shots and brought about the great Tests of 1961–3; the tie at Brisbane, the tightest of finishes at Adelaide and Melbourne, the tremendous drawn match at Lord's, and their conclusive win at the Oval. A cool captain, he knew that cricket was meant to be enjoyed. He has made as great a contribution to the well-being of cricket as any other cricketer.

Clyde Walcott was a different kind of batsman. All was power here. Six feet three and massively built he would stand up on his back foot and hammer the ball with all his strength. In 1953–4 England baited this strength by regularly posting a silly-mid-off to him when he first came in. The mighty Walcott could not avoid challenging their impudence, and would sometimes get out to a rash shot because of it. One of my favourite stories of Yorkshire solidarity is of Freddie Trueman during that tour. I need to explain that Harry Halliday was a useful county batsman, who couldn't quite hold a regular place in the Yorkshire team. You would have said that he was a strong back player. Someone during the West Indies' tour was praising the great Walcott: "He hits the ball harder than anyone in the world." "Aye," said young Freddie, "I don't think I've seen anyone hit the ball so hard off the back foot as him and Harry Halliday." Elephant and mouse!

But for sheer dominance and brilliance on good wickets my own choice in 1950 would have fallen on Everton Weekes. He was built small, very like Bradman, and I guess that he played more like Bradman at his best than perhaps any other player I saw. The hook and the cut were ferocious blows: he was so quick up the wicket to slow bowlers that Roly Jenkins at Nottingham (when Weekes made 129 and Worrell 261) said it wasn't fair and that he should wait at least until he bowled. Weekes was run hungry, but in his greatest days he would throw the bat at the ball with sheer exuberance and a succession of strokes streamed out which no one else would attempt.

He is a delightful man, whose friendship I have greatly enjoyed: there has never been a more popular professional in the Lancashire League than he was at Bacup. Now he has returned to his own island of Barbados as official cricket coach. I'm told that as he drives around the streets, where he played as a boy, in a bright red car, he is thought of as the uncrowned King of Barbados.

Barbados has a population of no more than 245,000. Yet
within two years of each other there were born in that island,
Worrell, Walcott, Weekes, three mighty men of cricket. No
people in the world is keener on cricket than the Barbadians,
and the list of some of their other post-war players makes
impressive reading: Goddard, Atkinson, Hunte, Cammie
Smith, Nurse, Sobers, Hall and Charlie Griffith.

The shock to England that year was that two slow bowlers
we had never heard of before the team was selected tied webs
round all our greatest batsmen. We had expected good fast
bowlers, but they played little or no part in the Tests. The
victory calypso their followers sung at Lord's did not mention
them but

The bowling was superfine
Of Ramadhin and Valentine.

Valentine took two or three paces, and bowled his left arm
spinners with a rather chest-on action not at all like my
classic picture of Hedley Verity. But in 1950 he had a mechanical
accuracy, a little outside the off stump. He spun the ball a lot
and he bowled rather quicker than most slow bowlers. Perhaps
his greatest triumph was on the hard, true wickets of Australia,
where he captured 24 wickets in the five Tests of 1951–2. Since
then he seems to have lost the accuracy, so that batsmen can
just stop the good ones and hit the one bad ball an over for
four runs. He is a simple, loyal and amusing team man. At
Leeds in 1957 Ramadhin went for a rather rash run, I threw
the wicket down, and he was run out. When he reached the
dressing-room, Valentine said, "Ramadhin he try to steal a run,
and the Reverend, he say, 'Thou shalt not steal!' Bom!"

Ramadhin brought a touch of magic to the bowling crease.
A neat little man, he always wore his sleeves buttoned at the
wrist. A few quick steps, a lively arm action, and then the
batsman was guessing. He had great power of spin, off breaks
and leg breaks, and I never met an English batsman that year
who had the slightest idea which way the ball was going to
turn. He varied his pace cleverly and I would certainly say that,

E

as he bowled that year, he was the best slow bowler I have ever faced. Any slow bowler bowls as well as he is allowed to, and the English tragedy of 1950 was that Denis Compton, who was the quickest on his feet of our batsmen, and the most likely to have 'chased' him, was unfit.

The Australians determined to hit Ramadhin as hard and as often as they could and he never bowled so well against them. In 1957 he took 7 for 49 on a good wicket in the First Test and it looked as though it would be 1950 all over again. West Indies replied to our 174 with 490 and Ramadhin took two quick wickets again. But May and Cowdrey set themselves to play him with great determination and put on 411 in a record English partnership. Having taken nine wickets very cheaply his next wicket cost him, I believe, 450 runs. By the time I came back into the England side for the Fourth and Fifth Tests that year, the magic had definitely left him. He was still bowling accurately but without any hope of reward. The last time I had played against him had been in 1950, and I needed to learn for myself that there was now no mystery. In 1957 he bowled mostly off-spinners. Suddenly he bowled me a very obvious leg-spinner; my mind was still in 1950 and I thought, "It can't be as obvious as that," and waited for the ball to pitch before assuming that it was a leg-spinner. But it was as obvious as that and there was no longer any difficulty in seeing what he was bowling.

Australians call most of their cricket grounds 'Ovals' but in England 'The Oval' means only one ground—Kennington Oval in South London, where the last Test match is always played. In my first Test match in 1950 we lost the toss, and I ran round the boundary for a day and a half while West Indies made 503. Jeff Stollmeyer, an elegant opening batsman, who was always good to watch, went for 36, but left-handed Alan Rae was like granite to break through: he scored 109 in five hours and Worrell made 138 without ever quite playing at his best. Rae went stubbornly along, with hardly a stroke for an hour at a time. Then suddenly he would jump in and hit Wright high, over his head two or three times in ten minutes.

Then he would go back into his shell again. Gomez and Goddard added 109 and we faced a high score.

Hutton and Simpson gave us a steady start, but, when I went in number three to join Hutton, Ramadhin and Valentine were wheeling away with great accuracy. Hutton was in no trouble himself and every now and then a cover drive or an on drive would flash out, and four runs would be added on to his score. I reached eleven and was beginning to feel at home: just as the last over before lunch was going to start the Surrey secretary announced over the loudspeakers the birth of Princess Anne. A large crowd of West Indians were sitting together in a block, commenting loudly and happily on every incident. "Let's have a wicket for the Princess," they shouted. "Let's have a wicket for the Princess." I was the Princess' wicket. Ramadhin bowled up a teasing long half volley. If it hadn't been the last over before lunch I should have tried to drive it for four. But something in my mind said, "Wait on until after lunch." I played an indecisive shot and was bowled.

Hutton went calmly on his way; Denis Compton played well for 44 and we were 229 for 2 when there was a tragic muddle and Compton was run out. Still Hutton was there at the end of the day with 160 not out. Then rain stepped in, the sun came out and the ball started to turn all over the place. John Goddard bowled himself, medium pace off-cutters, turning the ball quite a lot, while every now and then a ball jumped sharply from the pitch. The one vital question was whether we could save the follow-on. If we did, we might bowl West Indies out quickly on the pitch while it was wet and have a chance to win. If we failed, we should have to bat again on the bad wicket, and there would be no chance.

Hutton played superbly on the bad wicket: where for everyone else it was a struggle to survive at all, he seemed to score easily, and even managed to take most of the strike. But he ran out of partners only 10 runs short of our target—202 not out in a total of 344. In the follow-on Hutton was out for 2 to Goddard and we never looked like saving the game. I battled it out for two hours for 29 and was quite pleased as the ball was turning a lot. But we were all out for 129 and West Indies won the Test series three matches to one.

Few cricketers gave Freddie Brown's team any chance to beat Australia in 1950–1. We had taken a heavy beating from the West Indies and Australia were still king of the castle. Yet if the run of the game had gone differently we might have been two up instead of two down after the first two Tests.

The First Test at Brisbane was one of the craziest matches ever played. I was in bed with 'flu on the first day, and listened with increasing delight to the commentary on the radio. Moroney, playing his only Test match against England, was out for 0, and on a good batting wicket Bedser and Bailey were on top all day. Harvey made 74, but Australia were all out for 228.

Overnight there was a tremendous thunderstorm, the dread of all cricketers at Brisbane, and instead of being a small score 228 now looked an awful lot of runs. But we hoped against hope that the wicket might not be too bad. I was allowed out of bed and reached the ground about an hour late. I could see the score-board from outside: we were 49 for 1 wicket and my hopes grew that all was well. But, once inside the ground, I saw the fielders standing in a complete ring all round the bat. Miller and Johnston were bowling and the ball seemed to 'kick' straight up as soon as it pitched. Washbrook and Evans had been swinging the bat hard, and for a little all had gone well. But soon wickets started to fall, and during that fantastic day I saw 19 wickets fall for 81 runs. With great skill Hutton made 8 not out; the moment the ball pitched the least bit short he turned his back and took it between the shoulders.

At 68 for 7 Freddie Brown declared, in order to get at them while the wicket was still bad. The luckless Moroney, who had played extremely well on their tour of South Africa, duly completed his 'pair'. Three men were out before a run was scored. And at 32 for 7 Hassett declared. We only had to make 193 to win. If only we could last out the hour or so till the close of the play, the wicket would roll out well on the next morning. Hutton and Compton were held back: but wicket after wicket fell. Two seemed to be thrown away, one run out, going for a fourth run, another caught at mid-off. At 30 for 6 at last Hutton emerged from the pavilion, the lion lured from his den. He only got halfway to the wicket when the umpires decided that the light was too bad (an appeal had been made three wickets before), and everyone came off the field.

On the next morning we had 163 to win and four wickets to fall, but Hutton and Compton were two of them and the pitch had rolled out well. Hutton started with Evans as his partner, and 16 were put on before Evans was out. In came Denis Compton and the tension grew. Sam Loxton was fielding very close at forward short leg and as Compton arrived he took another step closer. First ball from Bill Johnston lifted a little and went straight into Loxton's hands. Compton out for o! Each of us felt something like a punch to the solar plexus. Only two wickets were left, but now Hutton and Freddie Brown went after the bowling. 31 were added before Brown was out for 17. Doug Wright was last man in, not a great batsman in Test company. He kept a straight bat in front of everything, and Hutton ran a single at the end of the over whenever he could. This was a unique innings of Hutton's. Gone was the usual caution, the typical forward defensive shot, head down over the line of the ball. He drove the fast bowlers so hard that Lindwall had no fielder within 30 yards of the bat. Then he drove him back over his head and high over the top of extra cover. It was magnificent, but it could not last long enough. Wright was caught off Iverson for 2 out of 45 they put on, and we had lost by 70 runs, with Hutton 62 not out.

It was plain that Australia's batting had become more brittle, and that, if only our batsmen could do their stuff, we had a great chance to beat them. Apart from Bradman, they had also lost Barnes from the tremendous batting array of 1948. Sid Barnes had moved into the Press Box along with his writing assistant. During this Brisbane Test Sid went up to Neville Cardus, doyen of all the cricket writers, and said, "Say, Neville, how about you put a carbon under yours for me today and

I'll do the same for you tomorrow?" He gave me an earnest piece of advice: "You don't want to run round the boundary all day. You'll kill yourself." "What shall I do, then?" "Throw your arm out. Do it big. Go off the field and let the twelfth man come on. Then specialise in some place—like silly leg." I fancied I caught an authentic note of autobiography about this. Sid Barnes always liked to be 'agin the government', but he has frequently been a most generous man in his own way.

Brisbane remains in the mind like a fantasy, with its tumbling wickets on the rather primitive ground, as it was then, with the roller pulled by an ageing horse, who had to be taken out of the shafts and led round after rolling each length of the pitch. The Second Test in the vast modern bowl of the Melbourne Cricket Ground is more like a nightmare in the memory. I think I was the only member of the team who was not playing who sat through the last agonizing moments. We had been 70 runs short at Brisbane; here we failed by only 28.

Again Bedser and Bailey broke through the Australian batting. Bedser took 4 for 37, Bailey 4 for 40, and Australia were all out for 194. Doug Wright had one of his most inaccurate days and eight overs cost 63 runs. Hassett hooked him for many of these without taking any risks and scored 52. We made a disastrous start and at lunch on the second day had lost six wickets for 64.

Freddie Brown now played a captain's innings which might have come out of a schoolboy story. Whenever he had the chance he drove hard and high. One of Ian Johnson's slow off-spinners disappeared into the crowd in the vast 'outer' stand. With his handkerchief knotted round his neck, growing redder and redder in the face until you felt a blood vessel must burst, Freddie Brown became an outsize edition of John Bull to the Australian crowds. His 62 that day was one of the bravest innings I've seen, and with 49 from Godfrey Evans we came right back in the game leading Australia by 3 runs. Australia reached 99 for 1 in their second innings before a brilliant throw from Cyril Washbrook at cover-point hit the middle stump at the bowler's end, and ran out Harvey. At once Bedser, Bailey and Brown put the grip on the Australian batsmen and they were all out for 181. Freddie Brown dropped the leg-spinners which he used to bowl and instead bowled medium-pace swingers with great accuracy and life. That innings he removed Hassett, Loxton, Lindwall and Tallon for only 26 runs.

When we set out to make 179 to win, everything seemed to depend on Hutton who was dropped down to number four for this match. Compton's knee had given trouble again and he was not playing. The bowling was tight, cracks in the wicket now meant that some balls kept very low, but we inched along closer to the target. Hutton reached 40 and then went to drive Bill Johnston high over mid-on. He did not 'middle' it and skied it to Loxton. Again we felt the sick feeling in the stomach, and after that we were never quite getting there.

At Sydney we won the toss and made a rapid start, Hutton and Washbrook whipping Lindwall and Miller all over the place. But Miller popped up in another way. Standing apparently disinterested at slip, he suddenly anticipated to his right, dived and took a fantastic catch to dismiss Washbrook from an edged slash off Ian Johnson. Now Hutton and Simpson with really good batting, carried the score to 128 for 1 wicket. Then Miller struck again. In one over he removed both Hutton and Compton.

There were many moments during that series when Keith Miller came on to bowl, and we felt that the whole match rested on the next three or four overs. He seemed to laze his way happily through a game and every now and then stir himself to some great effort. He was a tremendous figure on the cricket field with his supple, powerful figure, his unruly mane of hair which had to be smoothed down so often. There were some very hot-blooded moments about his cricket, particularly when he was bowling, but he was a warm and friendly opponent. Somehow his batting declined, as it became increasingly hard work against the great England bowling sides of 1953–6.

He had an unwavering fan on the Sydney Cricket Ground
in 1950–1. An enormous voice from an unshaven face would
boom from the Hill, "Miller, you are a great batsman; you
are the greatest cricketer in the world; Miller, I love you!"
I know the face was unshaven because one day I was fielding
on the boundary and the voice asked if I would shake hands.
I did, and in a moment my hand received a kiss which grated
like a scrape of rough sandpaper. I thought he wasn't going to
let go of my hand before the next ball was bowled. His comments were always generous to us. One day Trevor Bailey
ran round in front of the Hill, made a good stop, and threw
the ball back straight and full pitch to the wicket-keeper.
"Bailey," called the Voice, "that wasn't magnificent. It was
miraculous." But Miller was his favourite.

Freddie Brown again played well—79 this time—driving
with great force. We reached 258 for 5 but slumped to 290
all out. Bailey had his thumb broken by a short ball from
Lindwall, and, as if this wasn't enough, Wright pulled a muscle
in the course of being run out. I had been out in the nets with
him every day for long stretches while he bowled and bowled
to recover his accuracy after the Melbourne Test. I told him
where the ball pitched and threw it back to him so often that I
knew how well he was bowling again at that moment. The two
injuries were a cruel blow, and as thirteenth man I had to go
out to field, while all the bowling must be done by Bedser,
Warr and Brown. The three stuck to it gallantly, but Australia
forged well in front. Miller made 145 not out to the delight
of his own crowd, Johnson 77 and Hassett 70. The three
bowlers made them work very hard and during a slow spell
someone in the crowd behind me called out, "Look out, Hassett,
you'll get pinched for loitering."

If only we could make a good score we still had a chance
with Australia to bat last, but this was Jack Iverson's great
day. He had broken abruptly into Test cricket at the age of 38,
a heavily built, unathletic looking man. When he came in to
bat he carried his bat in the middle like a business man carrying
his newspaper to work on a Melbourne tram. Actually it

wasn't his bat: he didn't have one of his own but used a dark oil-stained club bat with the initials of his Grade club cut deeply on the back.

But he was not in the Australian team to bat: he was another mystery bowler to confound us, after a summer of facing Ramadhin. Where Ramadhin was perky and quick like a sparrow, Iverson lumbered smoothly up to bowl like a heavy rook gliding in to land. He had a freak grip and was able to bowl a leg break with an off-break action. But this would not turn on a good wicket, and he relied mainly on the off-spinner, which I thought he bowled as an ordinary spin bowler bowls a googly. He was very accurate and extremely difficult to score off as on a good wicket he bowled at the leg stump with six men on the leg side. I had to smile to myself when some Australian journalists attacked our off-spinners in 1962–3 for using an ultra-defensive leg-side field—of five men. I remembered not only Iverson, but also Toshack, who bowled medium pace, mostly outside the leg stump with six fielders on the leg side.

But at Sydney Iverson had a wicket which turned a little. He aimed at the off and middle stumps, bowled superbly well and took 6 for 27. We were beaten by an innings and Australia had won the ashes again. Iverson never played much more cricket: in the field he regularly stopped the ball with his boot and treading on the ball one day, he turned his ankle over. He had a lot of trouble with this later on.

A tour can be hard for the players who are not in the Test team. I went eight weeks in the middle of this tour during which I only played four first-class innings. They were all on the Sydney Cricket Ground against Lindwall, Miller and Alan Walker who were all quicker than any bowlers I had met before, and I did not reach ten in one of these innings. Between the big matches there were a number of games against country elevens. Sometimes we met good bowlers in these games, but though I was making a lot of runs in them, it seemed to count for very little when I came back to the big matches. In the State and Test matches no runs were given away and you could

wait for weeks at a time if you were hoping for someone to
bowl a full pitch or a long hop.

Against South Australia just before the Fourth Test I
played two long and slow innings. Eventually I lost patience
with Jack Wilson who was nagging away with great accuracy:
I tried to hit him over mid-wicket, and instead the ball went
straight up in the air. When I came off Len Hutton said, "I
don't think you should have tried to hit him over mid-wicket."
"Well, where should I have tried to hit him?" "I should try
to hit him square past cover, or straight back past the stumps."
In the second innings Hutton was batting when Wilson came
on to bowl. First ball he hit him for six, high over mid-wicket.
When he was out I thought it was my turn to have a go.
"What's all this?" I said. "You tell me not to hit him over
mid-wicket, and first ball you hit him there." He smiled, "Ah,
you must do what I say, not what I do."

To keep the whole of the side playing enough cricket, it
would be better to take, say, fifteen players to Australia, but
then that does not allow for some to fail, even though you could
replace injured men by air. We had seventeen players in
1950–1, but after the injuries to Bailey and Wright, two
more bowlers were flown out, Tattersall and Statham.
They came straight from mid-winter in England to play
their first match against a South Australia Country XI at
Renmark.

Renmark is a most dramatic place to spot from the air. In
the middle of a huge area of parched, brown country, suddenly
a dark green rectangle appeared, and we came down among the
orange groves and vineyards made by irrigation from the
Murray River. But it was hot. The temperature was 103 in the
shade and a hot wind was blowing, and, when Brian Statham
ran up to bowl his first over in Australia, I thought he was
never going to get as far as the stumps.

A four-day state match and a six-day Test match followed
at Adelaide and the temperature never went under 98° in the
shade. And cricket is not played in the shade. Roy Tattersall
played in all these first three games after his arrival—in a

borrowed pair of boots, as his new pair did not fit him—and this required great courage.

Arthur Morris made his first big score of the series in the Fourth Test. He had become Bedser's 'rabbit' so often that a determined attempt was made to shield him from our great bowler. Ken Archer took first ball and was out in Bedser's first over. Lindsay Hassett came in and stayed firmly at that end until Bedser had a rest. Alec was a tremendous bowler, and particularly dangerous to the left-handers: his in-swinger was an out-swinger to them and both Morris and Harvey fell to him a great deal. Few English county cricketers knew just how good Alec was: he certainly tried for Surrey, but always a little extra was brought out when he played for England. His great shoulders rocked as he took his nine easy paces to the wicket and the whole of his body went into his action. When the ball was new and shiny he would make his in-swinger dip in late, but this was far from his only weapon. He was always ready to 'get stuck in' and peg away with perfect length and direction just outside the off stump, making the occasional ball move a little either way off the seam. Then he would occasionally bowl his famous leg-cutter—less frequently than commentators sometimes suggested. On a good wicket it would not turn, but it was a little slower and would bounce higher, while on a wet wicket it was almost unplayable as it would turn and lift.

Alec Bedser was one of the hardest working bowlers I met, and also one of the most thoughtful. He improved enormously from his first appearance for England in 1946 to his great series when he took 30 Australian wickets in 1950–1 and 39 in 1953. He would have his little moan about how things ought to be run, but he would always play his part to the full. I often had a little go at him about taking more trouble over his batting. But he said, "I can't do all the bowling and all the batting too." He never practised batting much and it tailed away from the day in 1948 when he defied the Australian bowlers and made 79 most valuable runs.

On the morning of my first Test against the West Indies

Alec was lying face down on the table having his back mas-
saged. I must have been looking rather nervous, and he said,
"Would you like to have a knock? I'll come out and bowl at
you." It was typical of the kindliness of the man. He has
always been keen to help young cricketers, and he made an
excellent assistant manager of the 1962–3 team to Australia
and New Zealand. I hope he will be able to take time off again
from the very flourishing typewriter business, which he runs
with his twin Eric, to do this kind of job. It was difficult to
recognise one twin from the other until you knew them well,
and they had an uncanny way of thinking identically. I think
it was Doug Insole who told the story of playing at the Oval
against Surrey, probably soon after Alan Rae made that solid
century against England. Alec finished an over and remarked
to Doug, "Takes a bit of digging out, this Rae." Eric appeared
from deep third man, down the other end of the Oval and
promptly said to Insole, "Takes a bit of digging out, this Rae."

All this has taken us away from the Fourth Test at Adelaide
where Morris escaped from Bedser and made an excellent 206.
For us, Hutton was always in command, but without sufficient
support. He made 156 out of our total of 272. Jim Burke made
101 not out in Australia's second innings in his first Test match.
Miller made 99 when, going for his favourite late cut off Doug
Wright, he both hit his wicket and was bowled at the same
moment. Neil Harvey made 68 and we found ourselves needing
503 to win. It was all to win and nothing to lose, and Hutton
and Washbrook made a brisk start. A superb catch by Sam
Loxton wrecked any hopes we had. Hutton who was going
splendidly and had made 45 pulled a ball hard and high to mid-
wicket. But Loxton leaped and caught it. Washbrook was out
and Compton went for 0—all to Bill Johnston. Winning was
now out of the question, but a determined stand could still
save the game. Reg Simpson and I had a long partnership,
before he was caught for 61. I held on for nearly four hours for
41, but we were duly beaten.

At Melbourne in the Fifth Test Australia reached 111 for 1.

Morris made 50 and Hassett 92. But Bedser and Brown broke through and had five wickets each. They were supported by some good catching, and Australia were all out for 217. I can only remember Godfrey Evans missing once chance in this series; it was a little dolly catch which went straight up in the air, and for some extraordinary reason he dropped it. But he took some amazing catches: Neil Harvey seems to have been particularly unlucky with Evans' catches. In the Second Test he leg-glanced Alec Bedser with a firm stroke and was looking for it to go for four when Godfrey caught it, standing up to the wicket on the leg side. There was another Harvey leg-glance which he caught, diving full length, off Frank Tyson four years later. Godfrey Evans did a tremendous amount to liven up the fielding of an England team, and his energy always seemed to last the day and the night out.

Our bowlers had done it again. Could the batsmen at last match their effort? Hutton and Simpson had a fine partnership which carried our score to 171 for 1. But Hutton looked exhausted at tea and soon after was bowled for 79 by Graeme Hole having a rare over before the new ball. Lindwall and Miller took the new ball at twenty to five after a long day in the field, and right through till six o'clock they stormed back at us. Reg Simpson held firm at one end, without scoring a run for a long period. Denis Compton nearly saw the new ball off, but was caught off Lindwall at ten past five. The drinks came out as I went in to bat, and Keith Miller ran off the field. Whatever he chose to have instead of the lemon squash, certainly the result was tremendous. It was as fast a piece of bowling as I have seen. One ball to me I thought was going to knock the bat out of my hands. I was caught at the wicket. Freddie Brown was greeted with eight bumpers in the sixteen balls he had. He was out and Evans followed. We had gone from 171–2 to 216–6. It was a tremendous piece of fast bowling, and Miller signed off with a very fast bumper last ball of the day.

But Reg Simpson was still there and in the morning he really cut loose. Bedser, Bailey and Wright went quickly, but

Tattersall put an obstinate bat in the way of anything straight. Simpson drove, pulled and cut his way to a memorable 156 not out. He was always a great player of the fast bowlers and that day he made Lindwall and Miller look very ordinary.

Again Australia fell mainly to Bedser. Wright produced the perfect leg-break to remove their soundest player, Hassett. Graeme Hole, a graceful stroke-maker, played an excellent innings of 63, but we had only 95 to win. After eleven defeats since the war without a solitary victory, we hardly believed that we could do it even then. But Hutton saw us through and we won by eight wickets. That win was much more than a consolation prize: it was the turn of the tide for England's fortunes, and we did not lose a series to any team from then until 1958-9.

That series could have gone so differently if only our batting had not been such a one man band. The hardest part for all of us on this tour was Denis Compton's failure. There has never been a more popular cricketer: his feelings were always transparent, like a schoolboy's, and this was true now as he failed time after time, as it had been in his golden years when he seemed to be able to charm the ball away unfailingly. Undoubtedly his knee injury took away his great quickness of movement. He lumbered now, where once he had skipped. I had heard of how he had been woken up from a peaceful sleep to go in to bat in his first Test: now I saw him nervously trying to read a book to take his mind off the game, while waiting to bat. All the more credit to him that he came back after this disastrous series to play, not the dominant role, but nevertheless a most valuable role for his side. And after another knee operation he came back in the last Test in 1956 to play a much-needed innings of 94. I stood and cheered as he came in from this, with his hair still falling all over his face in defiance of his hair cream advertisement, as it had always done.

Cyril Washbrook had a poor tour, rarely surviving long after the slow bowlers came on, Reg Simpson was not consistent enough and the new boys like myself contributed little in the Tests. So match after match it was Hutton v. Australia when

we batted. I doubt if he ever played better than on this tour.
Prior to it there had been days when he had showed marked
dislike for the fast bowling. Before the First Test in 1950–1
he made a century against New South Wales: with the total
200 they took the new ball and Lindwall, Miller and Walker
gave him 'the full treatment'. For a few overs every other ball
was a bumper. He clearly did not like it, once sitting down on
the wicket with his bat over his head as I had seen in a photo-
graph taken in 1946–7. Eventually Lindwall bowled him ou
with a full toss. But I never saw this happen again: there were
of course individual balls which he did not like, but he was
always the fast bowlers' master. I have often wondered if that
brilliant 62 not out at Brisbane did not give him a new kind oɪ
confidence against them.

He was the complete opposite of Denis Compton as a player
and as a man. Denis was easy-going, forthcoming, his character
open as a book. And at his best there was always an air of
casual enjoyment about his batting, though this masked great
determination and skill. But for Len, batting was a stern
business. Fleetwood-Smith told me that he was bowling at him
when he made his world record 364. "When he was 290, I
bowled him a half-pitcher. He could have hit it anywhere for
four. But he got over it carefully and steered it away for a
single. I said to him, 'That was a terrible ball. You could have
hit it anywhere for four!' 'Aye,' he said. 'But there might have
been a trap in that.' " Len had learnt in a hard school where
they used to say, "We don't play this game for fun." He had
to remodel his technique after breaking his wrist so badly in
1940, that many said he would never play again.

In the post-war years he carried tremendous responsibility,
and, going in first, he met the full fire of Lindwall and Miller
at their greatest. Hutton has been called a hard cricketer and
a hard captain, but it needs to be remembered that Test
cricket was a very tough business for him. As a captain he was
comparable with Bradman, rather aloof from his team,
respected as the master player, knowing every trick in the
game, and ruthless in leading his team to victory. Colin

Cowdrey told me, "He never missed a trick" in the 1954–5 series.

My own opinion is that under both Bradman and Hutton Test cricket was a little too like total war. But when you start asking, "Who started it?" you find you have to go further back than you expected. When Bradman was a young man, he was so good that England could not get him out by normal means (I was going to say 'by fair means'). So they invented 'Bodyline'. Others were hit by Larwood and Voce, but it was directed primarily at Bradman. This was the roughest and most deplorable chapter in all cricket history. So it was not surprising that when he had two great fast bowlers as his spearhead he did not prevent them from handing out what they called 'The full treatment'. Nor was it surprising that Len Hutton, having been on the receiving end from Messrs. Lindwall and Miller, should have always longed to have two fast bowlers to lead his attack. When he had them, Alec Bedser's medium pace was shipped overboard at once, as Jardine had dropped Maurice Tate twenty years before. It must be said that Tyson and Statham never bowled anything like the number of bumpers which were bowled earlier at Hutton.

Len Hutton did not make friends easily: he was too closed-in a personality for that. But if you persevered beyond that sphynx-like front which he used in order to keep many at arm's length, you found real friendship and interest, based on a lovely home which his delightful wife Dorothy had made with him. He has a dry sense of humour which likes to talk in riddles and to produce whimsical theories. I was staying in their Pudsey home one day when he propounded at breakfast, "No one with a pink and white complexion, is any good in big sport. No one with a pink and white complexion has won the Open Golf Championship for forty years. Look at Godfrey Evans," he said. "He's got the right complexion, dark jowled ..." "But I've got a pink and white complexion," interrupted Dorothy. "I know, darling. But you're not meant to be a Test cricketer. You're a very good cook. We can't all be Test cricketers."

Samson Obiora
flew to greet Grace
and myself as
Eamon Andrews
hands over the
record of This is
Your Life.

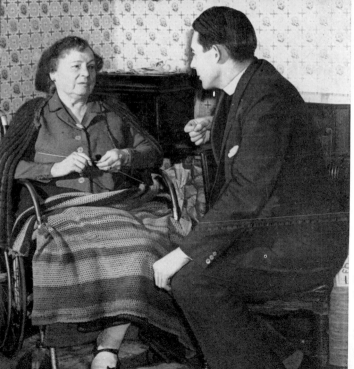

A visit to Mrs.
Withers in her top
floor room.

"The best England team I ever played in." England v. Australia at the Oval 1956. *Back row*: J. B. Statham, G. A. R. Lock, J. M. Parks (12th man), M. C. Cowdrey, P. E. Richardson, F. H. Tyson, J. C. Laker, Sandy Tait (masseur). *Front row*: D. S. Sheppard, D. C. S. Compton, P. B. H. May (captain), C. Washbrook, T. G. Evans.

When I first played for England I tried to persuade him to talk batting to me. At first he tried to push me away; "Go and ask —. He knows a lot about cricket." Eventually he decided he would take me under his wing, and he gave me a great deal of advice. During those later days — was mentioned: "— doesn't know about a cricketer's bootlace," he said.

He was a perfectionist as a cricketer and was perhaps too quick to write off others who did things differently. He found it difficult to share things with others, and as captain, driving himself very hard in his lonely eminence, he wore himself to a state of great nervous exhaustion, which meant that he dropped out of Test cricket when he could still have remained the Master for some time.

I learned a great deal from this tour though I made very few runs on it. Primarily this was the toughening experience of playing at the highest competitive level: learning to be calm in an arena like Melbourne where you feel the lions may be let out at any moment, is vital to becoming a successful Test cricketer.

Technically my batting needed much tightening up. I grew up as a natural off-side player, and was inclined to play my defensive shots away on the off side. I noticed how Hutton got so far over the line of the ball that defensively he always played it straight back down the wicket. Sometimes it would come out on the on side. I learned from him too what he called the V plan—that at the start of an innings you should play into a V only just wide of mid-on and mid-off, gradually bringing in the strokes square of the wicket as you settled down. All this made me set myself further over behind the ball, and, when I came home in 1951, I found myself making all my runs on the on side and unable to hit the ball on the off side at all. Gradually I recovered the old strokes and kept the new ones too.

Other lessons were learned in a different field on that tour. To live up to my new faith, away from regular Christian fellowship, with the constant travelling and the rather brittle, artificial life which international sport is bound to carry with it, was another kind of test. At one stage of the tour my faith seemed to be drifting away from me. Doubts rushed in: "You believe because you want to. It's all auto-suggestion." I had grown up believing that Christianity was true. But I had only thought about it in the way that I might have thought about Plato and his ideas—with distant admiration. Now it was the central fact upon which my own life turned every day and it mattered in a quite new way whether or not it was true.

I climbed slowly out of those doubts. Partly this was by some hard thinking and reading. The classic arguments for the existence of God never swayed me greatly: personally they seemed to me to end in a draw. But if only one could bring into a court the evidence which made the first followers of Jesus believe that he was God! They knew all the difficulties, had seen Him brutally put to death, and had failed miserably to stand by Him. What had changed their lives, making them men of new hope and courage, risking their lives as they answered the greeting, "The Lord is risen" with this ringing echo, "He is risen indeed"?

I came across a little book about this time which has helped me as much as any in answering questions about Jesus of Nazareth and his disciples. As a young man Frank Morison had believed that the Christian claims "rested upon very insecure foundations." Years later he set out to write a book which was to be called "Jesus, the last phase", to explain away the Christian notion that He was raised from the dead. But the harder he looked at the evidence, the more secure he found the Christian foundations to be. Eventually he became persuaded that this Christian belief was the sober truth. The book had to have a new title, for it was now different from the one he had set out to write. It is called, *Who moved the Stone?**

I realised also the importance of Christian friends. I had discovered at Cambridge that John Dewes was someone with whom I could talk naturally about the Christian life. This was something new to me as I had been brought up within a tradition which felt that it was almost indecent to speak about personal faith with another. Bishops you might discuss, or the

* *Who moved the Stone?* by Frank Morison, published by Faber.

choir, or the flowers in church, but Christ, and the daily matter
of trying to follow Him, would bring a strained silence.

One of the great answers to my doubts was to bring them
into the open with someone else who was sincerely trying to
follow Christ. John and I tried hard to make some time each
week to read something from the Bible together, to discuss and
to pray briefly together. And round Australia we met families
who gave us a welcome into homes where it was natural to
speak at times of our faith, and of the work of spreading God's
kingdom. We were both invited to speak to a number of
informal groups of young people, usually in someone's home,
and this too was a challenge which helped my faith to grow.
There is nothing like having to explain to another what your
faith is to make you think it out for yourself. Not infrequently
I meet someone who has a genuine trust in Christ, but whose
religion is a struggling, depressing kind of affair. Often I find
that they have never known the Church as a family which
brings friendships which are truly "in Christ" and which
gives them responsibilities to tackle.

Many of my Christian friends come from different races and
different backgrounds: sometimes we have started with very
little in the way of common interest. But when we find that
we have Christ in common—whether we belong to the same
denomination or not—we are able to meet at the deepest level.
John Dewes and I had met on the cricket field before either of
us had become committed Christians. We were not naturally
drawn to each other; in fact it was rather the opposite. But a
relationship which grew from our common faith developed
into a lasting friendship which extends to a great many parts
of life. I've seen him in action as a teacher with great skill with
boys in England and in Australia where he was headmaster of
Barker College in Sydney for some years.

A flying boat skimmed across the water from Rose Bay and
slowly the lights of Sydney Harbour became more distant. A
modern airliner does the trip to Auckland in three or four
hours, but our flying boat took nearer ten in 1951. A steady

course took us almost due East from Sydney, and the dawn was
a wonderful sight as the sun appeared straight in front above
the clouds. It was as though one vast white fleece was spread
out below us to welcome us to sheep country.

When we landed there was the warmest of greetings from
New Zealanders. The month's tour following five months in
Australia is a hurried affair. But although there was a four-
day match during the week's stay in each city the welcome into
homes meant the beginning of friendships which have lasted
for years.

A British team beating New Zealand at Rugby Union would
be the sporting event of the year. For the All Blacks represent
the peak of a game supported with fervour only equalled in
South Africa. But when the M.C.C. team reaches New Zeland
at the end of its tour of Australia it is quickly made aware
that its hosts do not give themselves a chance of winning. This
sense of inferiority has damaged their cricket: they very nearly
beat a strong England team in their first ever Test in England
in 1931. But they have never come so close since then.

To reach the top in Test matches there needs to be plenty
of tough, competitive, cricket. New Zealand cricketers play
few first-class matches in a summer, but so do the West Indians,
who can produce the finest side in the world from no larger a
population. I believe that were New Zealand to produce one
Test match team which really held its own with England and
the others, other Test cricketers would soon follow on. And the
problem here is perhaps primarily an economic one.

To keep three or four great cricketers playing regularly until
three or four more join them, and then to go on until another
three or four come on is difficult. The business or the family
demands that less time is given to cricket and the team we
played in 1963 had only five who had come to England in
1958. New Zealand had a good team in 1949 with Donnelly,
Sutcliffe, Wallace, Hadlee and Cowie, fine Test cricketers. But
it broke up immediately. Sometimes I have heard it said
cynically, "It's easier to get into a Test side than to get out
of it." But this is as it should be. A team of men who have

measured up to the Test atmosphere, and have some experience
of playing together in it, is much more likely to be more successful than one which is constantly being changed by a crowd
of young hopefuls.

Bert Sutcliffe looked a great player in 1951. He made an
excellent 116 against us in the Test match at Christchurch and
seemed the most complete left-handed batsman in the world at
the time. He played very straight, and was a crisp driver.
Wally Hadlee told me of how Bert first opened the innings.
Otago was playing Wally Hammond's M.C.C. side in 1946–7
and he had decided to ask Bert to go in first. But he thought he
wouldn't give him any time to be nervous about it; so he
waited until the morning of the match. When he saw him, he
said, casually, "I'd like you to come in first with me." The idea
worked so well that Sutcliffe made 197 and 128 in the match.

Many Englishmen would say that the greatest New Zealand
batsman was Martin Donnelly. He had two seasons for Oxford
University as well as playing for New Zealand in 1937 and
1949. He must have enjoyed batting at Lord's: I saw him play
a fine innings of 133 there immediately after the war for the
Dominions against England. In 1946 he made 142 for Oxford
v. Cambridge. In 1947 he made 162 not out for Gentlemen v.
Players and in 1949 206 for New Zealand v. England. For a
little man he hit the ball with great power. But his own country
saw him very little. He never played in a Test match in New
Zealand, and when we looked at the list of century-makers in
the pavilion at Wellington, we found he had only ever made
one century for his own provincial team.

If some claim that Donnelly was their greatest batsman it
would make a good quiz question to ask who was the greatest
bowler from New Zealand. I would unhesitatingly plump for
Clarrie Grimmett who took 214 wickets for Australia, but
came from New Zealand.

Donnelly, Wallace and Cowie had dropped out of Test
cricket and the 1951 New Zealand team leant very hard on
Bert Sutcliffe to provide the runs. But there was another
exciting player who had come at the age of 21 to England in

1949. John Reid was then a tremendous hitter of the ball, without producing runs very consistently. With maturity he has become one of the first three or four batsmen produced by his country. He is an exciting player bursting with power when he walks to the wicket. Against Sussex in 1958 he scored 118, reaching 100 in 86 minutes, mostly from thunderous driving. There was a time perhaps when he was the kind of hitter who needed to bat some way down the order. But he has learned to discipline himself and possesses all the strokes as well as unleashing those vast straight hits every now and then. His greatest triumphs were in South Africa in 1960–1 when New Zealand halved the series two matches all. Reid scored 546 runs in the five Tests at an average of 60 and 1,915 runs on the whole tour, averaging 68.

My last Test match was played against New Zealand in 1963, and a fine tussle it was on the fine ground at Christchurch. As always we had been given a wonderful welcome in New Zealand. The day before the match Alan Smith and I had a memorable day on a sheep station at Waiau in rugged hill country. So often on a cricket tour it is possible to see only the cities, but that day we were able to meet some countrymen. We heard a sheep shearer talk most coherently about country life as well as seeing him take a fleece firmly and expertly off a sheep. A shepherd came riding in with a vast flock, whipped in by his dogs. And we found a bulldozer slowly gnawing a track through the rough hills, which are fertilised from the air. Walter Hadlee came too, who had captained New Zealand when I first played there in 1951. He told us of a tour in Fiji, where there is great enthusiasm for the game. This was not dampened even by the fact that some games were played throughout with the water coming above the players' ankles. I understood scoring was not high, because the ball would not float too far over the outfield. 20 might well be a match-winning total.

We had won the first two Tests in 1963 by an innings at Auckland and Wellington and we made a quick breakthrough in the last Test at Christchurch when Trueman had Playle caught, who had made top score at Wellington. But Dowling and Sinclair then made a determined stand of 80, and it looked as though a big score was coming. Inexperience cost Sinclair his wicket: he hooked a short ball from Trueman very well for four. This often puts a fast bowler on his mettle, and sure enough, the next ball was a bumper, very much quicker. Sinclair went to hook again, but the extra pace got him in a tangle with himself and he hit his wicket. Different batsmen play bumpers in different ways. Some hook them, some duck out of the way, some who are tall play them as much as they can. I used to hook fast bowlers regularly until I went to Australia in 1950–1. I realised then that it was a very different matter against the quickest bowlers. The bowler puts everything in to the bumper and it is so easy to be caught off an edge or a glove. I decided that it was best for me to play the short ball defensively or, if it lifted too high to play safely, to duck out of its way, and hope that the bowler grew bored of bowling short. That was my way: I have seen batsmen hook the great fast bowlers successfully, but they have been very good at the stroke and have picked out the right ball to hook.

After Sinclair (44) and Dowling (40) went out there was a good stand between Reid (74) and Shrimpton (31), who looked a most promising player, full of fight and determination. They would have made a big score if it had not been for Freddie Trueman, who bowled splendidly—30.2 overs, 9 maidens, 75 runs, 7 wickets. There was great speed at times, but always accuracy and the ability to make the occasional ball move even after the shine was off, while with the new ball he made it swing away a lot.

New Zealand made 266 and their bowlers were for the first time given a reasonable score to bowl at. Motz, Cameron and Blair, all right arm fast medium, made batting hard work. Motz was the fastest of them, lively and hostile, and I could see how he had taken so many wickets in South Africa. Cameron was more Alec Bedser's pace and in each match of our short tour seemed to be bowling at one end all the time. This was the fourth innings in which he had bowled against us on this tour and he bowled 148 overs during them. Blair's pace was something in between Motz and Cameron and, like them, he gave nothing away. I made 42 and was feeling in good form when Cameron bowled me with a good one. Barrington, Dexter and Cowdrey all reached 40, but the bowlers stuck to their task and a large crowd saw an excellent day's cricket, with New Zealand fighting their way slowly on top.

When New Zealand batted again they led by 13. Our bowling gave nothing away, but Reid hung on, occasionally flashing out a powerful square cut which left third man standing. No one could stay with him, and though he fought his way to exactly 100, Titmus, Larter and Trueman slowly whittled the other wickets away. If one or two others had played an innings we should have had to make a lot of runs in the fourth innings. As it was we were left 173 to win. Ken Barrington came in first with me; at the end of a long tour in which he had made a tremendous number of runs, he felt he could not concentrate properly. He told me he was going to throw his bat at the ball. Some astonishing shots appeared and he gave us a very brisk start with 45. Alabaster, a good leg-spinner who, I believe, would be more successful if he played regularly on harder wickets, bowled me out for 31 with a beauty which pitched just outside the leg stump and hit the off. Cowdrey held firm with Parfitt and then some fine blows from Barry Knight carried us home by seven wickets. But we had been made to work hard enough to know that, if this side could stay together for a few years, and discover three or four more really good cricketers, they could take on all comers.

CHAPTER 5

LEARNING TO LEAD

AFTER the match against Oxford the Cambridge University team sit down together to elect a captain and a secretary for the next year. Usually the man who is secretary is made captain the following year. I had given this no thought during my first season at Cambridge, as I had assumed that Peter May was the natural choice for our year. It was a very great surprise to me when I was elected secretary. The following year I was made captain and I did some hard thinking about it before the 1952 season came round.

I felt that I knew the game well enough not to make obvious mistakes. John Warr had been a good captain the year before, and we had learned much together. But I knew that captaincy is not simply a matter of making sound tactical decisions: there needs to be a 'spark' which produces enthusiasm from the team, and the ability to make the players want to play for their captain. I reckoned that my biggest danger was that I was likely to be too easy-going, so that we would just drift happily through our matches without any driving purpose. I deliberately tried to react against this danger, and I am afraid there were days when I wanted to win so much that a sense of proportion got lost. With experience it became easier to reach a right balance: I believe it is right to play cricket as hard as possible in order to win. But *how* you play is equally important and it is possible to play to win and still to play absolutely fairly and as friends with the other side.

The Cambridge side in 1952 was an easy one to select and an easy one to captain. Often a university side has to be more than half built up with players fresh from school or the forces, who have played no first-class cricket. We had an unusual amount of experience. Peter May and I were playing in the England team that year, John Warr had played for England in Australia and Cuan McCarthy who had been South Africa's fast bowler, came up for one year. Raman Subba Row in his second season in the side was beginning to show the calmness and concentration which later made him an England player, and Robin Marlar was one of the two best slow bowlers Cambridge has had since the war, rivalled only by Gamini Goonesena. Then we had our Irishmen to bring a little more of the international flavour— Mike Stevenson, who could show as exciting a display of driving as anyone, putting the umpire in fear of his life with his straight driving against Lancashire, and Charles Kenny who was a lively medium-pace bowler who learned more skills all that season. Gerry Tordoff and Mike Bushby made up the batting and both had their days of success.

When the season started, finding a wicket-keeper looked like being our greatest difficulty. In the trials we looked at one and another. At last we remembered Gerry Alexander whom we had thought of as a good club cricketer, but no more. He had been playing college cricket at Cambridge for the last two years. He handled the fast bowling easily and improved all the time in taking the slow bowlers. He proved an excellent wicket-keeper and it was no surprise to me when he later played for the West Indies. Gerry captained the West Indies against England in 1960–1, and then surprised everyone by making a great many runs in Australia in 1961–2. Six Test match players was a remarkable number to have together in a university side.

We had our 120 undergraduates at the nets as usual that year, and, though it was plain that most of the side would choose itself, we still hoped to discover unexpected talent. One day I was sitting behind the nets watching some of the 'Seniors' practising: they had all been at Cambridge at least one season before, and it was unlikely that I would not have heard if there was an outstanding cricketer among them. As I watched I felt that one off-spinner kept bowling with uncanny accuracy. I looked at him more closely; his run up and action were almost identical with Jim Laker's and he was certainly spinning the ball a lot. His name was McGinty and he had bowled medium pace for Cambridgeshire the previous two seasons without doing anything remarkable. He had only just taken up bowling off-spinners in his last season at Cambridge. He was a heavily built man, with sleeves always flopping about, but he could certainly bowl.

He played for us for a number of matches and took 30 wickets, but Robin Marlar was still a better bowler and it did not seem possible to have two off-spinners in the same side. But McGinty would have walked into most University teams. I hope he will forgive me if I write my favourite memory of him. He was bowling his off-spinners around the wicket against Gloucestershire at Bristol and Graveney and Young were batting. Somehow they got themselves in a complete 'Yes—No —Yes—Go back' muddle over a run. The ball was in Peter May's hands at square leg. Martin Young was at the batsman's end and Tom Graveney was three or four yards from him. He had given up all chance of making his ground and was taking his gloves off. McGinty had very properly got behind the stumps, but May's throw was short. Mac stumbled round the stumps to reach it and knocked a bail off: I unwisely called from mid-on, "Take a stump," being afraid that he would forget that he had to pull up a stump once a bail had been knocked off. He certainly did take a stump: he pulled one out, and then set off to get the ball. By this time hysterical advice was coming from all directions, and, having finally got the ball, he finished up on hands and knees knocking both the remaining stumps out of the ground. By this time as you may imagine Tom Graveney had taken heart again and run safely home.

Gloucestershire had a burly and not-too-athletic off-spinner too—emphatically one of cricket's characters—'Bomber' Wells. I have the distinction of having provided him with his first wicket for Gloucestershire. Tom Goddard was injured when Sussex played at Bristol and Wells came in. He took exactly three paces up to the wicket, and bowled extremely accurately for forty overs. When he went back in the dressing-room, having played his first day's county cricket, he remarked to all and sundry, "Well, I can see I'm going to have to do a lot of bowling if I play for this side. I think I'd better cut my run down."

In 1960 when I was playing an occasional match for Sussex a number of cricketers had started calling me 'Rev'. I was batting against Nottinghamshire for whom 'Bomber' Wells was now playing. I edged a ball from him rather luckily past slip. He called down the wicket, "Said your prayers well last night Rev." "Why, didn't you say your prayers last night then Bomber?" "No, I trust to luck."

Cuan McCarthy was a tremendously fast bowler though perhaps he was too nice a man to be hostile as a Test match fast bowler properly should! Like Frank Tyson and Wes Hall he took his wickets by sheer speed and was not able to move the ball about very much. But given some pace in the wicket he could be very nasty: just before the Varsity match I gave him the match off over the previous week-end, and told him to go away and forget about cricket. He reappeared on the Wednesday for our two-day match at Lord's against M.C.C. He has always looked a tremendous figure, six feet three inches of him with an unruly mop of fair, wavy hair—even more bronzed now as he farms his acres down in Dorset. That day at Lord's he looked like a giant refreshed. We lost the toss, and slips and short legs went to our usual positions. But Cuan's first ball nearly went through Alexander's gloves and we all went back about five yards. M.C.C. had a scratch side, and first wicket down came in Harry Sharp an admirable cricketer and coach, but never a 2,000 run-a-year man. Cuan bowled him as fast an over as I have ever seen, including one bumper at which Harry waved his bat just as Alexander was catching it over his head twenty yards back. John Warr said, "Harry, that would have gone in the Mile End Road if you'd hit it." At the end of the over I said to Cuan, "Pitch it up a bit. It's not too serious a game, and he might get hurt." "Oh, someone told me he needed slipping out." he replied.

There had been arguments about whether McCarthy threw or not when he played for South Africa, and these were renewed now that he was playing in English cricket. Having 'declared my interest' that I was his captain in the Cambridge side, I can honestly say that before I knew that he was coming to Cambridge I had formed the opinion that he was not a thrower. He was a very stiff mover when he walked, and there was certainly something jerky about his action, but just before he delivered the ball he came sideways on as a fast bowler should, whereas some bowlers with 'doubtful actions' never get themselves into a bowler's position. After McCarthy was no-balled at Worcester I fielded most days at square leg and simply watched his elbow: in my opinion it went over as straight as a ramrod—but I admit that some of my friends do not agree with me. Cuan said, "I certainly don't want to bowl if my action is unfair."

Throwing is a touchy subject in cricket, and there has been something of a witch hunt for throwers in recent years. Though I have stated my own honest conviction at the time that McCarthy did not throw, I have strong doubts as to whether he would have been allowed to bowl had he come to England ten years later. Once before, in the early 1900's, there were some years of fierce controversy over the action of certain bowlers. I believe that this was finally settled by the counties all refusing to play against one team if a particular bowler was selected.

I have heard some speak as though the recent talk of throwing was a conspiracy of the Englishmen in order to remove good opposing bowlers from the game. And I have also heard it said that throwing does not give the bowler any advantage—that you cannot throw any faster than you can bowl. This is nonsense. I am about the world's worst bowler, but I can throw fast and straight, as I often have, to give batsmen practice in the nets. In addition throwing can give the bowler increased power of spin, a different kind of flight, and the ability to conceal great changes of pace.

This is not an academic question as I can think of Test match bowlers in my time who gained all these advantages from what the laws of cricket say is an unfair action. This is the real point. Any game is played under a code of laws or rules and it is unfair play not to keep them. The laws of cricket say that the ball must be bowled, not thrown or 'jerked' and that if an umpire is not "entirely satisfied of the absolute fairness of a delivery" he is to call, "No-ball." Few umpires do this. Many of them feel that they would be blighting a young man's career if they no-ball him out of the game. They forget that there is another young bowler who may never be given a chance because the thrower has his place in the side.

If you watch schoolboys playing in an area where a thrower is being allowed to play in first-class cricket, you will not have to wait very long before you see some boy with a similar action. This is perhaps the greatest reason why throwing should be stamped on. But an umpire has a horrible job in enforcing this law. Undoubtedly some 'suspect' bowlers are bowling entirely fairly nine balls out of ten. Imagine yourself the square leg umpire watching a fast bowler and trying to pick up the tenth, unfair ball. You have a split second in which to decide and to be sure enough to call, "No Ball". You realise that you need a lot of courage and an electronic computer's brain.

Suspect actions were allowed to get by for some years in England in the 1950's. The majority of English cricketers agreed in 1952 that Tony Lock's changed action was a throw, and he gained great power of spin from this. When umpire Fred Price no-balled him for throwing, he was selected for England two weeks later. Two of us had a long argument with an older cricketing friend in September 1952. We said that he should not be selected for Surrey or England until he changed his action. He replied, "You've no right to stop him bowling like this." A little later he added, "I don't care what we do to beat Australia." "Supposing you had been Douglas Jardine," I asked him, "would you have bowled bodyline to beat Australia." "I wouldn't have had the same field placing," he said.

So it went on until 1959 when Lock himself, persuaded by seeing someone's film of his bowling, decided that it was wrong, and changed his action. I admire Tony Lock tremendously, and I am sure that he would prefer to have been forced to change his action in 1952 rather than feel that a cloud of suspicion hung over seven years of his career. To his great credit he won his way back into the England side as an unchallenged bowler.

Our hands have not been clean, but we have done our best to put our house in order in the last few years. It is time that selectors all over the cricket world refuse to pick a bowler with a suspect action. And umpires should always be supported, if they no-ball someone for throwing. England has not considered a bowler for selection in the last five years if he has been no-balled in that season for throwing. There remains the problem of reinstating someone who has been wrongly no-balled or who has removed the unfairness from his action. Clearly a bowler must be given a chance to 'purge himself'. It seems fair that, if two umpires no-ball a bowler, he should not be selected for a representative side for the rest of that year. But the following year he ought to be regarded as a fair bowler unless he is no-balled again by two umpires.

Back at Worcester in 1952 it was a tremendous shock when Cuan was no-balled for throwing by Paddy Corrall from square-leg. His opening spell had been from Corrall's end, and he had come back for two overs before lunch at the other end. This was the first over Corrall had ever seen him bowl. In the second over no-ball was being called about every other ball. At twenty-five to two Dai Davies, umpiring at the other end, called, "Come on Paddy, man, we'll never get our lunch." When we went in to lunch I sat next to Cuan and naturally there was an atmosphere of some tension: the Worcestershire secretary came in and said brightly, "Well, if it doesn't do anything else, it may bring a crowd in this afternoon." Cuan said afterwards, "That man nearly got his ears poked back."

That match was memorable to me, because I made my highest score in first-class cricket. Worcestershire had outplayed us for two days. They made 295, Roly Jenkins making a bustling 85. He then had a field day against us with his leg-spinners and took 8 for 82. Apart from a whirlwind 53 in half an hour from Mike Stevenson we all collapsed and were all out for 185. Worcestershire made 262–6 declared in their second innings and we were left 373 to win in five hours. This time we made a good start and Raman Subba Row and I put on 202 for the third wicket. I was dropped at 69 but apart from that we sailed along and won by six wickets. We made the runs in four and a half hours and I had 239 not out.

I always enjoyed batting with Raman: he had great composure and determination and gradually added to his power of stroke, though he was never an exciting player to watch. But if we were in a tight spot I liked to see him come in. We had just that situation against Oxford that year, and he did not let us down.

With McCarthy and Warr to bowl for us the lightning wicket we had on the Wednesday and Thursday against M.C.C. would have suited us down to the ground. But when Oxford went out to bat on the Saturday we found the deadest of pitches to bowl on. Nothing would induce the ball to pounce above stump high. The Oxford opening batsman Bush dug in determinedly. Hardly offering a stroke he stayed there for four hours and ten minutes for 62. Alec Skelding, a great cricket character, was umpiring. He said to me after two hours or so of this, "Could you get me some Maclean's stomach powder." "Of course, Alec," I said, all anxious for his health; "aren't you feeling well?" "I've got the belly-ache," he said. "At least I haven't really, but this young gentleman's giving me one." He made another remark that afternoon which meant a lot to at least two of us. He had never watched McCarthy bowl before, and having stood at square-leg for two spells from him, he came over to him when a wicket fell and said, "I've watched you very closely, and I'm quite convinced you don't throw."

Oxford batted out the day at 233 for 6, the best innings coming from a freshman, Colin Cowdrey, who made 55. On the Monday we finally dismissed them for 272, Marlar taking 7 for 104. Our batting came unstuck and Bushby, May, Tordoff and Stevenson were out for 130. I *was* glad to see

From our flat when we first arrived.

CANNING TOWN OLD AND NEW

From the roof in 1963—new blocks rise from the bombed sites.

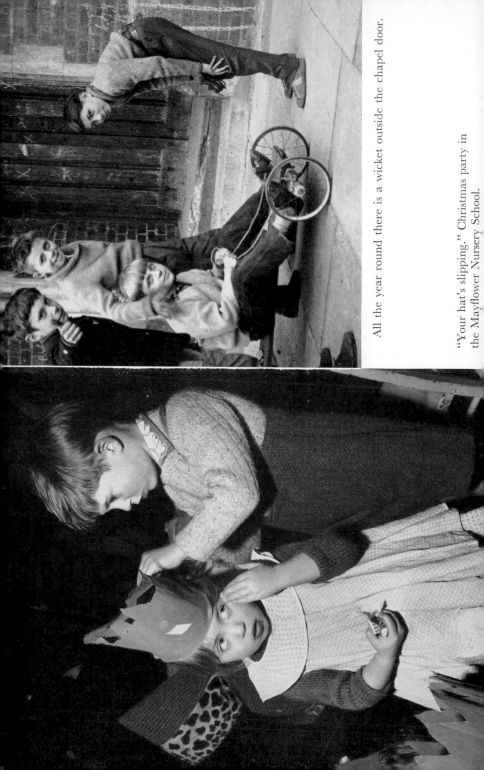

All the year round there is a wicket outside the chapel door.

"Your hat's slipping." Christmas party in the Mayflower Nursery School.

Raman. Neither of us played very fluently, but we fought out
of trouble and put on 119 before I was out for 127. Raman
went on to 94 and Robin Marlar hit well for 48 not out. I
declared before lunch on the last day at 408 for 8, so that we
had four hours in which to bowl them out.

It did not prove long enough. McCarthy made a break at
the start and wickets were falling steadily: but a vital catch
went down and we were held up by a fine innings of 52 by the
Australian Alan Dowding and by extraordinarily brave batting
by Oxford's fast bowler Coxon, who apart from anything else
showed the toughest skull I have ever seen. McCarthy bowled
him a short ball which he didn't like. So, with Cuan standing
at the end of his run watching him, he walked right up the
wicket to the other end and patted the pitch down at the point
where he wished the crowd to think that the ball had pitched.
Most cricketers would have guessed that the next ball might
be very fast and very short. It was, but Coxon had decided to
rush up the wicket before he bowled. The ball struck him on
the forehead: it was not a glancing blow, for the ball fell
beside him. We all rushed forward to see if he was all right,
expecting him to collapse at any moment. But he nodded his
head briskly, and went back to the wicket. We never got him
out, and his courage saved Oxford.

India came to England in 1952. In terms of results they were
not very successful, and India has still not defeated England
in this country. But Indian cricket makes me think of some of
the most talented cricketers the game has known. This is
natural for someone who grew up in Sussex, because probably
our two greatest players of all time came from India—K. S.
Ranjitsinhji and his nephew K. S. Duleepsinhji.

It is no good trying to persuade our oldest Sussex members
that batsmen have ever been as good as 'Ranji' and C. B.
Fry. Certainly they must have been a wonderful partnership—
the Indian Prince, silk shirt fluttering in the breeze, playing
strokes no one else had ever dreamed of attempting, charming
the ball to the boundary with cuts, glides and hooks as well as
the drives, and Fry, a superb athlete, carefully taught in the

G

English school, reducing the art of batting more to a science than anyone had done before. Of course I never met Ranji, but I did see C. B. Fry quite often: he was always a fascinating man, full of theories practical and impractical about every aspect of life, a tremendous advocate of free enterprise. I have long regarded his book *Life Worth Living* as the best cricketer's autobiography that I have read. I felt greatly honoured by his family when they asked me to take his cremation service after he died in 1956.

I met Duleep in Canberra in 1951 when he was Indian High Commissioner. He showed me several photographs of Sussex days, and spoke modestly and happily about his cricket. The senior Sussex players when I started playing had been in the team with Duleep, and always spoke of him with admiration. Everyone I ever heard speak of him talked of his modesty but along with this went a tremendous determination and skill. A favourite Sussex dressing-room story was of a match against Kent at Maidstone. In the middle of a dry spell Sussex found a wicket which had been heavily watered at one end. 'Tich' Freeman, bowling to that end, had Sussex out twice and beaten before lunch on the second day. Duleep said, "I will make two hundreds against them at Hastings." These things are easier said than done, but when the return match came he duly made a hundred in each innings, one of them a double century. Walter Robins once told me that he was the greatest batsman he ever bowled against, which was high praise indeed. Duleep captained Sussex in 1932 when we came within a whisker of winning the championship. It was that year at the age of 27 that he developed T.B. which finished his cricket career.

Vijay Merchant was the best opening batsman that India has yet produced and I watched him make 128 against England in the Oval Test in 1946. He was a graceful player and I remember his late-cutting the faster bowlers again and again. I also remember how England got him out. He was backing up at the bowler's end, and started for a run. Mankad sent him back, and Denis Compton running in kicked the ball hard with his left foot into the stumps. It was more like Compton the Arsenal left-winger, but Merchant was out.

India was the first overseas team that I ever watched, playing against Sussex in 1936. Merchant was their great player then and a cultured 52 started off the innings. Dilawar Hussain kept things going by a hard-working 122. But I have to admit that for a small boy the most exciting part of the day was when two tail-enders M. J. Gopalan and Amir Elahi swung the bat unscientifically but violently at the end of the day. A big hitter is always a great attraction and I often think that a number 9 batsman who laboriously struggles for 15 or 20 runs would do better for himself and the game if he learned to swing the bat.

When India came to England in 1952 two key men of the 1946 side were not with them. Merchant, who had averaged 51 in 1936 and 74 in 1946, had retired. Vinoo Mankad, who had made over 1,000 runs and taken 129 wickets in 1946, was playing in the Lancashire League instead of in the Indian team. They came to Cambridge early in the season having lost one and drawn two of their county matches. McCarthy bowled tremendously fast and we had 4 out for 49. Then came an unforgettable innings by Ramchand. He drew away almost a foot outside the leg stump to McCarthy every ball. But the fastest balls could not get past him, and powerful drives and hooks sent them flying all over the field. He seemed to be taking so many risks that I said to myself, "It can't last." But it did and he made 134 in three hours. Umrigar and young Manjrekar, whom we could not get out, were the only ones to help him and India were out for 285.

Peter May and I both made runs but found Divecha, Ramchand and Hazare with his low action, very difficult to score off. The best bowler, though, was the off-spinner Ghulam Ahmed who flighted the ball cleverly and was never easy to 'get at'. India led us on the first innings, and with Mantri and Umrigar playing well they had a chance to leave us a challenging score to chase. But Hazare did not want to take any risks and the game ended in a rather tame draw. Hazare was a great batsman and a delightful person, but I think he was over-cautious and his team seemed to think more of avoiding defeat than of winning.

However that may be India got themselves in a commanding position in the First Test at Leeds. Manjrekar playing in his first Test made a splendid 133 and Hazare scored 89. Hazare was out at 264, and at the same score Manjrekar and Gopinath went. But heavy overnight rain meant that England would have to bat on a turning wicket. It was a great chance for India. Laker showed what a spinner could do in these conditions by taking the last four wickets in nine balls. Ghulam Ahmed was quickly in the attack and Hutton, Simpson, May and Compton were out for 92. Then a determined stand by Graveney (71) and Watkins (48) swung the game back. Godfrey Evans hit brilliantly for 66 and England eventually led by 41 runs.

Then Freddie Trueman in his first Test, with all Yorkshire cheering him on, went tearing into action. Roy, Gaekwad, Manjrekar and Mantri were all out before a run was scored. Hazare (56) and Phadkar (64) fought very bravely but India could only leave England 125 to win. Hutton and May were out early, but Simpson, Compton and Graveney saw us through to win by seven wickets.

Mankad was released by his Lancashire League club for the Lord's Test match, and he produced the most outstanding all round performance. He bowled 97 overs, taking five wickets and scored 72 and 184. But there was little support except from the steadfast Hazare who scored 69 and 49. After a very slow morning Hutton made a superb 150. Simpson, May and Graveney all did well, but the show was stolen by Evans on the Saturday morning when he scored 104 in just over two hours. Then came Mankad's second great innings. First ball from Jenkins he pulled for six: on the first morning he had hit him clean over the sight screen with the game only half an hour old. But his great effort was not enough and England won by eight wickets.

I came into the England side for the Third Test at Old

Trafford. We batted, the first time I had opened for England with Len Hutton. The atmosphere was heavy and Phadkar, Divecha and Ramchand made the ball swing about. But we were getting on top when I was l.b.w. for 34 with the score at 78. Next over they came off for bad light and there were various interruptions. Hutton made 104, May 69 and there was another wonderful piece of hitting by Evans who made 71 in 70 minutes. We declared at 347 for 9.

Straightaway Tony Lock took a brilliant catch inches off the ground at backward short leg to send back Mankad off Bedser. It was the first time Tony had touched the ball in a Test match. Then came Trueman. With a gale behind him and an early wicket to encourage him, he bowled tremendously fast on a black-looking sort of wicket which helped him to make the ball lift. He took 8 for 31 and India were all out in 21 overs for 58. Only Hazare and Manjrekar made batting look possible at all. In the second innings Adhikari and Hazare held things up, but then Alec Bedser took over at Trueman's end; he took 5 for 27 and Lock, propelling the ball almost at medium pace and spinning it sharply, took 4 for 36. India were all out for 82 and the two innings had only lasted three and three-quarter hours.

We caught a lot of good catches in that match: in John Ikin, Alan Watkins and Tony Lock we had probably the three best short legs in the world, all in the same side. I caught one exciting catch which I shall always remember. Phadkar came in at 17 for 4 in the first innings. First ball from Trueman he rushed up the wicket, swung wildly and missed. I guessed that the next ball would be very fast and short and that Phadkar might draw away and slash at it. This was exactly what happened. I think my guesswork gave me the catch, and also saved my knee-cap, because he hit it right in the middle of the bat. I got both hands to it and it stuck.

Everything continued to run against India in the Fourth and final Test at the Oval. We batted first and their innings was on a wet wicket. I made 119, my first Test century, but it was very hard work, and for a long time I did not play very well.

Hutton and I had only scored 56 at lunchtime. Mankad bowled most of this time: he flighted the ball cleverly and bowled outside the off stump to a ring of fieldsmen. We drove the ball into the covers again and again, but the fielders cut everything off. Mankad was as clever a slow left-hander on a good wicket as I ever played against, though I think Lock, Wardle and Valentine (as he bowled in 1950) were better attacking bowlers when the pitch gave them some help. The runs came much more freely after lunch until Hutton was eventually out at 143 for 86 and Ikin and I put on another 118 before I was out.

On the second morning the accurate Indian bowling had its reward and England went from 264 for 2 to 326 for 6 at lunchtime. But then came a thunderstorm, an English declaration, and India faced Trueman and Bedser under very similar conditions to those at Manchester. This time the collapse seemed even worse when 5 wickets had fallen for 6 runs. Hazare, Phadkar and Divecha fought it out and India reached 98. But before they could follow on there was another storm and the match was left drawn.

Sussex played India immediately after the last Test and during the match Manjrekar followed a ball round on the leg side and hit our wicket-keeper, Billy Griffith, on the head, cutting it open. When Billy reappeared with his head swathed in bandages, Manjrekar said solemnly to him, "You are my fourth wicket-keeper."

When India came to England in 1959 they had an even worse time of it, losing all five Test matches. Manjrekar was no longer the slim young man of 1952: he was greatly overweight, was rarely fit and eventually had a knee cap removed. This was a great pity because he always looked a tough and skilled Test match player and India needed him in the Tests. Contractor played a courageous innings of 81 at Lord's with a cracked rib, and Baig, brought into the side after Manjrekar dropped out, and Umrigar both made excellent centuries at Manchester. The all-rounders Borde and Nadkarni were full of good cricket, but the great leg-spinner Gupte, who had been expected to rout England, only had 17 wickets at 34 runs each. Perhaps Englishmen play leg-spinners better than reputation has it!

India is a much tougher proposition at home than in England. Ted Dexter's team was beaten 2–0 in 1961–2: Manjrekar, Umrigar, Jaisimha, Borde and Pataudi all made runs consistently and the spinners Durani and Borde took 39 wickets between them. I had played with and against Pataudi when he was at school at Winchester. He stood in an altogether different class from other schoolboys: there was something ruthless about the way he took bowling to pieces and I felt that his nickname 'Tiger' was not inappropriate.

He had something of the intense concentration which divides a great player from the good ones and also a streak which wanted to live dangerously as a batsman. He looked the most exciting prospect, and when he came and played for Sussex where he lived in the holidays he seemed well able to find his feet in first-class cricket. He made a brilliant beginning at Oxford, but then came the tragic car smash in which his eyesight was badly damaged. It says much for his skill and determination that he has been able to win a place in Test cricket after this. His focus and field of vision cannot be what they once were, and though I have not seen him play since his accident I feel that cricket may have lost a great player who can only now be a good one.

England's record in India is not a very good one. Not since D. R. Jardine's team in 1933–4 have we won a series there. There are three reasons which partly explain this. First is the climate; secondly a full England team has never toured India; thirdly the type and pace of wickets enables Indian batsmen to play with far greater confidence at home. The climate undoubtedly makes life difficult for the genuine fast bowler, though Gilchrist took 26 wickets and Hall 30 for the West Indies against India in 1958–9. Extreme heat probably does affect the Englishman more.

Certainly I found problems I had never faced before when I played at Colombo on the way to Australia in 1962. I batted for nearly two hours that day, scoring 73, and sometimes after running between wickets I felt I could hardly breathe. It was very humid as well as being hot. I learned from Tom Graveney at the other end that the only thing to do was to 'take a breather', and spend an over not attempting to score until I had my breath back. If I had to do that as a batsman, how much more is a fast bowler going to find it difficult to keep going. That visit to Colombo reminded me of the enormous enthusiasm there is for cricket in Ceylon. Each time I passed through Colombo I met Ceylonese who knew more about the English County Championship than I did. In C. I. Gunasekera Ceylon has a great cricketer who would surely have played Test cricket if he had qualified for another country. He is a fine, forcing batsman, driving with great power, and a good leg-spin bowler. Leicestershire have reason to be grateful to Ceylon too, because Inman and Jayasinghe have brought character and skill to their batting.

Gamini Goomesena is another cricketer from Ceylon whom we respect in England: he played for Cambridge for four years and then for Nottinghamshire. As a leg-spinner he is not far short of the highest class and he could be a most effective batsman at number 7 or 8. In fact when he captained Cambridge against Oxford in 1957 he scored 211, the second highest score ever made in the Varsity match. Now he lives in Sydney, playing in Grade cricket and occasionally for New South Wales. My wife and I enjoyed meeting him and his delightful English wife Phyllida while we were in Sydney, and I baptised their baby son, David.

The fact that England has not sent their best team to India and Pakistan is a far more important reason why we have not done very well there. And both countries have understandably resented it when many of our best players have refused to go. Australia and the West Indies have both visited them twice since the war, and won on each occasion. Somehow we must find a way by which the full England team does go to India and Pakistan. But the problem for England is not an easy one: our players have far more cricket than Australians and West Indians, and we are committed to far more tours.

My third reason is one which I am sure both India and Pakistan should do something about. Their players grow up, never expecting the ball to bounce higher than the stumps; they learn to handle the spinning ball, but when they go overseas and meet fast bowlers on wickets with more bounce and speed, they are at an acute disadvantage. Lifeless pitches also mean that fast bowlers are not developed because it is all too discouraging for them. After their highly successful series against England in 1961-2, India went straight off to the West Indies and crashed 5-0. If they produced fast wickets, I believe that with all the keenness that there is for the game there, and with all the talent among their players, India could become the most powerful cricketing country in the world.

CHAPTER 6

SO NEARLY CHAMPIONS

AFTER the University season of 1952 Robin Marlar and I went back to Sussex, and in August Hubert Doggart joined us during the school holidays. We finished that season, Jim Langridge's last, in a blaze of glory, winning seven matches in a row. Robin Marlar bowled extraordinarily well at the end of the season, taking 34 wickets in the last three matches against Glamorgan, Lancashire and Derbyshire. In this form he was an excellent bowler, varying flight and pace, bowling a swinger as well as his heavily-spun off breaks. He was always setting batsmen problems, and I think he usually bowled better on the good batting wickets, where he had nothing to help him except his own resource, than on a turning wicket when he was expected to bowl the other side out. There seemed to be days when he was experimenting too much, and he never quite had the mechanical accuracy of Laker or Titmus.

That autumn I was asked if I would captain Sussex. I made it clear that I was hoping to be ordained and that I could only offer one season before I started my training at theological college. The committee said they were happy about this, and I was given every support as captain. At the first meeting of our selection committee Arthur Gilligan, its chairman, said, "You must have the team you want." Sometimes a county captain has been given little freedom by his committee. If they did not exactly send out a message to tell him when to change the bowling, there was no doubt that they told him who should play and what he should do. I felt that our committee trusted me to get on with the job they had asked me to do, while I knew they were there to encourage, suggest and support. And I believe a man does a better job if he knows that he is trusted.

Personally I started the season of 1953 very badly. The previous season I had averaged 62 and headed the first-class batting averages. But this May there was a solitary 93 to put alongside a whole series of low scores. This is an experience which keeps coming to every cricketer and gradually I emerged from it, and began to make good scores.

Sussex fortunes were somewhat similar: we won only one match in May, but were beginning to play good cricket. The team was in a transition stage and it was a most interesting moment to be captain, with a number of young players finding their feet. John Langridge and George Cox provided experience which was valuable for all of us. John was senior professional, and I was in the habit of trying out ideas on him before I made decisions. I encouraged the team to make suggestions, and normally these would come to me via John.

Some captains have felt, I think, that it is a sign of weakness to ask advice, and like to carry the whole burden themselves. I know that my worst mistakes were made when I didn't consult with anyone, and I do not think that it is weakness to share ideas. But I do believe that a captain should not run away from making definite decisions and sticking to them. A good team needs a leader, and being open to advice does not mean that there needs to be a team conference between every over. The opposing captain won the toss in one big match I played in. It was difficult to decide whether to bat or field, and eventually he came into our dressing-room, and said, "We've had a vote on it, and it's five all. So I've got to decide! You bat."

John Langridge was a great help to me in bringing forward suggestions and in listening to my notions critically, but not too critically. At many points in life I have found the value of a friend who can act as a kind of sounding board so that I have been able to bring ideas out into the open and see what they look like. At first slip he stood in a good place to be able to tell me what was going on. A remarkably good slip he was too. He hung on to some wonderful catches and he went on hanging on to them for a long time. In 1955, his last season, when he was

45 years old he caught 69 catches—more than any other fielder in the country.

I learned a lot about batting, and about cricket in general, through going in first with John. When I first played county cricket, I used to think, like many cricketers, that if I snicked the ball to the wicket-keeper I should never give away to the umpire whether I had hit it or not. I reasoned that a batsman is sometimes given out when he is not out, and that it only evens things out if he gets away with it sometimes when he is in fact out. Going in first with John I came to think differently. I never saw him not walk out immediately he was caught at the wicket. He never waited for the umpire's decision. After a while I started to do this too, as the great majority of county cricketers do today. In the last series between England and Australia there was hardly an occasion when the batsman did not walk out when he was caught at the wicket.

Some older cricketers think we are wrong about this. I walked out in a match against Victoria at the Melbourne Cricket Ground in 1962–3. A ball from Connolly had just flicked my glove on the leg side and the wicket-keeper caught it. I knew I was out and turned and made off for the pavilion, with the umpire, so I was told, shaking his head and saying, "Not out". One older friend of mine said this was making a fool of the umpire, but I don't agree with this. Several umpires have told me what a help it is, and their job is hard enough without making it any more difficult. The more pressure is put upon umpires, the more bad decisions there will be. An umpire thanked me once for walking out in a Test match, when he did not know whether I had hit the ball or not. Of all the parts to play in the game of cricket the umpire's is the one I should like least. He must be tremendously thick-skinned and able to keep his own counsel. John Langridge, my old partner, qualified in both these ways and has become one of our best umpires.

As a batsman John was ungainly with a number of little adjustments of cap and clothing every ball before he shifted finally into a very two-eyed stance at the wicket. But he was an

extremely effective player who made over 30,000 runs for
Sussex. He played fast bowling particularly well, and I always
found it interesting to bat with him against fast bowlers. Most
players make up their mind to move either on to the front foot
or the back foot against a fast bowler in order to be able to
react that little bit quicker. John was always coming forward
on to the front foot, while I was always moving on to the back
foot. We both had our system worked out, and I think we
both handled fast bowling well. This has always been a
reminder to me that there is no one method of batting which is
right for all: each player must work out what suits him best.

George Cox has appeared at various moments in this story.
In many ways he was my closest friend in cricket, and I
learned a great deal from him, not only about the technique of
the game, but about the whole approach to it. If cricket wasn't
fun you felt George would have no part in it. He has always
been intensely interested in people and their problems. He
used to go regularly to coach in South Africa, and it was he
who first started me thinking seriously about problems there.

As a batsman George could be exhilarating or nerve-racking
to watch according to whether he was in a good or a bad
patch. I cannot think of anyone who was as good a player as
he who seemed to lose form for such long periods. He was quite
often out very quickly. When he had his benefit season, George
Washer, the Sussex scorer, produced some statistics of his
career. They showed that he had made no fewer than 86 ducks.
"Just think," said Cox, "two whole seasons without scoring a
run!" Yet there were years when he made well over 2,000
runs, and many days when he was a top-class player.

There was always something dashing about his batting. In
1938 there was a trophy for the fastest fifty on the Hove ground.
In the last match but one Hugh Bartlett made 100 in 57 minutes
against the Australians. He was unfit for the final match
against Yorkshire. It was decided to present him with the
trophy at teatime on the first day. As they were walking to
tea Herbert Sutcliffe said, "I don't know about giving this
trophy today. Young George here can hit a bit." They were

prophetic words. Young George scored a hundred in sixty minutes that match, and one of the fifties was faster than Bartlett's. The trophy had to be given back. Hugh Bartlett was given a cheque in consolation for having to return the prize, Jim Langridge was given a tea service for being an unselfish partner to each of them, and George only had the trophy which had to be given back next year!

Before the war he was a fierce straight driver. Later on he was more likely to find his runs by square drives or slashes and by a late cut or delicate deflections. He remained very fit and enjoyed fielding at cover point, quite often running the batsman out with a fast throw to hit the bowler's stumps when they went for a quick single.

He has always been encouraging to young players and this is a big reason why he is an excellent coach. We were camping in Sussex one year and took some of our fourteen-year-old boys over to Hove for an afternoon in the nets. By the end of the afternoon George had persuaded at least two of them that they really could bat. It was done by sheer encouragement. At the same time he had picked out the laziest of the group and had chivvied him into making an effort which surprised us and the boy himself.

Left-hander Ken Suttle played his first full season for Sussex in 1953. He is a good example of someone who breaks a lot of the rules of batting, but is yet a most effective player. I said to the selection committee at the start of the season, "I want Ken in the side every match. I know I'm going to be furious with him sometimes for getting out stupidly, but he's going to play some innings no one else can," He made six centuries for us that season. Like many small men, he is a good cutter and hooker, and I've seen him drive many bowlers frantic by drawing away and cutting a straight ball for four runs. He made a brilliant hundred against Middlesex at Lord's in 1953. When Alan Moss took the new ball, and came thundering in irom the Pavilion end, just before he let the ball go, Ken rushed up the wicket and pulled him for a glorious six on top of the grandstand.

Ken Suttle was selected for the M.C.C. Tour to the West Indies that year: he did not make the Test team and had few opportunities on the tour. He has never played for England, but he has been a great competitor for Sussex. He is a great conversationalist as well, and whether he is showing off his conjuring tricks (for which I am the perfect audience, admiring and never being like one of those nasty small boys who say, "I know how that's done") or partnering you at the wicket, he keeps a lively patter going in case anyone is bored. One day Alan Oakman (six feet five inches) was batting with Ken at Eastbourne. Alan, a peaceful, apparently sleepy, sort of batsman, was leaning quietly on his bat at the end of one over. Suddenly a perky voice came up from Ken's five feet six inches. He had come down the wicket as usual for a little chat: "Well, here I am," he said, "What are we going to talk about?"

Alan Oakman has had his great days for Sussex, and played for England against Australia in 1956 without quite making the grade in Test matches. Later on he took over John Langridge's role by going in first and fielding at first slip. With his great reach he has held some wonderful catches though perhaps he nods a little more than John did. As a batsman he is at his best when going hard for his drives along the ground and over the top. During the winter before I captained Sussex I went round a number of cricket dinners and lunches, and among other things I said that I thought Alan might one day become a batsman in the mould of Frank Woolley. Perhaps this was a little too optimistic, though I think not a stupid prophecy; but we had to wait a little longer for his best batting years. He was then our one slow bowler until Robin Marlar arrived. Though he could spin the ball a lot, he did not quite produce the sustained accuracy to reach the top as a bowler. But I am sure it was a mistake not to use him as a bowler for several years. Against Yorkshire at Hastings in 1953 he went for a very hot catch at slip: the ball hit him on the joint of the thumb. He came over to me with the bone sticking out of the flesh at right angles and made the understatement of the year: "Skipper, I think I'll have to go off," he said. He missed the rest of the season.

Don Smith was a left-handed batsman who had to struggle for years before he gained real success in county cricket. As an opening batsman he did not perhaps play quite straight enough when he first started, but he was a great fighter, and he eventually became a very good player. In charity matches and less important games he was always a big hitter, while for a long time he was very cautious in first-class cricket. Then I think he deliberately brought some of that aggression into his batting for Sussex, picking the right moment to tear into the bowlers. There was a famous day against Gloucestershire at Hove when a message was sent out from some members in the pavilion that it was too dangerous there: he hit nine sixes that day.

I think it was Robin Marlar who suggested to him that he should try to bowl medium-pace swingers in 1955. He at once became a formidable bowler, settling into a rhythm of great accuracy, and always using his brains as he bowled. In 1957 he had a tremendous season with the bat and played in three Tests against the West Indies.

Jimmy Parks was the most talented of the players who were making up the new Sussex team. In fact I do not think there has been a more fluent stroke-maker in England since Denis Compton. When he goes to make a drive every part of the body seems to flow into the stroke: every stroke in the game is at his command. Again I would say he plays leg-spin-googly bowlers as well as any Englishman since Denis Compton. I remember seeing him bat in a charity match when he was no more than seventeen or eighteen. Doug Wright was bowling really well, and I, for one, always found his googly extremely difficult to spot. The moment he bowled it that day, Jimmy would see it, and promptly despatch it over mid-wicket for six.

Our opponents said he couldn't play fast bowling and for years every fast bowler in the country has been unleashed against him as soon as he came in. And he has played them all, making 2,000 runs a year with great regularity. When he was

pitched into the vital Fifth Test in the West Indies in 1960 he
scored 43 and 101 not out, saving the game for England. But
some ingredient has been lacking in his approach to the game
or he would have made the position in the England team secure
which belonged to his skill. Sometimes the joy which ought to
match his ability seems to have been missing and we have seen
him fiddle with little deflections and dabs instead of playing his
full, straight strokes.

He took up wicket-keeping seriously in 1958 when he had
already been playing first-class cricket for years, and has
become England's wicket-keeper. He has had many critics
here, and he does not look the part as, say, John Murray does.
But the thing in a wicket-keeper is not whether he looks stylish,
but whether he holds on to all the chances, and by this standard
Jimmy is a very good one indeed.

We had a good batting side in 1953 and, though we did
not make many large scores, someone would usually come up
with a score at the right moment. But the most important
addition of strength was the arrival of Ian Thomson. The
previous year, playing for Cambridge, I had batted against
him, and he swung the ball a good deal. But one ball would be
wide on the off side, the next wide on the leg side. In 1953 he
had learned to control direction as well as length. He was
always wanting to learn and almost every over I would make
some suggestions of how to bowl at a particular batsman,
knowing that 'Tommy' would try them out. He never had vast
natural ability, but by intelligent change of pace allied to
tremendously hard work and great accuracy he became one of
the half dozen best opening bowlers in England outside the
Test match bowlers. He would pretend to be more pleased at
making 30 runs than at all his successes with the ball. If you
said, "Well bowled Tommy!" when he had taken five wickets,
he would probably say, "I didn't get any runs though."

Ian gave just the extra penetration that the bowling needed.
Ted James was always accurate, able and willing to keep
going all day; he had some days when, with some help from
the wicket, he could be almost unplayable. Jim Wood was a

H

great trier; like every left-arm over the wicket fast bowler, he seemed to have a lot of bad luck when the batsman would play and miss instead of getting that little edge to the wicket-keeper. Jim Wood bowled fast left arm round the wicket before the war without great success. After the war he tried bowling slow for some time. Then one day in 1948 some of us were practising in a net. Billy Griffith said to Jim, "Why don't you try bowling over the wicket like this Toshack." He promptly ran up and bowled quick—nothing like Toshack's slow-medium nagging at the leg stump. But that was how he started bowling over the wicket, and his success dated from that time.

Good catching can make all the difference to the bowlers, and we fielded well that year. Rupert Webb made a calm, philosophical wicket-keeper, never taking the eye with Godfrey Evans style of movements, but holding on to most of the catches. Many good catches were picked up around the wicket, and the outfielding was smart with Ken Suttle in particular very fast round the boundary.

At the end of May we struck a winning streak and started to play with great confidence as a team. Leicestershire declared and left us 346 to make in under four hours; it was one of those golden days; I made 186 not out and we won with the loss of only two wickets and with half an hour to spare.

The win at Leicester was the beginning of a run in which we won seven out of ten matches, and climbed to the top of the championship table. The victory which meant most was over Surrey at Guildford: Surrey were in the middle of their great run of championship years and were eventually the champions in 1953. Stuart Surridge won the toss, and surprised me by saying, "I think I ought to put you in, but we're going to bat." When I had played at Guildford before it had been a very true, easy batting wicket. But this one was a 'green top', and remained helpful to the swing and seam bowlers throughout the match.

Jim Wood bowled magnificently that morning. From left arm over the wicket he often made the ball swing in from the off, and then move away off the pitch. He had Clark and

Fletcher out early, and then had three catches missed off him in close succession. All went fast and none was easy, but "dropped catches, lost matches" is all too true, and we came in to lunch feeling that we had lost our chance. Peter May and Eric Bedser were playing well and Surrey were 80 for 3. Immediately after lunch Jim Wood made two fantastic catches to get rid of May and Bedser. He was standing at leg slip to Ted James who made the ball swing late, and Wood threw himself full length first to his right and then to his left to hold on to snicks which went very quickly. Ted had two more quick wickets, Jim Wood dismissed Ken Barrington, just starting in the Surrey side, and Surrey had gone from 86 for 3 to 93 for 8. Then a typically pugnacious innings of 40 from Tony Lock rallied their score to 145.

Alec Bedser was the danger man on this pitch and John Langridge was caught Lock, bowled Bedser 0 straight away. We lost 3 for 70 and then Jim Parks and I put on 117. He made 68 and I got 105 which was about the most valuable innings I played that year. It was never easy to score and we never went very fast, but the crowd was always interested because a real fight was going on. Our last six wickets went for 66, and Bedser finished with 5 for 94.

106 runs behind Surrey batted much better, but a series of great catches kept removing batsmen when they looked dangerous. Fletcher and May took the score to 81 before the third wicket fell, but after that only Eric Bedser stayed very long, making a determined 65 not out. We had 106 to win, but the excitement was not over yet. Stuart Surridge could be very hostile with the new ball, making it swing away a great deal, and he had me out for 1 and Cox for 0. It was the moment for a bold innings and Ken Suttle provided it. Just as he had done to the Middlesex fast bowlers he ran up the wicket to Surridge, and pulled him for six over mid-wicket. John Langridge fell for 19, but Suttle and Parks laid in to Lock when he came on and we won by 7 wickets.

If a team is going to win the County Championship it has to keep on winning, and catching or missing the half chances can make all the difference. We outplayed Yorkshire completely at Hastings, but missed a vital catch, and could not dismiss them a second time despite excellent bowling by Marlar who had 9 for 100 in the match. We had to be content with first innings points against Kent in the other match at Hastings and rain meant no points for either side at Northampton.

Then we ran into real trouble for four successive matches. Against Middlesex we were 228 behind on the first innings, against Derbyshire it was 241, against Gloucestershire 176 and against Warwickshire 158. In each game we fought back and played some really good cricket to save the match: but we played well at the wrong moments and we went without a point for five matches.

In the Test match at Leeds that year Trevor Bailey had bowled six overs down the leg side with almost all his fielders on that side in order to stop Australia winning the match. We had discussed this, like all cricketers, and it is interesting to see the effect that tactics in a Test match have on cricket elsewhere. This is bound to happen, and it is never true to say that tactics are legitimate in a Test match which are wrong elsewhere. Early that year I had argued with another county captain that such tactics were unfair. Now that England had done it, I decided to do it myself. Against Derbyshire at Hove our second innings recovery (Parks and Suttle making hundreds) meant that we left them 85 to win in 55 minutes. For part of the time we bowled down the leg side: they hit at everything, our home crowd cheered us on, and a desperately exciting match ended with Derbyshire 82 for 7.

The next match was at Cheltenham: again we were in dire trouble; again we batted well in the second innings, Suttle and Cox doing best. Gloucestershire had to make 169 to win. Wickets fell regularly and both sides had a chance of winning. But at one stage they were scoring too fast for our liking, and I wanted to put the brake on. So for a few overs we bowled down the leg side again. This time we were not in front of our home crowd, and the Gloucestershire supporters let us know noisily that they did not like it. When we switched back to bowling

ordinarily we took some wickets quickly and the match finished
with Gloucestershire 154 for 9.

Although the two matches produced exciting finishes I am
quite sure that I was wrong to use defensive tactics like these.
They are my most unhappy memory of cricket, and I have only
included them in this book because I do not want to give the
impression that I have always done the right thing on the
cricket field. When we played Gloucestershire again a week
later the first thing I did was to make an apology to Jack
Crapp, their captain, who accepted it most graciously.

We registered our first points for three weeks at Cardiff
when we led Glamorgan on the first innings. But rain prevented
the match being played out, and we came back to Eastbourne
with hardly a chance of catching Surrey. When we were at the
top of the table in July we had a discussion about the Eastbourne wicket. John Langridge said that when we nearly won
the championship in 1933 we got no points from the Eastbourne week because the wicket was so good that no side could
be bowled out. We wondered how we could inject life into it.
Nothing was done in the end and as it turned out no one could
blame the Eastbourne wicket that we did not win the championship in 1953.

The first match, against Nottinghamshire, was one of the
most exciting I remember. The wicket was its usual, true self
on the first day and we did well to bowl them out for 252,
Hardstaff making 66 and Simpson 58. We had thirty-five
minutes to bat overnight—the kind of session when opening
batsmen usually try only to survive until morning. The opening
bowlers used an 'umbrella' field, with everyone up for the
catch, and Don Smith and I went for our strokes. At the close
we were 51 for 0 and were glad enough of this when heavy
rain came down in the night. Eastbourne may be a beauty to
bat on when it is dry, but when it is wet it can give the bowler
a great deal of help. Unlike most wickets, the wetter it is the
worse it is. We remembered a match three years before when
we had 98 to beat Hampshire and were all out for 38.

We could not start until after lunch on the second or the

third days because the ground was too wet after rain in the night. When we did start on the second day we batted as aggressively as we could and for a long time we got away with it: Don Smith got 56, I made 79, and George Cox a dashing 50 not out. As soon as we passed their score I declared and after Simpson and Clay made 34 for their first wicket Nottinghamshire collapsed. Ian Thomson made the ball lift sharply and took 6 for 37, while Robin Marlar took 4 for 56, and they were all out for 101. We had to make 100 to win.

Jepson made the ball lift and took two wickets early, and Stocks turned his off-spinners sharply. We lost 4 for 43. Then Jim Parks and I took the score to 71 when Bruce Dooland had me caught for 40 off a leg-spinner which turned and lifted. The rest of the game I only have from hearsay as I could not bear to watch any more. Dooland immediately had Thomson caught and Stocks had Ted James out. Now we had 74 for 7 and the odds were heavily against us. But Robin Marlar went in and immediately hit Dooland, against the spin, over mid-wicket. He repeated this several times, Parks held firm, and we scrambled home by three wickets.

It rained again during the second match at Eastbourne against Gloucestershire. We won by ten wickets and only lost one wicket in the match. Marlar had 7 for 42 in the first innings and James 6 for 19 in the second. So Eastbourne did us proud and gave us still an outside chance of winning the championship. We met Surrey in the next match, and if we beat them it was just possible for us to do it.

The biggest crowd I had seen at Hove came to see the match, and as quite often happens, I'm afraid the cricket did not live up to the occasion. Surrey lost 3 for 49 and were always fighting out of trouble: David Fletcher made 81 in four and three-quarter hours and they crawled to 220. We were no better: all the batsmen made between 15 and 38. Just as someone really felt he was 'in' and started to take command, he got out. We just passed their score and declared as soon as we had done so. But Peter May was too good for us and batted out the match, making an excellent 136 not out.

We had one more chance, for the last match of the season was against Lancashire and whoever won would be runners-up. This time we made no mistake about it. Robin Marlar had bowled them out in other years, and now he took 10 for 129 in the match. Hubert Doggart played a strong, disciplined innings of 100: George Cox drove and pulled his way gaily to 96, and Ken Suttle played excellently for 89. We declared at 340 for 5, won by an innings, and finished second in the County Championship. Sussex has never won. We were second once in the days of Ranji and Fry, and for three years running in the Duleep and Tate era. Now I hope Ted Dexter's team will pull it off at last.

CHAPTER 7

TRAINING AND TESTING

"THE front gate shuts at 10 p.m., and after that you are not to wake the porter up, as he has to be up early. If you come home after ten, the way into the college is over the wall at the back of the chapel." The Principal was explaining life at Ridley Hall to us on the first day of our theological training. It seemed a very commonsense way of carrying on, and was a good omen for two very happy years that I spent there. About sixty men were training for the Ministry of the Church of England at Ridley Hall: it was a small community in which there was much common life. All of us fed together, went to lectures together, worshipped together morning and evening in the chapel every day. There was much to crowd into those two years: theology is a subject with a vast literature: men once called it 'the Queen of Sciences'. I found it fascinating and important, but tried to keep firmly in my mind that all this was a background to meeting real needs of real people, and not simply some unending intellectual argument.

I had arrived slowly at the conviction that God wanted me to serve Him in the Ministry: there was no sudden sense of calling. I believe that God guides in great things and small if we want to know His plan. I met a group of teenagers in Western Australia in 1962, and in our discussion one girl put the most important point about finding out God's guidance when she said, "You've really got to want to know His will haven't you?" Sometimes He does this in dramatic ways, sometimes through more ordinary things—people we meet, circumstances in which we find ourselves, books we read. And if a man sincerely wants to follow, he will find the personal relationship with Christ, which is at the centre of every deep Christian experience, growing stronger. Then increasingly he will know

Christ's mind about the world around him, and His plan for his life.

There is a promise in Isaiah which says, "Your ears shall hear a word behind you, saying, 'This is the way, walk in it,' when you turn to the right or when you turn to the left." Some young Christians spend hours and hours thinking, worrying and praying about what they ought to do in the future—even when decisions do not have to be taken for years. The verse in Isaiah says that the word is "behind" us, and I think this means that quite often we shall only "hear the word" of God's guidance as we get on with His work here and now. There is plenty to do for Him today and tomorrow, even if it seems unimportant work. In the parable of the Talents, the master says to the faithful servants, "Well done, my good and trusty servant! You have proved trustworthy in a small way; I will now put you in charge of something big." Wanting God's guidance may mean being willing for some great life-long sacrifice. It certainly means being ready to find out His will and do it in everyday life.

There is a mistaken idea that if you become an enthusiastic Christian the only way you can serve God is in the ministry of the Church. A stevedore, who works in the docks near us in London, said to me in our Fellowship Hour after the evening service, "I envy you your job. You can serve God all the time. I can only serve Him an hour or two a week at the most." But he had misunderstood. Our Lord worked with His hands until He was thirty years old, doing His Father's will as he earned His living, and He brought His Father's love to those He met.

I realised that He wants His servants in every walk of life, including cricket. In fact there were so many opportunities of talking about the faith with individuals, and quite often to groups of young people, that I felt there was a strong case for finding a job which would allow me to stay in first-class cricket for some years. Cricketers and cricket followers, many of whom never went near churches, seemed able to talk about their questions and problems because I was involved in the life they understood. In 1952 I wrote myself an 'Appreciation of the

Situation' as I had been taught to do in the Army, which proved to me, I thought, that I should stay in cricket unless I felt positively that God was calling me out of it. Of course I was praying that He would pull me back from this course if it was not His will. And pull me back He did: every circumstance of the next few months seemed to show me that each job which I could really see myself doing in the future, meant being ordained. I think I was rather afraid of putting on a dog collar, thinking that it would keep some from talking to me. Perhaps that has been true, but I know that it has opened the door for many others to come and talk. To be set free from earning an ordinary living to serve Christ and His Church is the most exciting and rewarding job I know—if (and it is a big 'if') you are sure that this is God's calling.

Many young men have a problem which I didn't have when they are deciding about entering the Ministry of the Church. The same applies to men and women who feel that God is calling them to serve Him as overseas missionaries, or doctors, nurses, teachers, youth leaders or other jobs of this kind. Often their parents stand in their way for a variety of reasons. Sometimes it is because the parents have long-held ambitions for their children to get on in the world or to come into the family business. They think of these jobs as wasting their lives. There was a well-to-do mother whose two sons went as missionaries to China in the nineteenth century. This kind of thing really 'wasn't done' in her circles, and she avoided the shame of it all by speaking airily of her sons' "travelling in China".

Other parents stick firmly to the old Greek philosophy, 'Nothing in excess'. They would be very upset if their children 'went wrong'—became communists, were in trouble with the police or lived immoral lives. But they seem to be equally upset if their children become too enthusiastic for something which they themselves agree is good. They feel that 'Everything in moderation' applies to the way in which they should follow God. My mother was like many of her generation in wanting the good to triumph, in teaching us about God, yet in feeling that Jesus Christ was someone we simply couldn't talk about.

It was as though we took Him for granted. But in taking some-one for granted we can forget him, and for her the war years, as for many others, were years when in the busy-ness of other demands Christ and His Church increasingly were forgotten.

When I first came home from Cambridge, enthusiastic about the new faith I had found, I guess that she was puzzled and possibly a little anxious. But we have always been very close to each other, and soon we were learning together about Christ, and together meeting other Christians who have helped us. Very gradually her faith became more and more real and personal. When I felt that I should be ordained, and in all my work since then, I have known that her thoughts and prayers have been right behind me. This has meant a great deal to me.

At theological college there was a great deal of thinking to do about people and their needs. We would go out in pairs, one term going regularly to visit a ward in a hospital, another term teaching in a school, or going to an old people's home, or taking services in some of the village churches around Cam-bridge.

Some terms we would belong to a sermon class. This was made up of eight men, together with one member of the college staff, and each week we would go to a church where one of the eight would be preaching. On the Monday we sat down to-gether to dissect what had been said. It was painful, but very useful. Every preacher needs an honest critic from time to time. My best critic is my wife, but I also find some very useful comments from members of our congregation, for we speak our mind quite freely in Canning Town. During my second year at the Mayflower I had my first confirmation class, of half a dozen adults. One week at this a young man said, "I couldn't understand a word you were talking about on Sunday. What was it all about?" An elderly lady rushed to my defence, "Well I'm sure I like your sermons." At the door at the end of the evening the young man said, "I hope I didn't say anything I shouldn't have." "Certainly not," I said. "How can I know if I am being understood or not, unless someone tells me."

There were many evenings at Ridley when I came in over

the wall. I still had many friends in the University and believed that I would have a better and not worse grasp of theology if I was 'earthed' by a certain amount of contact with friends who did not share my beliefs. Both while I was at University myself and when I was at Ridley it seemed to come about naturally through friendship that I found myself often talking about my faith with others. There were several young men who had come to Cambridge, very much as I had done, with a belief in a distant God, longing for Him to become one who would stand in the middle of their life. It was a great step to put aside shyness and try to speak honestly of God's claims to a friend. Sometimes it was resented and I could always shut up; generally I think that it was welcomed by men at Cambridge and in cricketing days who very much wanted the opportunity to talk about God and Christ but did not know how to put their questions into words. So many hold back from speaking of their faith because they feel that they do not have sufficient training to explain it adequately. Others say they are not good enough. On that score none of us would ever be able to speak about Christ. But the Christian is not saying, "Come and follow me and my friends. We are the good ones." He says, "We are sinners. Don't follow us, but join us in following our Master, who helps and forgives us." As for lacking training, the first disciples were not college trained. There is great conviction about the stumbling words of an honest Christian who speaks out because his faith is a real power in his life. And when I made the excuse to myself, "I wouldn't know what to say," I found very quickly that our Lord was saying, "Then find out what to say". Laziness keeps us from doing things for Him as much as cowardice.

Some friends came as I had done to a definite trust in Christ. But I learned that 'getting down off the fence' on His side does not solve every problem. Often it caused men to look life in the face for the first time and to realise how many questions there are to be asked. Some went steadily on to become strong Christians, themselves helping others. Some became half-hearted about it, though they have seemed to continue to want to be on God's side. Sometimes years later on I have met someone who appeared to have drifted away from any interest in Christian things: he has met up with other Christians and the spark of faith has been fanned into strong life. Others again appear to have turned their backs on everything Christian. It taught me to look at Jesus' story about the sower and the different results after the seed fell in the ground. In the story it was only one part of the seed out of four which yielded as the sower had hoped. I knew how much help my Christian friends had been to me when I was starting out in following Christ. So I did not feel time was wasted in offering friendship to younger Christians whose faith had begun in Cambridge, or who had come up to University to face many new questions and challenges to a faith which dated from boyhood.

I met others who were ready to argue about belief in God, and others who rejected my ideas out of hand. But often our friendship continued with mutual respect for one another's views. I remember an afternoon in an Indian's rooms when for the first time he tried to understand what the Christian faith meant. I remember too trying to stand by a friend who was going through a very deep mental disorder. I knew nothing about that subject then but I probably gave him as much help as I could ever have done by listening for hours on end as he talked and by making him realise that I was not condemning him.

Most of us at Ridley Hall were involved in some kind of Christian work in the vacations: I used to help regularly at a Public Schools camp in Dorset. Once a year we all went together on a mission. Four parishes in some city would be found who wanted us to come, and we would form four teams for the mission. There would be much visiting during the day and in the evenings a home meeting in someone's living-room, or a visit to a youth club or a special service in church. We were billeted on different families in the parish. One year I was leader of a team in a parish in Liverpool. There was the promise of hospitality from several homes, most of them offering a room for two men: there were two who would take one man each.

One of our team was older than the rest of us and I naturally thought he would like a room to himself. When we arrived in Liverpool we found that one of the singles had fallen through, and those two, both stouter than average, must share a bed. It was too late to do anything about it and a friendly enquiry in the morning brought the complaint from Ken that Tom had been pulling all the bedclothes off him in the night.

I imagined that first-class cricket was behind me apart from perhaps a month with Sussex. There was an occasional game for Ridley Hall, when I found that Little Shelford at home on Bank Holiday were more difficult to make runs against than Middlesex at Lord's. I was also persuaded to play for our Rugby team who had five or six matches a term. I was never any good at Rugby but I understood the rules of the game. Not so my friend Albert who was press-ganged into making up the fifteen one afternoon. I felt the selection committee was gravely at fault in picking him as hooker (a) because he had never played the game before, (b) because he couldn't understand the rule that the hooker must not have his foot up before the ball was put into the scrum, hence giving away a penalty every scrum, (c) because he couldn't wear his glasses and therefore couldn't see when the ball was put in anyway.

One morning I went into the common room just before breakfast: the papers had come and two of them were waved in my face. Banner headlines proclaimed that moves were being made to persuade me to come back into cricket and captain England for the tour of Australia that winter. I knew all about it, and so did my college principal; but no one else was meant to know.

There had been some unhappy moments on the West Indies tour, and some blamed the captain Hutton for these. At any rate, Ronny Aird, then secretary of M.C.C., did approach me. We went to conspiratorial lengths to prevent anyone knowing that we were discussing anything. I was to go to his home rather than to his office and he would leave the door open so that I could walk straight in. But a few weeks later there it was in the newspapers.

I was put in a very difficult position that year. Was it right to break my training for the ministry for two terms? Was it right to offer myself as a rival as captain to Len Hutton, whom I counted as a friend, and honoured as our master cricketer? As I thought about the first question and discussed it with older friends, it seemed that, if I were asked to captain the side, this was an altogether different contribution to make to cricket than simply going as a member of a team. I had received much from cricket, and I ought to be willing to put what I could back into the game. My Principal agreed that it would be right for me to go if I was wanted as captain. Rightly or wrongly I decided that it would only be right to break my training if it was a question of the captaincy. This put me in a very difficult spot for half the summer when I was constantly being asked by the Press if I was available for the Australian tour. "No comment" is a very lame answer at the best of times.

The question about rivalling Hutton as captain was an equally difficult one. In 1952 before he was made captain of England he came round to my room in Cambridge one evening when Yorkshire were playing us. During the evening he said, "I think they're going to ask you to captain England, and I hope you'll accept." A few weeks later he was made captain of England. In 1954 other things made me feel that he would be glad not to have to shoulder the burden of captaincy as well as being our leading run-maker.

I mentioned my dilemma one day to Professor Norman Sykes who was Dixie Professor of Ecclesiastical History in Cambridge and later Dean of Winchester. I had introduced him to Len two or three years before because he was an ardent Yorkshire and Hutton fan. Len was brought up in the Moravian Church which most people know little about. So he enjoyed meeting someone who could tell him far more about the Moravians than he had known before. I knew Professor Sykes had seen him, and I asked him what he thought Len's feelings would be. He encouraged me to feel that he would welcome my taking over the side. Perhaps the simplest thing would have been to ask Len himself, but the opportunity did not present itself. Eventually I agreed to make myself available to go to Australia if I was wanted as captain.

When Len Hutton was ill after the First Test match, I was made captain for the Nottingham and Manchester Tests against Pakistan. It was an unpleasant position to be in, because I felt quite unsure of my position, as though I was more of a care-taker than a captain. Almost as soon as I was appointed captain I sensed the tide of feelings was running the other way. Walter Robins, who was a selector, came to my hotel room in Notting-ham during the Test match and said, "I feel we've been unfair to Len. He was in a very difficult position in the West Indies." The Manchester Test was an affair of a flooded ground and inspecting the pitch every day. They were selecting the team for Australia that week-end, and I already knew I wasn't going to go. For the only occasion that I can think of in Test cricket I breathed a sigh of relief when I was out of it after that match.

Pakistan's first tour of England in 1954 is remembered chiefly because of their great win in the last Test at the Oval which drew the Test series 1–1. But their achievements through-out the tour were remarkable for a first visit. Five batsmen made over a thousand runs, four bowlers had over 60 wickets, and they won nine and lost three of their first-class matches.

The First Test did little more than show the bowling skill of Fazal Mahmood and Khan Mohammed: everyone had sat watching the rain for three and a half days: Pakistan was all out for 87: England tried to force the pace but lost nine wickets for 117 before declaring. Pakistan then safely batted out the match.

I took over as captain for the Second Test at Nottingham. I had known Kardar, Pakistan's captain, quite well when he was at Oxford: he had shown himself then to be an aggressive left-handed batsman and a slow left arm bowler who could spin the ball sharply. Now he had the job of building up his country's first Test team. Kardar won the toss and decided to bat on a good wicket and after an hour of Statham and Bedser Pakistan had made 37 for the loss of Alim-ud-Din.

Then I brought on Bob Appleyard, playing at the age of thirty in his first Test match. He had Hanif leg-before with his second ball; in his third over he had Maqsood caught at the wicket; first ball of the fourth over he bowled Waqar; second ball of his fifth Imtiaz' off-stump went flying, and Appleyard had 4 for 6. His presence in the Test side at all represented a great fight back. In 1951 he had taken 200 wickets in his first season for Yorkshire. Then he was seriously ill with T.B. and it was remarkable that he should now be fit enough to bowl for England.

I rated Appleyard very highly indeed: in fact I think I would make a place for him if I had to select a post-war England team. Tall and heavily built, he varied his pace from a fast-medium swinger to quite a slow off-spinner. He had great control of length and direction and his constant change of pace made it very difficult to get on top of him. In Australia that winter his job was to keep the game 'tight' while Tyson and Statham prepared for another onslaught, and not only was he our most economical bowler but he also headed the bowling averages with 11 wickets at 20 runs each. I have sometimes wondered whether the great length bowlers of years ago, J. T. Hearne, Albert Trott, Hugh Trumble, M. A. Noble, may not have been a little like Appleyard.

That first spell of his really won us the match at Nottingham, because it was a beautiful batting wicket, and someone was bound to score heavily. Pakistan were all out for 157, and Reg Simpson and I scored 98 for the first wicket. I was caught at the wicket on the leg side off Khan Mohammad, who then bowled Peter May for 0. But no more wickets went cheaply: Simpson made 101, Graveney 84 and Compton 278. Graveney played an innings of beautiful, flowing strokes, and even overshadowed Denis Compton in their partnership of 154. Then Denis really cut loose, and a stream of square drives, straight drives, on drives, sweeps, late cuts, and strokes with no name poured from his bat. He added 192 with Trevor Bailey in 105 minutes of which Trevor made 27.

We had quite a problem in the dressing-room because they

I

had very kindly lent us a television set for the match. That Friday afternoon there was the Wimbledon Lawn Tennis Final between Drobny and Rosewall: we wanted to watch, but no cricketer could fail to watch the kind of innings Compton was playing. So, when he had the bowling, we watched the cricket, and when Trevor was taking strike, we went back to the tennis! When we came off the field at the end of the day the television was still on and we saw Jim Swanton giving a summary of the day's play. He said that he thought Compton tried to get himself out for a time after he reached 100. "But then," he said, "I saw him look up at the dressing-room balcony where his captain was sitting, and, as a result of the signals exchanged, he got his head down, and went on to make this enormous score." The facts of these balcony signals are quite simple, and I'm afraid there was no subtle, tactical, decision being passed on. In fact they were nothing to do with cricket at all. Denis Compton looked up at the balcony because he wanted to know how Drobny was getting on at Wimbledon, and someone signalled with his fingers, "Drobny 2, Rosewall 1."

I declared 401 runs in front and Pakistan had to bat for an hour that night. Instead of capturing any wickets we were treated to some bold and brilliant batting by Hanif, who at the age of nineteen was already something of a veteran in this side. Statham let go two or three 'bumpers' at him, and he hooked each one hard and safely for four runs. His 51 was a delightful piece of batting, and gave us a glimpse of the ability which has made him such a heavy scorer. Maqsood played some brilliant strokes but fell to a rash one when he had made 69, and Pakistan were all out the second time for 272.

The rain won the Third Test at Manchester and we had less than two full days cricket. Compton (93) and Graveney (65) were the best of our regular batsmen and Johnny Wardle hit three sixes and five fours in his 54. When I declared at 359 for 8 at lunchtime on the Saturday, Pakistan had a wet wicket to bat on, and though Hanif played well for 32, Bedser, Wardle and McConnon presented too many problems for them. They were all out for 90, and in the second innings had lost 4 for 25 by the end of the day. But then the rains came again, the ground was flooded each day, and so the match was left drawn.

There was also plenty of rain about for the last Test at the Oval. I was not there, but of course followed the game over the radio. Pakistan lost 7 for 51 in their first innings, Tyson, Loader and Statham doing the damage, but Kardar made 36 and put some fight into the 'tail'. Their 133 gave them a lead of 3 runs over England who always had to struggle on a wet pitch against Fazal and Mahmood Hussain. Again Pakistan collapsed, this time to Wardle, 8 wickets falling for 82, but Wazir Mohammed (42 not out) and Zulfiqar Ahmed (34) saw that the total reached 164. With 168 to win England passed 100 with only two wickets down and May and Compton in control. We seemed in a hurry to try to win that evening: when May was out for 53, Evans was sent in. He failed, and so did Graveney, and when Compton was out just before the close England were in real trouble. The last day started with England needing 43 to win with 4 wickets to fall. When McConnon was run out, Pakistan had won a famous victory by 24 runs. The hero was Fazal Mahmood who took 12 wickets in the match for 99.

On their own wickets Pakistan have been very difficult to beat. When Richie Benaud's team beat them twice in 1959–60 this was the first time any visiting country had won there. Since then Ted Dexter's team has won a series there, but Australia, West Indies and New Zealand have all been defeated in Pakistan. As with Indian cricketers they find it much harder going when they go overseas and play on livelier wickets. They have been very wise to send many of their players on a Pakistan Eaglets tour of England several times. But I believe their cricket would be strengthened if they played on faster pitches at home.

After such a first tour it was difficult for the next Pakistan team in 1962 to live up to expectations. The batsmen never surrendered tamely, but the bowlers, frankly, never looked like dismissing England for a small score. The lowest England total in five Tests was 370. I came into the side for the Fourth and

Fifth Tests when England were already leading 3–0. Cowdrey, Graveney and Parfitt (twice) had already made centuries, and the captain Ted Dexter, was in tremendous form. Mushtaq Mohammed, Saeed Ahmed, Imtiaz and Alim-ud-Din had all fought well at times and the captain, Javed Burki, and Nasim-ul-Ghani had each made 100 in a wonderful fight-back at Lord's.

For the Fourth Test Pakistan had flown Fazal from his police duties to add some punch to the attack. He bowled unchanged through our innings of seven and a half hours with the exception of a rest of less than an hour. It was a remarkable feat of stamina, but I had the impression that he was expecting to bowl all the time. He was bowling to stop us scoring rather than to try to get us out. Ted Dexter came in in tremendous form when Geoff Pullar was out early, and this helped me to find my touch in my first Test Match for five years. Ted made 85 and I got 83.

After Fazal had been bowling non-stop for two hours I said, "I don't think your doctor would approve of all this." After three hours or more without any change of bowling seeming likely, I said, "Now why don't you go and have a rest? I'm sure your doctor would advise it." "All right Reverend," he said surprisingly, "If you want me to, I will." And he took his sweater and went off into the field. I happened to have chosen the exact over at which he and his captain had agreed that he should come off. Tom Graveney and Peter Parfitt both made hundreds and we declared at 428 for 5. Mushtaq, Saeed and Nasim all fought gamely when Pakistan batted, but they had to follow on 209 behind. Two wickets went quickly but Burki and Saeed stayed with little Mushtaq who played splendidly, earned a draw for his side and made 100 not out.

If Hanif's failure (at least partly due to his knee trouble) was the greatest disappointment to Pakistan in 1962, his 18-year-old brother Mushtaq's batting was the greatest triumph. Mushtaq was just 13 when he first played first-class cricket, and 15 when he first played in a Test match, while at 17 he was the youngest man to make 100 in a Test match. His four brothers Wazir,

Raees, Hanif and Sadiq have all played first-class cricket. Mushtaq is full of courage and determination and played the fast bowlers extremely well. As the bowler was about to bowl, his right foot was edging across to the off stump so that he would get right behind the ball, but he never seemed to get himself into trouble on the leg-stump through doing this: in fact he was very strong on the leg-side, frequently whipping the fast bowlers away. To the slow bowlers he was quick on his feet, and drove and cut well.

The Oval Test was a very similar story to Nottingham. Again we batted first, and again I felt that Fazal and D'Souza, who opened the bowling this time, were trying to stop us scoring rather than get us out. Fazal is the type of medium pace bowler, rather like Alec Bedser, to whom I would normally think it suicide to play back. But after a few overs I went and looked at the marks the ball made on the pitch, and decided that he had not bowled one ball to which I need have played forward. So I then went exclusively on to the back foot, and runs became easier to find. This sort of bowling makes scoring a very difficult matter, but, particularly when the ball is new, the swing bowler ought to pitch it well up to the batsman if he wants to get him out.

Colin Cowdrey, fit again after an unpleasant illness, and I went in first and we made 117 together before I was out for 57. I thought Intikhab bowled his leg-spinners very well and was amazed that he had been given so little bowling on the tour. But no one was allowed to bowl very well after I was out, because Cowdrey (182) and Dexter (172) really took all the bowlers to pieces. Cowdrey did it by beautiful timing, and wherever the ball was pitched it seemed to keep on disappearing wide of mid-on. Dexter's method was more violent, and the high straight drive was often in use. They added 248 in two hours and three-quarters, and Dexter was able to declare at 480 for 5.

Our bowling 'staff' was very different in this match— Coldwell, Larter, Knight, Allen and Illingworth—and a stand of 82 by Imtiaz and Mushtaq made us feel that we were going to spend a long time in the field. But the bowlers all kept at it with great accuracy, gave nothing away and the batsmen duly made mistakes. The hardest part of batting in Test cricket, once you have established yourself at the wicket, is to keep concentrating, to pick up one's and two's by placing and good running, and to develop enough power of stroke to score when the bowlers set themselves to bowl 'tight'. If you only expect to score when the bad ball comes along, you may have to wait a very long time. There was a good partnership later between Saeed and Hanif, but this also was broken when they were getting into their stride. Pakistan were all out for 183, our giant fast bowler David Larter taking 5 for 57 in his first Test match. Dexter gave him short spells of about three overs at a time, and he kept at it on a wicket which had little life in it.

When Pakistan followed on, Imtiaz and Mushtaq were again the best batsmen, and in two and a half hours they put on 137. Both are fine stroke players, and drives, cuts and hooks often beat the field. This was real Test match batting, and everyone was sorry when Imtiaz missed his century by two runs. Mushtaq was out for 72 and quickly the score slumped from 171 for 1 to 186 for 5. Burki and Wallis stood firm and added 64 and Pakistan totalled 323. But we were left only 27 to win, and duly won the match by ten wickets.

Pakistan had had a disappointing series, but they had never given up and there were some fine cricketers in the side. They are sure to become a powerful batting side and I thought Nasim and Intikhab might develop into good spin bowlers. They needed most some attacking opening bowlers. So I come back again to the subject of wickets: fast bowlers—and good leg-spin bowlers—are encouraged by fast wickets.

CHAPTER 8

LONDON HOME

On Michaelmas Day 1955 I was ordained by the Bishop of London in St. Paul's Cathedral. I had been most unsure of where I ought to serve my first curacy until Maurice Wood, who was Vicar of St. Mary's, Islington, asked me to join his staff. I visited the parish, a densely populated area in North London, and saw a mixture of large, once middle class, houses now mostly split up for three or four families and modern blocks of flats. As I got the feel of the area and came to know Maurice Wood, I felt quietly that this was where I wanted to serve.

There is much that is new when you put a clerical collar on, and it makes a great deal of difference to be working with an experienced man whom you respect. In the apparently simple matter of wearing the collar I, or it, came unstuck on my first day in the parish, and it parted company from the stock so that I was left with collar alone high up my neck in the main street. There were more important lessons to learn than how to dress; I was meeting others in all kinds of need, sick, facing death, in a marriage breakdown. I needed to learn how to use the opportunities of meeting those who are at the great moments of life, as well as know how to conduct services. I believe that in all this we need most to pray for a real caring about people. An inexperienced young man can have that, but it was a great help for me to have Maurice to discuss it with.

One of the regular difficulties is to handle men who come to the door wanting money: no one wants to turn away a man in genuine need, but there are so many who simply wander from one charitable hand to another: a gift of money is not really helping someone like this, as it is keeping him from facing the challenge to tackle a regular job of work. But it is far from easy to tell the genuine from the phoney. Maurice Wood told of a man coming to him when he was a curate before the war in London. He said he needed the money to tide him over the week-end, because he had just come out of hospital, and to prove it he pulled his shirt up and displayed several lurid scars on his chest. They were enough to move the most hard-hearted curate. After the war, when Maurice was in an Oxford parish, the man appeared on the doorstep with the idential story. He pulled up his shirt, and there were the same scars! They appeared again some years later at the vicarage door in Islington—valuable scars! I had an Irishman who came cheerfully to ask me for some money. I asked him if he had been to the National Assistance Board; "Oh no, I like to support myself," was the surprising answer.

Maurice Wood once told us that he had gone back to speak at his previous parish in Oxford; a member of the Youth Fellowship came up to him and said, "Oh rector, everything's gone so well since you left!" This was really a great compliment, and I think it has been repeated at Islington, when after ten years his energy and enthusiasm were withdrawn. He rightly believed that the work of a parish should not all depend on its vicar, and saw a large part of his work as training laymen and giving them real responsibility. A small, but loyal congregation was gradually growing up again, after the parish had almost totally collapsed during the war, when the church was bombed, and so many church members moved away.

We have a picture in our flat, a copy of Holman Hunt's famous painting *The Light of the World*, which is a happy reminder of our years in Islington. It was given to us by a couple who came to understand in their own lives the meaning of the verse from the Bible which that painting of Jesus tries to illustrate—the same verse which had helped me in Cambridge: 'Here I stand knocking at the door; if anyone hears my voice and opens the door, I will come in and sit down to supper with him and he with Me.' They had first been set thinking about the claims of the Christian faith on their lives through contact with a woman across the street who was often unwell and could get out very little. She had made friends with the children and with them, and had told them about St. Mary's. The wife began to come to our Young Wives Fellowship, and he eventually came to a special Cricketers' Service in the Town Hall. This broke the ice, and he now felt free to come and to think seriously. Later they told us that they had prayed and asked Christ to come into their lives and be their Friend and Master. After some months I remember their making their outward stand as Christians in confirmation in the rebuilt church. I remember finding them on the floor in their home working out the notes which one had taken at the confirmation class that week. They took it in turns to stay with the children while the other went to the Vicarage. Then they would go through it all together.

I learned much from many of the Londoners whom I visited in Islington. Mrs. Withers was one whose whole life strengthened my faith in God. I used to knock three times on her door: the top window would open and down would come a stocking with the key wrapped in it for me to let myself in. She had lived alone there for years as her husband had died very young, and so had her only boy. She used to go out once a year when she was taken for an outing. She had lost a leg and spent her days in a wheelchair sitting by the window. She later lost the other leg after much pain with it.

During the last years of her life she was taken out a little more, and had regular visits from a number who made it their business to go and see her. All of us found that we were more cheered up by her strong faith than the other way round. She took a lively interest in everything she could find out from her friends and I know that she prayed for my wife and me every day. She was dressing a little doll for our baby Jenny at the time she died. When I visited her in hospital after she had lost her second leg I found that she was the life and soul of the party in her ward. I saw in Mrs. Withers such lack of self-pity and such genuine interest in others as to put me to shame.

There are a large number of West Indians and Nigerians living in Islington, and we spent many hours visiting them.

One day a young Jamaican woman came to our church service clutching a letter. It was from her Vicar at home introducing her "To any priest in the Church of England". She lived a stone's throw from the church, but when she had asked about going to a service, other West Indians had said, "You can't go to a church in England. They'll throw you out." Every incident of colour prejudice which happens—and too many do happen—is repeated a hundred times until that sort of statement is made. Mildred, not knowing what to do, wrote back to her vicar. Hence the letter, which gave her the courage to come, still very nervously, to a service. We were worshipping in an upstairs hall, while the church was being rebuilt: at the foot of the stairs she met a member of the congregation who said, "You're new here, aren't you? Please come and sit with me." The fears ebbed away and she soon came right into our fellowship.

Quite a number of overseas families do now go to St. Mary's; but many others stay at home, brooding over every white insult and huddling back into their own community. Many who came from overseas were shattered that England 'where the missionaries came from' should be so godless. I would say to them, "But I think of England as a mission field. We could do with missionaries from Africa or the West Indies." They laughed and did not lose their sense of bewilderment. But I was serious: we were surrounded there as we would be in many parts of Britain with a solid ignorance and indifference, which could not care less, and which never thought for a moment that Christianity might be relevant to adult life. We could reach children, but unless we could break through into some families and older groups, the children would drift away at thirteen or fourteen.

I came to know one family living in the well done-up basement of a house. The elder boy had been in trouble, and when he came back from Approved School I was put in touch with him. One day I was sitting in their home when the younger boy came in. "Brian's the religious one in this family," said Mum. "He goes to your church. At least we send him." I looked at Brian, whom I had never seen before in my life, and his face went a kind of purple. It was obvious that, though he had been sent, he had never arrived. I did not blame Brian for working out that if it wasn't important enough for his parents to make time for God and the Church, it wasn't important enough for him. The longer we stayed at Islington the more we felt the determination to try to make friends with our neighbours whom I describe as "Happy pagans", and bit by bit to show them that following Christ could be the most important and exciting adventure of their lives. When the chance of taking over the Mayflower Family Centre in Canning Town came, we seized it with both hands, because it seemed to offer just that opportunity of meeting and making friends which is so important.

"We" has crept into the story, as we were married while I was a curate at Islington. I had grown up accepting that, if I was to enter a profession like the Bar, which demanded a long training when I would not be earning enough to support a wife, I should not marry until I was about thirty. This seemed to be equally sensible when I decided to enter the ministry of the Church, so marriage did not come into my calculations while I was at Cambridge. I met a number of girls with whom there was good friendship in a group but there was no special 'girl friend' in those years. But while I was at Ridley Hall I wanted to introduce a girl I knew to a Christian group in Cambridge. I asked another friend to suggest who would be the best girl for her to meet. He promised to think and let me know. The following day a note came suggesting that the best person would be a girl training to be a teacher at Homerton College.

This historic note—for two of us—ended "Grace Isaac's the name." Grace Isaac came to tea the following week to meet the other girl, and that night I never slept a wink. I still felt that it was too soon to think seriously of marriage, and thought I should not enter into a really close friendship with a girl until marriage was not too remote a possibility. So I did not follow up this first meeting. But one thing after another seemed to

cause us to cross each other's path. We discovered later that
we were both worshipping from afar, each of us thinking that
we had no chance. I saw others talking easily with her and
thought they must all be in love with her; she tells me she
heard me speaking at a meeting, saw me playing for Sussex
and thought that there must be many in the queue for me. The
first time I asked her to come out to anything was to a cup of
coffee after a meeting we had both been to. Along with a
mutual friend we had hardly settled down to the coffee before
she had to go as she had no late pass for getting back into
Homerton. With a few crumbs like this and the occasional
chance meeting we made do for nearly a year. When I had
been ordained a while, we started to go out together and four
or five months later I asked her to marry me—a moment which
made me more nervous than any in the pulpit or at the wicket.
We were engaged for sixteen months, and as Grace was
teaching in Sussex, and my weeks and week-ends were very
involved in Islington, a day or half a day a week was usually
the most we could manage to be together.

It has become a partnership which means more than I can
express on paper. Our decisions have been made together, and
we have found ourselves able to discuss every kind of subject.
I'm sure that one of the greatest reasons for this has been that
our faith in Christ has been shared from the beginning; and
that we have always known that the deepest purposes of our
life have been at one. This doesn't mean that there have been
no clashes or disagreements: we are both too strong-willed for
that. But our faith has been a help here too. I heard a Christian
say once, "The first thing I pray for my son is that he'll be able
to admit when he's wrong." Admitting that we are wrong
should be one direct result of facing God honestly.

We also made each other a promise before we were married
which has helped greatly. We promised that we would pray
together every night before we went to sleep: like many
couples we read a few verses from the Bible, and one of us
prays for those we've met that day, for our staff and our
families, and about any particular problems we face. It has

been a great safeguard because we find we can't look Him in the face if we can't honestly look each other in the face. So occasionally we have had to talk some difference out before we can pray.

Another factor has drawn us much closer together. It was a very unpleasant experience, and my hardest decision in writing this book was whether to include this or not. But we have felt that speaking of it honestly may be a help to others who have the same sort of tunnel to go through. We went to Northern Italy for our honeymoon, and just before we were due to come home Grace developed a very bad attack of chicken pox. No girl dreams of ending her honeymoon in an isolation hospital in Rapallo. She came home the day after she was allowed up; almost straightaway she came up to the Test match at Leeds and too quickly was caught up in the whirl of life again.

All this triggered off a serious nervous illness. In September she collapsed in an underground train and for some weeks was in bed with regular bouts of violent shaking. The doctors came and went. She was taken into hospital for three weeks for observation. Every test brought the same answer, "Nothing organically wrong." They stood at the foot of her bed, shook their heads, and said, "Don't worry." In fact she was quite unable to take that advice, for the basis of her illness was a breakdown of confidence in herself: this meant that actions like crossing a road, or going to a shop became as fearsome for her as crossing Niagara on a tightrope would be for most of us. The fact that her fears were unreasonable was known to her, but it did not make them any less real. It was all like a long, black tunnel with no light at the end in which she felt desperately alone, and horribly different from everyone else.

Since then we have met many others who are going through comparable tunnels, and the fact that someone understands, has been through it, and does not condemn them for being in it, can perhaps help them more than anything else. We can be very cruel, because we are very ignorant about the whole world of nervous and mental illness. I was tempted at times to tell Grace roughly to pull herself together and snap out of it,

but I came to understand quite quickly that these were symp-
toms of an illness. What she needed was not blame but support.

Slowly, after six months, with psychiatric help, she became
well enough to cope with most ordinary situations. Certain
problems remained as formidable and unreasonable obstacles.
Some of them have been left behind over the years, usually
without making any great issue of overcoming them. We have
found that we can genuinely thank God for this experience.
It is not only that we can help others involved in this sort of
illness as we never could before. It has drawn us much closer,
because we have had to face together in the open so many
things about ourselves. Through Grace's more sensitive eyes I
have noticed much that I passed by previously. I do not in
any sense want to present either of us as tragic figures. There's
an enormous amount of fun in our home—fun which received
a great addition when Jenny was born on March 17th, 1962.

A number of questions arose in my mind about the Christian
attitude to this kind of experience. A fine Christian young
woman came to me one day and asked, "Why should Christians
worry? My vicar preaches about peace of mind, but I don't
have it." It has often been taught that, if someone is trusting
Christ and obeying Him, he will know no worries or fears. In
fact, so it has been said, we should think of them as sin.

But a good deal needs to be said about this. First God has
given us different temperaments, some of us being thick-
skinned, some, as a friend put it to me, 'with one skin less', more
sensitive, more subject to strains and pressures, but more alive
also to life around them. I am more thick-skinned than Grace,
and we are both richer in experience for sharing our life with
someone who has a different temperament. I was talking about
this recently with someone who taught me at school. He said,
"You weren't thick-skinned at school." I think school, the
Army, University and the world of cricket made me much
tougher skinned—which is probably a good thing. It may also
have made me more insensitive—which is probably not a good
thing.

Some are tempted to feel that the stiff upper lipped English gentleman, who never shows his feelings, is God's ideal pattern for men. But it is a mistake to think that there is a pattern of temperament and outlook which all should try to copy. God meant us to be different from one another and so He made us different. In fact God's ideal man seems Himself to have had a most sensitive nature: He wept at the grave of His friend and over the hard-hearted city of Jerusalem. There were moments too when He showed His anger at men's stubbornness and selfishness.

Secondly it needs to be recognised that there are about our make-up things which God did not intend to be there. Sin and selfishness leave scars, whether we committed the sins ourselves, or whether they are the result of what our parents or our neighbours did. It will not necessarily be as easy for one man to be as balanced and at peace with the world as another. One who was never wanted and never treated with respect by his parents, or whose parents were out of work and always on edge because of it, or who was always given everything he asked for by spineless parents, will not have the same advantages as one who has always known that he was wanted and had the security of a stable home. My wife and I both thank God for happy homes, and we see something of the problems which face every child who grows up denied that security.

Someone who grows up with an extremely sensitive temperament or a make-up which has been scarred by one cause or another needs to find unjudging fellowship in the Christian family. The best illustration I have heard of what the Church should be like is found in that great organisation Alcoholics Anonymous. A man can only belong to A.A. if he is an alcoholic —not just a heavy drinker, but suffering from alcoholism and therefore always weak in that direction. They tell me that quite a percentage who join crash after a while, and go back to heavy drinking. But there is a strong pull about A.A. And the greatest element in this is that when someone goes back to join again he knows that no one will judge him. This is because they are all weak and know it. They belong only because they are alcoholics. The Christian Church is Sinners Anonymous:

we are all weak in different directions, and we have no right to point a finger of judgment at others.

The peace which God offers is not a promise of protection from storms and difficulties. In the Bible the word peace is first a translation of the Hebrew *shalom*, the same root word as the Arabic greeting Salaam, and its basic meaning is peace with God, wholeness, being right with Him. A good question to ask yourself is whether Jesus had God's peace in the Garden of Gethsemane, when He wrestled in an agony of mind over the cup which He must drink in death on a cross. We are told that His sweat was like great drops of blood: yet I believe He had God's peace in that agony because He was at one with Him, wanting to do His will.

Perhaps I can explain best what I mean about God's peace by comparing two miracles of Jesus. Both involved a storm on the Sea of Galilee: both may be related to storms in our minds. On the first occasion the disciples were crossing the Sea with Jesus asleep on a pillow in the back of the boat: they could see Him near to them, but their faith snapped as the storm grew stronger until they woke Him up and appealed to Him, "Master, we are sinking! Do you not care?" At once He commanded the wind to be still, and there was a dead calm. This is how most of us think God ought to answer our prayers, and we are inclined to say that He has not answered them unless it happens like this.

The second miracle is different. He tells His disciples to cross the Sea while He sends the crowd home. Then He goes up into a mountain and for hours stays there in prayer. They battle through the storm. He isn't there; perhaps He has forgotten them. Somewhere between three and six in the morning He comes towards them, walking on the water through the continuing storm. They are terrified, thinking He is a ghost. When He calls to them, Peter replies, "If it is You, tell me to come to You over the water." "Come," says Jesus. The storm still goes on, and Peter has to walk through it. When he begins to sink he cries out for help; Jesus catches him and brings him into the boat; and then there is a calm.

The second miracle is not less than the first. And for us sometimes storms happen when we do not feel that He is there; but He comes to us through the storm; and helps us to go on through it together with Him.

While I was a curate it was agreed that I should have a month off to play some cricket for Sussex from late July. I had no thought that I might ever play in a Test match again, and I doubt if anyone else had. In April I went to Lord's for a practice net on a day when the Australians were there, and Keith Miller came over and off a run of a few paces really put me through it. At the end of that week I captained the Duke of Norfolk's team in a friendly match to start the Australians' tour. The Duke has as beautiful a cricket ground at his home at Arundel in Sussex as any that I know. Two-thirds of it is ringed with magnificent beech trees and the natural banking makes it possible for a large crowd to watch although there are no stands. I remember the match for the way in which the attempt to 'arrange' a friendly match can come unstuck.

I said to Ian Johnson, the Australian captain, "The only result which mustn't happen is that you lose," and I virtually promised him that I would see we did not win. We agreed that we would try to see that everyone made at least 15 so that the crowd would see everyone make some runs, and that anyone who made 50 would get himself out. I went in first with Len Hutton, and Lindwall opened the bowling to him. Instead of the usual hostile opening, he bowled a series of gentle, straight, half-volleys—trying to 'get him off the mark'. But Hutton had retired the previous year and had had no practice: he missed two out of the first three and the fourth ball bowled him easily for o.

When the Australians batted, needing 189 to win, we nearly wrecked our nicely arranged, friendly match. We had five wickets down for 38 and I had to take Bedser and Wright off because they were bowling too well. Eventually they duly recovered and won by three wickets. But I never thought I

K

would see a day when we should try not to get the Australians out.

Australia drew first blood in the Tests with a win on a fast bowlers' wicket at Lord's. With Lindwall and Davidson both unfit, Miller rose to the occasion as he so often did. At the age of 36 he bowled 70 overs in the match and took 10 wickets for 152.

Early in July I went to Lord's on one afternoon of the Oxford v. Cambridge match. I was busy and wouldn't have gone if I had not accepted an invitation from Jim Swanton to have tea in his box. In the end I don't think I watched a ball of the match: as soon as I arrived Jim said, "I think Gubby wants to talk to you." Gubby Allen was chairman of the selectors that year. He came over and said, "Everyone's been telling me that I ought to press you to play, but I feel that if a man decides to pull out of cricket that's his affair and you should leave him to it." I said that I was in fact planning to play a month's cricket for Sussex. "Now you're talking," he said. "When are you starting?" We took out our diaries, and saw that if I followed my plan of starting to play on a Saturday it was only the day before the team for the Fourth Test was selected. "Couldn't you play the match before that?" he asked. "It would give us more of a chance to pick you."

I was preaching to a school-leavers service in Portsmouth on the Tuesday and Sussex were playing at Worcester on the Wednesday. We reckoned that I could get up at 5 a.m. and drive there in time for that. I said that I was sure that they wouldn't want me: England had had a bad match at Lord's, but I felt that our batsmen would 'come good' at Leeds in the Third Test. Anyway, I was going up to Leeds for the first day and we agreed we could see how things went there before organising my early morning drive to Worcester.

I met Gubby at Leeds soon after our third wicket fell with the score at 17. "I think you'd better play at Worcester," he said. So I preached to the school-leavers, arrived quite late to stay with the Bishop of Portsmouth who had been dean of Trinity Hall, and greeted him by saying, "If you don't mind very much, I'm leaving at five in the morning."

On that first day of the Leeds Test there was one of the best examples of gamesmanship that I have ever seen. Alan Oakman went in number 3 in his first Test match, feeling no doubt a little nervous. The Australians waited until he had taken guard and was ready to bat. Then they started calling fieldsmen in from all corners of the ground to crowd around the bat, while Alan stood waiting and watching. When the third wicket fell and Cyril Washbrook came in, they went through exactly the same performance. He waited until they had finished moving the fielders, and when they were ready, he strolled slowly up the pitch, found some minute piece of dirt and flicked it away. Then he walked slowly back, surveyed the field, adjusted his cap, flexed his arms, and settled down to bat with an unspoken, "Now *I'm* ready." He certainly started one up—and finished with a famous 98.

In the game at Worcester before I had made ten I lobbed a poor shot just over silly mid-off's head. But I got away with it, settled down, and played quite well for 59. It rained and we had no second innings. On the Saturday I made 42 against Kent at Hastings, and on the strength of this and a 97 for Sussex against the Australians in my one other game earlier that year I was asked to play in the Fourth Test at Old Trafford.

It made the perfect newspaper story; one journalist was able to be the first to tell me that I had been selected while I was with the children in their Sunday School during the afternoon. The *Sydney Morning Herald* wrote in the best *Boy's Own* style about the curate being whisked from the youngsters of the parish, and with almost no practice walking out to take 100 off Lindwall, Miller, Davidson and company. The *Daily Sketch* took a coach-load of our Islington boys up to Old Trafford for the first two days.

It *was* like a fairy tale. I had one more innings after the team was selected and was run out for 0. This meant that I had played only four innings in first-class cricket that season. When I walked out to bat I think I was in rather a light-headed mood. From my point of view Lindwall did the best possible thing by bowling me a bumper first ball. It made me realise that it was a serious game, and I buckled down to it.

There was more talk about this match than a dozen others. The wicket was very bare of grass, and there was little pace in it for Lindwall, Miller and Archer. The Australians had been bowled out twice by Laker and Lock on a crumbly wicket in the Third Test at Leeds; the Fifth Test was at the Oval where Laker had taken all ten wickets against them for Surrey, and they expected another turning wicket there. Manchester had seemed their last chance, but even on the first day Benaud and Ian Johnson made the ball turn quite often. Peter May was caught at slip off a ball that turned and lifted from Benaud. Some Australian supporters felt that the wicket was deliberately prepared to suit our spinners. I doubt if it was as simple a case of villainy as that, but more grass was taken off than usual, and something had clearly gone wrong with the preparation of the wicket.

Everything went our way. Richardson and Cowdrey led off with 174 for the first wicket, and Richardson reached 104. Peter May and I put on another 93 and we were 307 for 3 at the end of the first day. The following morning Godfrey Evans had a hit just when the innings was beginning to slump, and made 47 in 29 minutes. I was ninth out for 113 and we totalled 459. Benaud and Johnson each bowled 47 overs and took 2 for 123 and 4 for 151 respectively.

Macdonald and Burke began steadily, but just before tea Laker had Macdonald caught at short-leg by Lock, and promptly bowled Harvey with a perfect ball. Lock had Burke out first ball after tea and Laker did the rest very quickly. It was the only time that I have ever felt that the Australians threw it in without a fight. They were all out for 84 and Laker had 9 for 37.

Several of them tried to hit Laker off his length without much success. England's batsmen had often been told when we had tried to battle our way through when the bowlers were on top, "The Australians always hit their way out of trouble." This was a reminder that different approaches are needed for different situations.

McDonald retired with a knee injury with the second innings score at 28. Harvey rushed up the wicket to Laker first ball, made it into a full pitch, and hit it straight to Cowdrey at mid-on. Burke and Craig fought it out till the end of the day at 51 for 1. Manchester's weather then took over, and there was less than two hours' cricket on Saturday and Monday. Australia was 84 for 2 at the start of the last day, and the wicket was wet and sluggish. Colin Macdonald played a great fighting innings of 89 for his side, which was forgotten in the praises for Laker. The extraordinary thing was that Lock bowled 69 overs, and only took one wicket. Relentlessly Laker worked through the Australian batting. His accuracy never faltered and all the time there was a slight change of pace and flight, while some balls turned and some went straight.

Like most slow bowlers he took years to learn his craft, and he had come a long way from 1948 when the Australians deliberately set themselves to hit him out of sight. They hit eleven sixes off him in a day in the M.C.C. v. the Australians match that year, and scored 404 for 3 on a dusty wicket against him on the last day to win the Leeds Test. He was not selected to go to Australia until 1958–9, when various Australian batsmen were keen to get at him on their own hard wickets. Certainly he did not rout them as he had done in England, but he took 15 wickets at 21 runs each, and topped the England bowling figures.

I enjoyed playing with Jim Laker: he was a master craftsman, and he had a dry wit. Unfortunately there seemed to be some grievance in his mind which made the book which he wrote when he retired a very bitter one which did no good to cricket, cricketers or himself. I believe he has regretted this very much since.

His performance at Old Trafford in 1956 broke every bowling record in the book. His full figures were:

16.4 overs, 4 maidens, 37 runs, 9 wickets;

51.2 overs, 23 maidens, 53 runs, 10 wickets.

It meant that England led by two matches to one when we went to the Oval for the last Test. The selectors completed an

astonishing year by bringing Denis Compton back for this
match. Selection committees usually come in for more kicks
than anything else, but everything that they touched in 1956
turned to gold. The surprise new choice for the First Test was
Peter Richardson who scored 81 and 73, and went on to have
a thoroughly good series. In the Second Test they left Lock
out on the morning of the match; the same day he was taken
off to hospital, and would not have been able to play at all.
At Leeds they recalled Cyril Washbrook after six years out of
the England side and he rescued the side by making 98, the
best innings I ever saw him play. At Manchester I was brought
in and made 113. At the Oval Compton came back and
played an excellent, and much needed, innings of 94.

As in almost every England innings that year Peter May
was getting runs at the other end to Compton. He hardly
seemed to be with you that year while he was at the wicket,
so intensely did he concentrate on his batting. He averaged
90 for the five Tests. After reaching 222 for 3, England collapsed
at the Oval and were all out for 247. In Tyson's first over Lock
took one of his most fantastic catches. MacDonald glanced a
very fast ball right off the middle of the bat, and an inch or
two off the ground. Lock picked it up right-handed with the
ease of a housewife shelling peas for lunch. One of the secrets
of his brilliant catching is his fanatical keenness which makes
him treat every ball as a matter of life and death. Another
factor is sheer courage; he has had his share of knocks, including
a terrible crack behind the ear against Sussex at Hastings. But
he always comes back, standing a yard closer than most short
legs do. This was possible with Laker because he was so accurate.
If a slow bowler bowls the occasional long-hop it gives the
batsman a chance to frighten the short legs, and the fieldsman
hasn't quite the same eagerness to move forward.

I spent a large part of that Oval Test ducking and weaving
at short-leg as Miller, Archer, Benaud and Lindwall all
decided to swing the bat hard and often at Laker. I only just
had time to move my head out of the way of a low skimmer from
Ron Archer, before Frank Tyson came tearing in from deep

square-leg to hold a wonderful catch by his boots. A little later a powerful sweep from Benaud hit me on the forearm, and it seemed like an anti-climax after so many had just gone past my head.

Australia were only 45 behind us and on the Saturday morning a wet pitch and a hot sun meant a genuine 'sticky' wicket for us to bat on. Davidson made one jump from a good length to Cowdrey, and he was caught off his glove. It was a great chance for Australia to take their revenge, but their bowlers hadn't the same skills for these conditions as Laker and Lock. Peter Richardson and I took every chance to hit the loose ball and I think this was probably the best innings I ever played for England. After an hour on a sticky wicket we came in to lunch at 64 for 1. Keith Miller said as he came off the field, "If we had batted on that, we'd have been 7 for 12—and I'd have got 10 of them!"

Rain interrupted the rest of the game: we tried to push the score along and I made 62. We declared at 182 for 3, leaving Australia two hours to bat. This was making the series doubly sure as we already led 2–1, but I felt we might have declared sooner and given the bowlers a chance to bowl them out. As it was they lost 4 wickets for 10, but hung on and finished at 27 for 5.

I think the England team at the Oval that year was the best that I ever played in: the batting order ran Richardson, Cowdrey, Sheppard, May, Compton, Washbrook, Evans, Laker, Lock, Tyson, Statham. When you remember that Trueman, Bailey, Appleyard and Wardle were in reserve you realise the strength of English cricket at that moment. The only rival among teams I have played in was the side at Manchester against India in 1952 which was Hutton, Sheppard, Ikin, May, Graveney, Watkins, Evans, Laker, Bedser, Lock, Trueman. This was certainly the best English fielding side I remember.

The West Indies came to England in 1957, and all the big names were in the side. John Goddard was captain again, and Worrell, Weekes, Walcott, Ramadhin and Valentine, the

heroes of 1950, were there. In addition came Sobers, Collie
Smith, Kanhai, Gilchrist and Hall. Yet England won the
series by three matches to none. As a member of the 'Opening
Batsmen's Union', I may be accused of having an axe to grind,
but it seemed to me a classic example of the importance of
having a sound pair of opening batsmen. Again and again
England's fast bowlers broke through and were able to attack
these talented stroke-makers while they were still fresh. At one
stage Worrell and Sobers had to go in first. Also the team was
not quite so strong as the names make it sound. Valentine was
not the menace of 1950 and Hall and Kanhai had not yet
'arrived' as great cricketers.

But my first impressions were of a very formidable side. I
played for M.C.C. against them at Lord's and both Walcott
(177) and Sobers (101 not out) played tremendous innings.
Then I saw the first day of the First Test at Birmingham.
England batted on a beautiful wicket and were all out for
184. Just as in 1950 little Ramadhin looked a magician and he
took 7 for 49. By Saturday night West Indies had scored 474
with Collie Smith making a wonderful 161; Walcott had 90,
Worrell 81, Sobers 53, and Ramadhin had snatched two more
wickets. He was only to take another 5 in the whole series, for
now came the biggest swing-round that I remember in Test
cricket. May and Cowdrey determinedly played forward to
every good ball he bowled, and they broke his heart. May made
285 not out, Cowdrey 154, and they put on 411. The match
finished as a draw, with England crowding round the batsmen
and West Indies 72 for 7.

At Lord's on a fiery, fast bowlers' pitch England won by an
innings. Bailey had 11 for 98 in the match, Cowdrey scored 152,
Richardson 76 and Evans 82. The best batting from West
Indies came when their position was almost hopeless: Weekes
played brilliantly for 90, having a finger broken in his right
hand in the process, and Sobers made 66.

The Nottingham Test provided a feast for the batsmen.
Graveney was really greedy, making 258, Richardson had
126, May 104. Worrell carried his bat right through the innings

for 191 not out but in spite of this wonderful effort West Indies had to follow on. When five wickets had fallen in their second innings, they were still 158 behind. Then Collie Smith played his greatest innings. Denis Atkinson helped him put on 105, and John Goddard joined in a stand of 154.

There was an air of anticipation when Smith came to the wicket always with a large, happy grin: he would take guard and then flex his muscles, showing the tremendous strength of his shoulders. He liked to play with freedom from care, and never lost his liking for hitting sixes. But he learned also to play with discipline when things were difficult. He was a delightful man and a very popular team member. I remember with pleasure a service in St. George's Church, Leeds, during the Fourth Test, when I preached, and Collie came and read the lesson. It was a shock to all cricketers when he was killed in a road smash at the age of 26.

I was brought into the side for the last two Tests. Leeds produced a good wicket, but it was overcast, and the ball swung about all through the match. Peter Loader, whom I have always admired greatly as an opening bowler, took 6 for 36 in West Indies' first innings. He had fine control of swing, changed his pace cleverly, and, without being as fast as Trueman or Statham, could be very nasty. West Indies were all out for 142. England lost 3 for 42 and always had to work hard for runs. Worrell took 7 for 70 with medium-pace swingers. May made 69, Cowdrey 68, and I got 68 too. We led by 137, and though Sobers and Walcott fought hard we won by an innings and five runs.

I had some trouble in my left hand just before the Oval Test, which goes by the name of tinosinovitis. I was finding that I could not grip the bat properly. In the written invitation to play in a Test match you are always asked to send a telegram to Lord's saying that you are available and "completely fit". I rang up to tell them exactly how my hand was, and went along the day before the match, wondering whether I should withdraw from the side. My doubts were settled when I went into the England dressing-room: the first thing I saw was Tony

Lock busily bandaging his knee and Trevor Bailey having plaster wound round every possible muscle that he might pull. I decided that I was fit.

For fun I had often imitated Len Hutton's grip of the bat with the left hand round the back of the handle, and I used this now. It meant there was no jar on the hand, although it restricted one or two of my scoring strokes. Thinking of plaster and pulled muscles reminded me of a delightful Canadian, Henry Basil Robinson, who played for Oxford in 1948. He went on a Free Foresters tour of Holland with Gubby Allen, then 46 years old. After seeing all the different bandages and plasters which were supporting Gubby on the field, Robinson referred to him. in broad Canadian tones as 'The Regius Professor of Elastoplast'.

The wicket for the Oval Test was an extraordinary sight. At Sydney in 1963 Grace said, "It seems extraordinary that they should keep the whole ground green, except the part you play on"—which was a pale brown. The Oval pitch in 1957 looked much the same, and on the day before the match I ventured to say I thought we ought to have another wicket cut. I was told that it might play much better than it looked.

During the first over of the match Worrell bowled a ball outside the leg stump. It knocked a piece the size of a half-crown right out of the pitch and went past the off stump. The spinners did nearly all the bowling and the ball was always turning, though slowly. Peter Richardson and I (plus my new grip on the bat) put on 92 for the first wicket before I was out for 40.

I enjoyed batting with Peter: he was always looking for short singles. A tap wide of the fielder, a look, a nod, and off we'd go. He has never been among the great players as a stroke-maker, but the bigger the occasion the more he seemed to score runs with pushes here and there—and always those short singles. He came badly unstuck on the 1958-9 tour of Australia and seems to have been put out of regular reckoning for the England side since then. The higher bounce of the ball on Australian wickets may have accounted for his being caught behind the wicket so often, but on English wickets I should like to see him given much more of a chance. He made 103 that day, but everything was overshadowed by Tom Graveney's innings: everyone else kept the ball out of their wickets, and by placing the ball kept the score ticking along with an occasional full-blooded stroke. But Graveney stroked the ball all round the field with perfect timing, as though it was coming fast and true on to the bat. Tom in this mood leaves most players in the world standing. The pity is that he has rarely produced runs against Australia when the 'heat' has been turned full on.

When West Indies batted Lock and Laker soon got to work, Lock being the chief wrecker on this occasion with 5 for 28 and 6 for 20. Sobers batted splendidly to make 39 and 42 out of totals of 89 and 86. In my view this wicket was a worse one than that at Old Trafford when Laker took 19 wickets.

Wickets play a greater part in the game than is often realised: in the 1930's in England they were very true with little grass on them, and it was very much the batsman's game. In 1937 a committee under Mr. Findlay set the pendulum swinging the other way: in 1948 the bowler, instead of having to wait until 200, could take the new ball after 55 overs. The invention of sprinklers which could automatically creep round the outfield, doing the watering at night, meant that the shine would stay on the ball much longer, and improved materials for making cricket balls had the same result.

For some years which came to an end about 1957 a number of counties produced wickets with far less preparation on which spin bowlers flourished. Wickets tumbled and the spectators were expected to be pleased. Recently the swing has been back to try to produce hard pitches, and the fast bowlers have to wait until 85 overs have been bowled before they can take the new ball. But the typical English wicket now has a cushion of grass on it, and is surrounded by a beautiful, green, park-like outfield. It was a natural thing to want to make grounds look pleasant, but its effect has, I believe, been a bad one. Now every county has its squad of three or four fast bowlers, polishing or licking away to keep the shine on the ball. The effect has been to lose the hard-earned skills of a slow bowler who can tease batsmen out on a good wicket, and equally the young batsman does not have enough confidence to go through with the finest shots in the game.

Great batsmen are normally bred on good wickets, and a bowler who is going to hold his own in Test cricket must learn to bowl without expecting too much assistance from the wicket. Much of the remedy lies in the groundsman's hands. He must cut his outfield really short, even at the risk of killing grass, for his job is to produce a cricket ground, not a park. And he must rake and roll the wicket until he has a packed-down surface which will remove the shine from the ball. If the ball hurries through, it encourages the genuine fast bowler and the batsman who plays strokes.

CHAPTER 9

QUESTIONS WHICH HURT

FAR and away the most difficult personal decision I have ever had to make, which concerned cricket, led to my publicly refusing to play against the South Africans in 1960. I should like to explain as best as I can what brought me to this decision.

At no time was it a question of personal dislikes; quite the reverse. I had greatly enjoyed playing against the South Africans; I was never selected for a Test match against them, but made a century for Sussex against them both in 1951 and 1955. I counted several of their team as personal friends, particularly Jackie McGlew who was captain of the 1960 team. They were friendly cricketers and played good cricket. The 1955 series in England was one of the best in recent years. May was at his best for England, but Adcock, Heine, Goddard and Tayfield made a very strong attack while McGlew, Goddard, Endean, McLean, Waite, Keith, Cheetham and Winslow made a long batting line up to bowl out. They were well captained by Jack Cheetham who had led the young and inexperienced team which so surprisingly halved the series in Australia in 1952-3. They came to the Oval Test two matches all and went down there to some fine bowling by Laker and Lock.

Very much the same teams met in South Africa in 1956-7 when Clive van Ryneveld, later a Progressive Party Member of Parliament, captained South Africa in a great come-back to draw the series after being two matches down. This was the only time that Johnny Wardle was given his head to bowl his wrist spinners—off breaks and googlies. He took 26 wickets in the series, and produced the best bowling overseas by any English slow bowler since the war. I have never known who really made the decisions about this, Yorkshire, England or

Wardle himself. But he rarely bowled this method, usually sticking to his orthodox, and very accurate, slow left-hand leg-spinner, less expensive, but less dangerous.

For South Africa Heine and Adcock were a very hostile pair of fast bowlers: Peter Richardson went in first for England on that tour with Trevor Bailey. Peter told me that one evening Heine and Adcock started to ask him about what kind of man Trevor was. "He's all right. You'd like him," said Peter. "Come over and have a talk with him." The conversation went all right for a little, then Neil Adcock asked Trevor, "Who would you say was the fastest bowler you have ever played against?" The teasing reply was typical of a man who was not afraid of anyone. "I don't know that I've ever batted against what I'd call a *fast* bowler," said Trevor. For my part I've always thought it wise to be nice to fast bowlers.

Tayfield was a great slow bowler, possibly the best of all the off-spinners on good wickets where the ball will not turn. Perhaps English batsmen were too slow to move up the wicket to him, but he had every trick of the trade. He followed two fine slow bowlers Athol Rowan, right arm off-spinner and 'Tufty' Mann, left-hander, who died tragically as a young man. They bowled England out in the Nottingham Test in 1951. The following day I played for M.C.C. at Sherborne against my old school. Playing in the M.C.C. side was Colonel Robins, R. W. V. Robins' brother. He had much of the same aggressive approach to the game as his brother, and though I hadn't played at Nottingham he attacked me as soon as he arrived, as though I was personally responsible for modern English batting. "England bowled out by two slow bowlers!" he exclaimed, "I look in the paper to see if anyone was out stumped, going up the wicket to them. Nobody stumped! Then I look to see if anyone was out run-out, trying to steal a short single. Nobody run-out!"

At the time that the M.C.C. Team to tour South Africa was being selected in 1956, I was playing in the England team in the last two Tests against Australia. One day Crawford White who was then cricket correspondent of the *News Chronicle* rang me up. He wanted to write a piece about why I was not available for the South African tour. I had then been ordained less than a year, and I reminded him of this, and said, "I am not available because I have a lot of work to do in my job as a curate." "Yes," he said, "I know that, but I can't help feeling that the way non-Europeans are treated in South Africa must have had something to do with it. Knowing you, I think you'd have quietly packed your bags and gone home half way through the trip." He asked me if I minded if he wrote an article along these lines. I said, "You can write whatever you like about what you think my reasons may be, but the one reason which has counted with me is that I have a job to do in Islington, which makes it quite impossible to be away for the winter." A few hours later he rang back and read me what he had written. It was perfectly fair, putting nothing into my mouth which I had not said, but hazarding a guess as to what my thoughts might be.

But newspapers have a tradition, a dangerous one in my opinion, that headlines are always written by someone quite apart from the writer of a piece. The writer himself has no power over the headlines, which can alter his whole meaning. Crawford White's piece appeared the next day on the front page with the headline, "I WON'T PLAY IN AFRICA". This did not represent what he had written, and of course it changed its sense. The headline was quoted elsewhere, and I received a cutting from an African paper *The Drum* praising me for my refusal to play in racially dominated cricket. While the tour was on, a juicy newspaper story appeared in a Johannesburg paper. It said that the team on the way to South Africa had each been given a copy of Father Huddleston's book *Naught for your comfort*, and had dropped them over the side of the ship at dead of night, while I had not been selected because I would not give M.C.C. an undertaking not to talk politics on the tour.

It is very difficult ever to keep something in cricket secret from the Press. There are so many correspondents trying to beat each other to a story, that, like a corps of detectives, they usually smell out what is going on. It was nice to keep one little secret from them that winter. During the South African tour there were injuries and loss of form, and Peter May wrote to me to ask if I would fly out for three Test matches. I had to say No, and carefully sent a cable which would not give this away. I even went to the length of signing it with a nickname I had for a time at Cambridge.

Gradually I was forced to think more deeply about South Africa. Cricketing friends went coaching there every winter and they often talked about South African attitudes to non-whites. George Cox went regularly for years to a school in Port Elizabeth. One day he was batting in the nets, and kept playing the typical Cox slash. One of the boys said, "Sir, you bat like a native." "Perhaps that is because I *am* a native—of Sussex" came the reply. Alan Oakman went on the M.C.C. Tour in 1956–7. One day he was driving a car, and had the misfortune to knock an African off a bicycle. He stopped and ran back to see if he was all right: a crowd of white people gathered round, not doing anything for the man who was hurt, but clamouring for Alan's autograph. He found it very difficult to persuade anyone to fetch help for the injured man. And another friend, sitting with a senior South African cricketer at a Test match, asked him if the Africans played cricket: "Man, they're savages," was the reply. These incidents sound like scurrilous stories: but I have included them to show that apartheid is not only a Nationalist party policy; it reflects a way of thinking which takes in the majority of white South Africans including many who are enthusiastic sportsmen, and carry their thinking into their sport.

Of course I never believed that this was the only attitude, and I have met many white South Africans who have cared tremendously about non-whites and their opportunities. I do not think for a moment that there is some simple answer to their very complex problems which would solve everything in ten or even twenty years. I have never been to South Africa, but some things are right and some are wrong at any distance. Sometimes indeed it is possible to see great issues more clearly

A pause in decorating the club. Members with their leader, George Burton.

CLUB EVENINGS AT
THE MAYFLOWER

Sir John Hunt shows us how it's done.

We want service—from the canteen.

George Burton's flat is an informal meeting place.

"THE SUNDAY GROUP".

Some senior leaders discuss a point.

from afar. There is an illustration of this in cricket: Test cricketers are very inclined to say of the newspaper critic, sitting up in the Press Box, "What does he know about it? When did he ever play Test cricket?" Down there in the middle we know all the difficulties. But, let it be whispered, sometimes it is easier to see some of the great issues of the game better from the detachment of the Press Box.

Apartheid has often been misunderstood, so its defenders tell us. There could be an honest policy of Apartheid, or separate development of the races. In June 1956 a Volkskongres was convened at Bloemfontein by the Federation of Afrikaans Cultural Organisations, the three Dutch Reformed Churches and the South African Bureau of Racial Affairs.* Between 600 and 700 people attended the congress, about two-thirds of them being ministers or missionaries. There were almost no farmers or industrialists present—and no Africans. They reaffirmed their belief in apartheid—but total apartheid—no more African servants, no more African labour in industry. This was at once disowned by the South African government who said, correctly, that Bantu labour was essential to the country's economy.

The point at which the government's hand was really shown was in the Bantu Education Act of 1953. This provided education up to a certain level: beyond that the Bantu is *never* to go. Alexander Steward of South Africa House in London wrote a book called, *You are wrong Father Huddleston*. In it he quoted the increased amount of money spent on educating Bantus—rising in the first eight years of the Nationalist Government from £4,250,000 to £8,500,000. "These are imposing figures," he said. What he did not do was to compare the expenditure each year on white children and non-white. In 1960–1, the expenditure per African child in state and state-aided schools was calculated† at 12.46 rands (having slowly *decreased* from 17.99 rands in 1953). A rand is worth approximately ten

---

* *A Survey of Race Relations in South Africa* 1955–56 compiled by the South African Institute of Race Relations.
† *Survey of Race Relations* 1962.

L

shillings. The expenditure on white children in 1961 was as follows:

In the Transvaal
For Primary education   R90.66   Government   R31.74
                                               providing
For Secondary education R141.74   do.   R49.61
In Natal   R131.95   do.   R29.13
In the Free State   R136.00   do.   R59.84

In other words, the government in 1961 was spending from two and a half times to five times as much on each white child as on each African child.

When I refused to play against the 1960 South Africans, I was accused of bringing politics into cricket. It was said that I was beating cricketers, who maybe disapproved of the policies, in order to get at the government. But I was protesting against apartheid in cricket. Of course it would have been far easier to play and to argue that the South African selection was nothing to do with me. Some of their cricketers had made a point of playing with non-whites when they could. But the fact remained that politics had long since entered South African cricket just as they affect every part of life in South Africa. Before the Nationalist Government came to power cricket in South Africa was played on a racial basis. And the team we were being asked to play against clearly did not represent the whole of South Africa. Basil d'Oliveira, a coloured man from the Cape, had already shown that he was a better cricketer than men who were selected, and the selection was plainly made on a racial basis.

Cricket can be a wonderful bridge for drawing together men of different races. I was delighted when I went to the Oval Test match last year to see England v. West Indies. Perhaps half the crowd came from the West Indies. Sitting next to us was a couple from British Guiana; with us at lunch was a group from Trinidad. Here was cricket playing its part in bringing men together. Standing out from all the other cricketing countries is South Africa where only racial cricket can be played, white with white, coloured with coloured, Bantu with Bantu.

I did not think that the action of a cricketing clergyman in England would be likely to sway Dr. Verwoerd from his iron policy. That was not my motive. I certainly hoped that it might help jolt some white South Africans into new thinking. But far the strongest motive to me was to try to encourage African Christians. Both in South Africa and all over the continent the Christian Church is attacked as an institution which supports white dominance. It seems to me that every Christian, in whatever way lies to his hand, should show that he does not believe that white men are better or different in God's eyes. And the ball was in my court, for the Duke of Norfolk asked me to play for his side against the South Africans in the first match of their tour. I asked him to excuse me, but I still had to decide whether I would make this public.

In January I wrote to the Archbishop of Capetown whom I had known when he was previously Bishop of Stepney. I told him I had decided not to play but wondered whether he felt it would do any good for me to make this public. He replied that if I felt I could make this known, he believed "it would do a tremendous amount for our cause here." In March I wrote to the President of the M.C.C., Harry Altham. I was a member of the M.C.C. Committee, but was retiring after three years early in May. It seemed to me right to tell them what I was going to do, and wait until I was no longer a member of the Committee before I made it public. Harry Altham wrote back saying he hoped I would be able to reconsider making this public.

This made me think it through all over again. I wrote to five or six Christian leaders to ask their advice: they all knew much more than I about the issues involved, but, except in one case, I could not guess what their opinions were likely to be. All but one said that they thought it would be right to make this public. The one came from South Africa. He said he thought it would not help, and added that the only thing we could do was to pray. I would not dispute for a moment the need for Christians to pray, but I believe that there are times when it is right to speak out.

Just at this time, when I had just about decided that I should speak out about this, I drove up to the centre of London early one morning. I had a committee meeting over breakfast, and I came up from Canning Town quite early in order to miss the worst of the traffic. I sat in the car on the embankment and read some verses from the Bible as I try to do regularly. I was reading Isaiah at the time and I started to read that day at Isaiah 58, verse 1; "Cry aloud, spare not, lift up your voice like a trumpet; declare to My people their transgressions," I read. And as I went on I saw that the prophet was to tell God's people to "loose the bonds of wickedness, to undo the thongs of the yoke, to let the oppressed go free." It was not a case of opening the Bible at random and putting my finger on a verse. It was my regular reading. There have been several days when particular words in my Bible reading have stood out with great force to meet my needs. I felt that no passage from the Bible could have spoken more clearly about my question of the moment.

Some of those who said that I should have kept my mouth shut held that a parson should only speak about 'religion'. This is a view of religion which is totally foreign to the Bible. Such men want to think of life in a series of watertight compartments. "Don't let your home life affect your business life. Don't let your business life affect your sport. Don't let religion affect the way you run the other parts of your life." But the whole point is that, if Christ is Lord, there are no *other* parts of life. He claims to be the Lord of every part of life.

It is possible to go to the other extreme and to spend the whole of life protesting about one abuse or another. I certainly have never felt called to do that. Since I spoke out about South Africa, I have been asked to join in protests on all manner of subjects, about which I knew nothing. I have steadily refused unless it has been a subject in which I felt strongly that I must be involved. Looking back, I see the South African cricket issue as a thing I could not avoid, and I am thankful that I did not side-step it.

Harry Altham and I had an hour together in which I told him what my motives were: though he did not agree with me, he respected my position, and could not have been fairer to me. He gave me the opportunity at the end of an M.C.C. committee meeting to explain what I was going to do and why.

In the event it was impossible to keep this secret until May: English newspaper interest in South Africa was at boiling-point: at Sharpeville only a few weeks before 67 Africans had been shot dead by the police after a demonstration. On the eve of the South African team's arrival the Press guessed or got wind of my position, and came to ask me all about it. So that my refusal to play was headlined over all the newspapers as they arrived. I wrote to Jackie McGlew to try to make plain that there was no personal feeling of any kind, and to apologise for the hurt he would feel, but saying that I believed greater issues were at stake.

AMATEURS AND PROFESSIONALS

During my first county match the local Hastings paper made a caustic remark about 'The anaemic amateurs' in the Sussex side. There were four of us, and we did not contribute very much to the Sussex cause. If some suggested that the amateur was anaemic, others regarded him as a blue-blooded left-over from a former generation. It is true that years ago amateurs and professionals came on to the field by separate gates on many grounds, and that even in my time there have sometimes been separate dressing-rooms for them. But by and large cricket has followed common-sense about this. Amateurs and professionals have played together in the same teams; I always regarded myself as being on the same basis as any other member of the team.

There have been exceptions: when I was at Cambridge we played against Gloucestershire at Bristol. I made some runs, and, as we came off the field, Tom Graveney with whom I had made friends in 2nd XI matches said, "Well played, David."

A few minutes later the Gloucestershire captain for that match walked into our dressing-room and came over to me. "I'm terribly sorry about Graveney's impertinence," he said. "I think you'll find it won't happen again." I found Tom as soon as I could, and said how sorry I was, and we have laughed about it often since.

There are those in the Pavilion at Lord's who probably agreed with Lord Hawke's famous wish, "Please God, no professional will ever captain England." But they are far from being the majority, and we have long been far in advance of other sports where professionals are not allowed to compete in great national events, although amateurs frequently draw their living from the sport. The M.C.C. Committee has often been depicted as the most reactionary bunch of diehards: my experience in three years on that committee, and in several more years of belonging to other committees at Lord's, has been that, though there is a strong conservative element, there is a readiness to listen fairly to what the young men have to say.

The post-war facts of life for first-class cricketers have been that no one can afford to play cricket for six days a week throughout the summer unless someone pays him. If he received a salary directly from the County Club to play cricket for them he was called a professional: if he was paid by them as an assistant secretary, who was expected to play cricket, if some firm allowed him four months off because they felt their prestige grew by having a first-class cricketer in their ranks, or if he earned money by writing for newspapers on cricket, or for advertising his name on cricket equipment or for a breakfast food, he could still be termed an amateur.

The time came when many of us wondered if the name meant anything any longer. Young men like myself could play for nothing while we were still single or at University. But it would not be long before we had to earn something. It seemed to me that the line between earning a living from cricket directly or indirectly had become very difficult to define. Yet when Paul Gibb became a professional cricketer, having previously been

an amateur, he felt obliged to ask that his membership of
M.C.C. be held over until he had finished playing as a professional. Though the game has largely been played by professionals, none has been a member of the M.C.C. committee,
though groups of professional cricketers have been consulted
on occasions. I hope that this may be put right now that the
distinction between amateurs and professionals has been
removed.

The strongest part of the case for retaining the distinctive
status of amateur, was that it is good to have players, and
particularly a captain, who are independent-minded. It was
felt that a man who does not earn his living by the game might
play with a freer approach, and that an amateur can more
easily snap his fingers at his committee, when that is a good
thing to do, than someone who is a 'servant of the club'. Yet I
can think of an amateur county captain who was the complete
slave of his committee and of professional captains who have
had a most independent spirit.

The personality of the man himself rather than his status is
what counts. And if we start thinking about status, the men
whom we should consider first are those who are the backbone
of the first-class game—the professional cricketers. The professional cricketers of today are not the same as those who once
were expected simply to bowl and not to be able to think. I
wondered what the old Yorkshire professionals would have
made of the young professional whose book I noticed when we
were sitting in an aeroplane in Australia. One day he was
reading *Dr. Zhivago*, and the next time I looked it was the
Annals of Tacitus.

I was a member of a committee to discuss Amateur Status
in 1957-8. I was one of only two who then voted for the
abolition of any distinction: the committee's report said that it
"considered that the distinctive status of the amateur cricketer
was not obsolete, was of great value to the game and should be
preserved." At the same time it was agreed that broken time
payments should be made to amateurs who went on M.C.C.
tours overseas. I did not agree with the committee's decisions,

but I did not think it right to resign as I felt that it was an opinion honestly held, and that there might be a chance later to put our case again in commitee. Mercifully we had a discussion one day about what a member of a committee should do if he was asked about a committee decision which he did not agree with. We agreed that, unless he resigned, he ought to be loyal to the decision of the committee.

A few weeks after this I was 'Guest of the week' on the B.B.C. television programme *Sportsview*. I arrived in rather a hurry, without any idea of what we were going to talk about. Two sporting journalists were interviewing me, and they started straight away on the decisions of the Committee on Amateur Status. They may well have guessed that I did not agree with its decisions, but I remembered the discussion of a few weeks before, and answered, "What the Committee had in mind was . . ." and "It was felt that . . ."

Duly the subject came up again in committee: it was too difficult to draw the line. A tribunal had to say to one man, "We accept that you are a *bona fide* amateur," and to another, "We declare you to be a professional." When another committee was formed to look into the state of first-class cricket, amateur status came up again. There was more support now for removing all distinction, calling all players 'Cricketers', and making their financial arrangements a private affair between them and their clubs. Some committee members still said, "I'm sure it's going to come eventually," but did not want it now. One said, "I'm sure it's going to come, but I can't vote against the amateur."

But finally opinion swung towards 'abolition'. It was honest: it offered flexibility to a club who might want to give someone a run before he signed a regular contract with them, or to a professional who no longer wanted to play full-time, or to someone who didn't want to sign on for the whole summer, but could afford time for a month or two of cricket if he was paid match money. It will take time for clubs to work new methods out, but it could make it possible to have a wider circle of players, as there was in pre-war days. No doubt this would be less efficient than to have a small, regular, playing squad, but it might well bring new colour and interest to the game.

SUNDAY CRICKET

New solutions to the way first-class cricket should be organised are always being propounded. One of the most frequently put forward is the idea that every week there should be one week-end match only, on Saturday, Sunday and Monday so that players should be able to do an ordinary job of work for the rest of the week. The practical politics of this are very doubtful: the strongest asset most county clubs have are their regular members (greatly increased in numbers since the war). They would not want the number of matches they can watch cut by half. Certainly they would not want to make it half as likely that they would see Yorkshire and Surrey play. Again many counties have the heavy overhead expenses of running a county ground. If they do this, the most economical thing to do is to use it as often as possible.

Apart from this radical suggestion there are many who think Sunday should become one of our regular big match days. They suggest that the only thing which stops this coming about is the prejudice of a small group who wish to impose their pattern of Sunday upon the majority.

But it would be mistaken to think that the only 'defenders' of the English Sunday are those who feel that no one should ever kick a football or hit a cricket ball on Sunday. The Report of the Wolfenden Committee on Sport, published in 1960, has a section on Sunday sport. It says that there is a difference between "private or semi-private enjoyment and organized, commercial sport". It does not condemn the former, but believes that the majority of fair-minded men would want to prevent the growth of commercial sport on Sunday. Gate-keepers, ground staff, public transport, caterers, would all be involved as all would have to be 'on parade' on what would presumably be one of the big match days.

We were discussing this in the England dressing-room one day. I said that, for example, a Test match would involve a tremendous number in work. "Oh I wouldn't want to have Test matches on Sunday," was the reply. But it is naïve to think that, if the law was changed to allow county cricket on Sundays, we should not have Test matches, plus horse racing, professional soccer, and all the other sports.

The Church of England took a definite line about this in 1947. The Convocation of Canterbury and York accepted a report called *Your Sunday in Danger*. This report represents a very large constituency of moderate Christian opinion. It appealed "To all men of goodwill to co-operate in all such steps as can wisely be taken to safeguard Sunday as a day of rest from avoidable labour, and in particular to resist the increasing menace to the character of Sunday from the commercialisation of Sunday amusements."

It is true that the 'defenders' have sometimes said some very intolerant things. They have sometimes presented Christianity as a code of rules rather than as a personal and joyful faith in a living Lord. And the pattern of Sunday at home, with a walk in the country, or a stroll round the garden, is scarcely possible in the middle of a great industrial area such as I live in in East London.

But what most of us want to fight for is a *different* day, when no more than necessary are forced to work, and families are left free to spend the day as they will. When Christians argue for what they believe is best for the whole country they are regularly accused of interfering in other people's lives. But every citizen has a right to fight for what he thinks is best for the whole country, and I believe it would be a tragedy both for Christian and non-Christian if Sunday were commercialised further. There are really not many Christians who want to impose the details of how to spend Sunday on those who do not share their faith. We have come a long way from May 1622, when the cricketers of Boxgrove in Sussex were presented to the Bishop of Chichester, charged

"First, for that it is contrary to the Seventh Article, secondly, for that they use to breake the church windows with the ball; and thirdly, for that a little childe had like to have her braynes beaten out with a cricket bat."

When my faith in Christ became a real thing, I started to think differently about Sunday cricket. Until then I had frequently played in Sunday club matches or charity games. Now I wanted my faith to grow: I needed time to worship God, but not only that. My weeks seemed to race past at ninety miles an hour, and time to read, time to think, time to relax and talk with other Christians, time to visit or write to others in need, was not easily found. I accepted the Ten Commandments as being God-given, and in the commandment about the Sabbath there is clearly a great principle that man needs one day in seven for rest and worship. While I was playing cricket six days a week, the fact that I kept Sunday as a different day, when I could unhurriedly turn my mind to God, was the most important single factor in keeping my faith strong. I happen to think that it also meant that I played cricket with a fresher approach.

First-class cricket on Sunday would put an unfair pressure on a young man who had this kind of feeling and who also had cricketing ambitions. If there were only one match a week, played partly on a Sunday, he would be totally shut out of cricket if he followed his conscience.

And for all cricketers I doubt if such a change would be for the good. We have rarely, if ever faced up to the question of how much we take our top cricketers away from their homes: long winter tours abroad and six-day-a-week cricket in the summer mean that players are not very often at home. If the idea is that they should do an ordinary job for four days a week, no doubt with some evening practice, and play a three-day match at the week-end, the strain of living would mount one degree more. Whether a man is working with his hands, running a business or playing cricket, I do not believe that he can give of his best if he is at it seven days a week.

CHAPTER 10

BRIDGES BY THE DOCKS

A NUMBER of friends tried to persuade me that I ought to find a job which would enable me to travel round, and speak to the widest possible numbers. To put it bluntly they said that I should cash in on the reputation cricket had given me. Provided my motives were right I do not think there would be anything wrong in that, for it would be using a gift God has given me. A young man came to me at the end of a University meeting in Wellington, New Zealand, and said, "Frankly I only came because I was interested in you as a cricketer." But he went on to tell me that he had become interested in what I said, and felt that he must really think about the claims of Christ.

But the longer I stayed in Islington the stronger grew my desire to be able to meet and explain the Christian faith to the families of 'happy pagans' around us who had no contact of any kind with the Church beyond baptisms, weddings and funerals. The word 'happy' is important because the problem of the great industrial areas of our cities is no longer, thank God, that of poverty-stricken slums. Bruce Kenrick has written a brilliant book about East Harlem in New York which is full of good thinking about the Christian approach to the industrial areas of our cities.* But East Harlem is full of unhappy families in a way which is almost unknown in London except in small pockets which exist in several areas. This is not our main problem. The problem in the industrial areas of England is that the majority of those who go to church go only at a time when they feel unhappy. Those who are lonely or depressed, the youngster who is in trouble with the law, the

---

* *Come out the Wilderness* by Bruce Kenrick published by Collins.

ill or the hungry—these will very often turn to the Church for help, and certainly it is part of our task to help them.

But we must never be content with helping simply those who come to us. Most of our neighbours in London are quite well off; their lives are happy enough and they see no reason why they should come anywhere near the Church. However good our services or our preaching may be, they will have little effect on our neighbours, because they can see no reason why they should attend them. When young people have come to a thoughtful faith in Christ, they have frequently developed new ideas and new standards (which may have been learned from Christ or maybe simply from another social group they have begun to mix with). When they have married they have usually wanted to move out to a suburban district, for the sake of the children. I am not at the moment trying to say whether they were right or wrong to move out. Often housing shortages seem to force them out. All I am trying to show is that most of our neighbours have rarely, if ever, seen a thoughtful Christian couple living in their district. The Christian gospel has been presented to them by 'outsiders' who have travelled in to tell them about it or who have come to live for a few years in the district while they were young and single. No wonder so many working men think of Christianity as something very admirable, but only for 'them', for those who wear collar and tie, work in an office and travel in from the suburbs.

After two years in Islington we saw that if we were going to meet them effectively we had to be prepared to live for a long time as their neighbours and offer long-term friendship. What we needed was some bridge of neutral ground upon which we might meet and make friends. We wanted a bridge for another purpose too, so that young men and women who wanted to serve God with their lives should be able to come and live in an industrial area. They could see some of its needs, share in Christian work there, understand what abilities they had, and go away and tackle similar, or maybe quite different needs elsewhere.

One day in 1957 I went to speak to a group of youngsters

at the Dockland No. 1 Settlement in Canning Town. This was a
large block of buildings which had grown up since the 1890's
when it started life as the Malvern College Mission. Malvern
College had broken their links with it a few years before,
principally because it was such a long distance to keep up
effective contact. Now the Dockland Settlements Committee,
who managed several other settlements, were on the point of
deciding to sell the Canning Town buildings for factory use.

This much I gathered during my visit that Sunday afternoon: I also felt that this was just the kind of place where the
dreams I had been dreaming about 'bridges' might come true.
I had a contact which made me bold enough to approach the
Bishop of Barking, now Archbishop of Sydney, who was *ex
officio* a member of the Dockland Settlements' Committee,
and I wrote to him that evening. He rang me up the next day,
and on the Tuesday I went to see him. After that negotiations
took some time but eventually the Dockland Settlements
handed the Centre over to an undenominational Committee,
which later decided on the name Mayflower Family Centre.
We felt that 'Mayflower' had a ring of Christian adventure
about it: 'Family Centre' described what we wanted to be.
Of course there would be groups for 'youth' and groups for the
'elderly' but we wanted to reach the whole family.

In January 1958 we moved into our flat in the centre and
started off on a new adventure. Douglas Minton, who had
been a club leader in East London since 1920 stayed with us at
the Centre until he retired at Christmas in 1961. He passed on
an unrivalled store of knowledge about our neighbours and the
district, plus an equally unrivalled fund of tall stories. David
Gardner, who had first asked me down to Canning Town,
stayed two years with us as Chaplain, Miss Truscott stayed a
year or two as housekeeper, and Margaret Fish, who came to
Canning Town a year before us, is still our 'lady worker'
doing a great job with groups of 'Mums', 'Wives' and children.

I needed to find Christian youth leaders to join the team,
and the two who came were I believe literally a 'godsend'.
George Burton is a Scot in his forties, who has learned a great

amount of wisdom about people in knocking about the world, and at the same time a deep and practical faith in Christ. Before I came to Mayflower I said that I thought that in the ideal club for our kind of teenager there should be a bit of a riot going on, and the leader leading the riot. This is not a bad description of what George is able to do. There is always a lot of noise in our teenage club, discipline is not paraded, but he has control in his hands. He has built up a strong club of older teenagers, which had just about ceased to exist when he joined us at Easter in 1958. Jean Lodge Patch is our assistant Youth Leader, and she also came with us in 1958. She had been working as an almoner before, and came to grips with her job in our team with great courage and skill. We have spent much time together discussing, praying and planning, and Jean's patience and shrewdness has played a vital part in helping us to come to a common vision for our work.

To complete our present team, Hilary Harman came with us at the beginning as our secretary, upon whom the efficient running of the Centre largely depends. She knows how my mind works, and I am able to lean heavily on her in organizing my life. Joan de Torre came in 1962 as Head Teacher of the Nursery School which has sixty children of three and four years old; like each of the staff Joan does not regard this as a job which finishes after certain hours. She is interested not only in the children but in the families, and spends many evenings visiting homes. Her assistants in the Nursery School are Sheila Harvey and Pat Deadman, one of own own local young leaders. Dilys Gething joined us as housekeeper in 1961 and has a family of thirty to look after. She makes them, and all the others who drop in at every awkward moment, feel relaxed and at home. Apart from our staff the thirty are made up of young men and women who want to help at the Mayflower, and are working or teaching in the district or training for the ministry of the Church, for youth leadership, probation work or the like.

There is a great value in working in a team; where the local Church is strong I believe the Vicar should make a team out of his most loyal Christians, take them into his confidence, plan together with them, pray with them, and share the work with them; where the local Church is almost non-existent as it was at Mayflower in 1958, a team has to be imported at the beginning if the Church is to tackle its task in strength. One man alone can all too easily feel lonely and depressed. Out of the clash of different ideas in a team hard thinking is borne, and we do not simply try to work according to the pattern we have seen work somewhere else.

I do not believe there is one way to run youth work: there are many different kinds of young people and there should be a variety of different approaches to them. Nor do I believe there is one way to run a local church; we serve a living Master who is actively loving people. We have to love them too, and learn from Him what is the best approach to them.

I had long thought it a good idea to have a men's club in a church. I started one in Islington, and, when we came to the Mayflower, we duly had a men's club. It became little more than a clique who wanted to play snooker or swim, and offered very little welcome to any others who came in. I am ready to wait a very long time for the chance to talk about God and Christ, but I would not think it right for a Christian Church to run a group in which over the years it did not become easier to discuss the Christian faith. But after two and a half years we seemed to be making no progress in this direction. I am not saying that a men's club may not be a very good idea elsewhere, or that it may not be a very good idea one day at the Mayflower. But in our situation we came to feel that the home was a more natural meeting-place, and that it was good to try to meet as couples.

My wife and I have one evening in the week which we keep free for quite a small circle of couples of our own sort of age, who don't come to church. Often their children come to the Centre and this is our point of contact. Sometimes they tell us their own children's faith is a challenge to them. We visit their homes, and about every other week a small group meets in our flat or in another home: we have a friendly, light-hearted

A home meeting provides a chance for discussion.

The Grandfathers' Club provides another place of friendship.

My first jellied eels were a present from Mrs. Olley, one of our members.

evening together, and towards the end of it we have a discussion. Usually we start on some problem which touches each of our lives; a row at work, or in our street, the rights and wrongs of a strike, the difficulty of forgiving and forgetting, why God allows suffering, what it might be like if Jesus came tomorrow to our factory or home. We've never yet had an evening when more than two have not joined in. Christ's name is mentioned often, because it isn't possible for someone who is sincerely trying to follow Him not to bring Him into the events of every day.

If we start on a 'religious' topic I find that newcomers will sit politely and listen to us. But when we have talked about more familiar subjects a few times, they will raise 'religious' questions. If we are ready to build the bridge of friendship, the time generally comes when genuine questions are being asked about our faith. And I believe I have learned much from these friendships, for all true friendship is a two-way thing.

After these 'home meetings' had been going for nearly a year, I went round to some of the couples and said, "We're good friends now. We are in danger of going round and round in our discussions. Would you be prepared to join what I'm going to call a 'Searching Group', and sit down for six evenings when we can fit them in, and try to understand what this Christian faith really means?" Five couples, who two years before never came near Church, came regularly, and I would think that at least five people out of that circle have now come to a definite personal faith, while all but two are coming to our church. On the first evening he came to our home, Ken, who is an electrician, said, "This Christianity would never work in my job." Soon after we came home from Australia he told us what a difference Christ now made in his life. He had come very slowly and cautiously to the place where he thoughtfully committed himself to Jesus Christ.

Adults have come to the church in ones and twos, never so far as I know from seeing a notice board, but always through personal contact. There is a couple whom George Burton first met in their home. They had long talks about Christ, and

M

Charlie prayed and asked Christ to come into his life for the first time, while Rose came back to a faith she had known when she was a girl. It was some weeks before they came to the church, but now they both have real responsibilities at the Mayflower. Another Charlie was set thinking when I spoke at a meeting at his factory. After weighing it up on his own, he committed his life to Jesus Christ, and soon afterwards found his way to our church. For Tom and Grace it all began through their son coming to the teenagers' Sunday group. They began to come to church and after they had been coming a long time, they saw their need to commit their lives personally to Christ.

All ages come to us at the Mayflower but the greatest number are in the 12–21 age group. There are those who claim that if they are given a child in his earliest years, they can win him for life. Without for a moment belittling the importance of doing things for children, I do not agree with this. There are many who go to church as children and drift right away in these see-sawing, rebellious, years between 14 and 20. And these are the years when decisions about career and marriage, which affect the whole of life, are made.

Many think of youngsters' needs primarily in terms of providing facilities and activities for them. Boy's clubs and youth clubs were born in days of poverty and it was natural to think this way then. But today in Britain the need is not to 'keep them off the streets': my belief is that what youngsters want most from adults is unjudging friendship. This does not mean that there must be no discipline. Different leaders will win control in different ways, but they must have control. It does not mean that there must be no beliefs or ideals. Jesus gives the perfect example of unjudging friendship when He says to the woman caught in the act of adultery, "No more do I condemn you." Yet she is in no danger of thinking that He is approving her sin. After He has shown that He is not turning her away, He adds, "Do not sin again."

To bring Christian impact into a club, we need a good number of helpers who have a real faith, and want to share it. They are ready to turn up faithfully, and out of the large numbers in the club to offer friendship to a handful of members. This is difficult. It is so much easier to believe that you have done something for God if you have taken a Bible Class, or if you have instructed them in a game or a skill. But a club is built round friendships, and with some youngsters these can only be made literally by 'sitting where they sit', or standing where they stand. Most of them want to spend a fairly lazy evening.

The helpers who win through are those who stick at it, and come regularly. There are many who talk about the lack of 'stickability' of teenagers. When I think of the number of promises adults have made to them and then broken, promises of a club which closes down after a year because the leader hadn't realised it was going to take so much of his time, promises made for 'every Monday' broken because the youngsters didn't turn up last Monday, I am not surprised that teenagers in their turn do not stick at things. We need first to prove that there is such a thing as adult 'stickability'.

One of our girls wandered back into the club after being away for several months: "Where's Pam?" was her first question. The thing she was looking forward to in coming back to the club was renewing her friendship with a helper. Thank God, Pam was in the club that night and she wasn't disappointed.

At one time I was quite embarrassed when friends asked me, "What do you do in your clubs?" The answer was, "Well, we sit around, and talk." Those who want to hive off to other rooms for judo or weight training, or washing and setting their hair (not a 'mixed' activity!), or outside to our playground for football or cricket. But the club centres round one big room with a canteen in the middle, plenty of noise from the records, snooker tables, table tennis and darts. There are these, but they don't create the club, for the club is people.

Similarly I believe that the role of a Christian Youth Leader is not first the organising of teams and the collection of subscriptions. Normally someone else should do this so that he can give time to his members either in groups or as individuals.

George Burton has a genius for making club members feel they are noticed and wanted. It is an education to walk round the club with him, and see how in a few moments he can draw each member into the circle with a remark about his clothes, his girl friend, or last week's outing. I know also the time he gives to following through the needs of one boy—finding him a job, going to court with him, visiting his home. And I have sat with him late at night while a young couple talk out their problems with him. One of the dangers of status being given to Youth Leaders is that they may begin to reckon their job in terms of so many sessions done in the week. For the Christian Youth Leader much of the most important work is going to be done out of the club and out of hours.

When the Albemarle Committee's report on the Youth Service was published they said that *Association* was the first purpose of running a youth club. I believe they were right; learning to get on with other people is the most important single strand in Education. *Challenge* and *Activities* are real parts of youth work, and they will naturally spring out of the association of members with one another, and with leaders and helpers who have ideas. If we make too many demands upon would-be members as soon as they put their head round the door, there are many who will immediately back away. A club leader once said to me, "You must demand a standard and expect a standard, and you will get a standard." This approach is right for some young people: equally I am sure that there are many other young people who would never give this sort of club a try, and the more free-and-easy way is right for them.

It has often been suggested to me that my cricket must be a tremendous help in our job. This is much less true than might be imagined. I am not the Club Leader and our youngsters know me only as someone who drops in on their evenings. My job is first in bringing together and leading a team, and in reaching homes and building up the family of adult Christians which is gradually growing up. Some of our club members say to me, "You have to go to a posh school to play cricket." I tell them that I wish they could come with me to the cities of

Yorkshire and Lancashire, and they would see that this is untrue. But it is not a game much thought about in the East End of London, though a few are very keen about it. I feel that cricket has its value in our job, as other interests do, in bridging the gap which men think separates Christ's Church from everyday life. It takes a useful place as one of the activities which spring out of the life of the Mayflower.

Facilities are not very good for cricket: I've already described West Ham Park's wicket where our older boys play. One day we took a team of younger boys, whose cricket ground is Star Lane, to play another boys' team elsewhere in London. It was a good grass wicket. Our boys were soundly beaten, and some of them said to me, "You wait till we get them on cinders." Star Lane ground is cinders—not just the wicket, but the whole ground.

One of the more difficult moments was with the older team, when unfortunately—or fortunately—I was not present. Our wicket-keeper caught someone out, and the umpire, as umpires sometimes do, said, "Not out." There happened to be a hammer lying around which had been used for knocking in stumps. The wicket-keeper threw this at the umpire and then gave the batsman a punch-up, which held the game up for ten minutes. Cricketers aren't all the 'poshest' sort apparently.

We are under no illusions about how far we have to bring most of our club members before they will even look at Christianity seriously. I have been several times on a television programme geared for teenagers, called *Sunday Break*. This has been a brave attempt at 'building bridges' between the Christian faith and many young people. One Sunday I discussed with some teenagers on the programme who Jesus was and what they thought about Him. On the Monday I walked into the club. A girl said, "Saw you on the telly last night." "Oh? Did you listen to what we were talking about?" "Talking about cricket, weren't you?" "Yes, and did you listen to the other part we were talking about?" "Talking about God, weren't you?" "Yes. What do you think about Jesus?" "I don't know. I never saw Him, did I?"

This conversation probably represents what a good many of our teenagers would say. On the 'bridge' of our clubs they meet those who have a faith, and argue and discuss with them; once a week they listen to one of us talking about God and life; and most of all we pray that they see something of Him in our lives. We expect it all to take a long time.

The expert who wants to come into the club simply to put over his subject, reckoning to find a group waiting eagerly to be instructed in it rarely gets an audience beyond two or three for more than once. This holds true whether his subject is football, wood work, painting or Christianity. The man they are ready to listen to is someone who has spent time with them in the ordinary life of the club; after a while he can gather his own group, and they will be interested in his subject because they are interested in him. This is doubly true of the man who wants to talk about the Christian faith. If he is simply an expert, dropping in to talk about his subject, there is little chance that young people will give much weight to what he says. Occasionally a visitor can 'ride in on the backs of' those who are regularly there. But normally young people will start to listen only to those they know.

One of the few outsiders who was listened to with real interest was Sir John Hunt. He showed some slides of mountain climbing, then dressed up as for Everest, and showed us how to climb up the wall of the club. He spent the evening moving among club members. Barry came up to him, and said, "I could have climbed it, but my feet would have played me up." It ended with various members tearing round the club with ice-axes, and a good time was had by all. But it was not essentially his story which made them accept John Hunt. It was his deep and genuine interest in our young men and women. They were plainly people who mattered to him, and his humanity and simple faith made the bridge to them.

We are inclined to let other visitors wander round the club with us so that members meet them in an informal way, rather than asking them to speak to everyone as they sit in rows. Richard Attenborough came into the club late one evening.

He was quickly recognised and a crowd of teenagers were soon round him. He took out his cigarette case and offered it to the boy nearest to him. In a moment the case had vanished into the crowd. Roars of laughter eventually subsided with a slightly awkward silence when the case failed to return. It had been full, and when it finally came back it was completely empty. At last another boy said, "Here, you'd better have one of mine," so that the generous visitor did have one for himself.

The big clubs are not our only activities with teenagers. For four or five years George Burton has had a 'Sunday Group' who meet in his flat. They were drawn out of the club, and as a group agreed to come to church on Sunday evenings and to discuss Christianity from time to time. They spend a lot of time together every week, and organise and carry through week-ends and holidays together. This group, and others which have since come into existence, is limited in size, and somehow seems to set its members free to think about God, when in the large club they seem to be more aware of others looking over their shoulder and laughing at them. It is as though they have taken one step towards Christ together by forming the group. They still have to think for themselves and respond to Him for themselves.

I have a tape recording of several members of this group talking to some other young people. They told them something of how they had come to a Christian faith. Pat said, "We used to have quite a few discussions and arguments and films. I just couldn't believe in it. Well, I don't think I really wanted to . . . They had something I hadn't got. I felt that I wanted this thing, but I was slow, dozy, couldn't be bothered." Later it became different as she 'really wanted it'. Her fiancé, Len, also took a long time to think seriously about Christianity: "I didn't like talking about it, because I didn't want to be involved." After a year or more in the group he said that he prayed, "Jesus Christ I believe in You. Will You accept me?" Bill said, "Christianity to me was just a fairy tale. But I began to watch and listen and to try to argue it out. After a year or two one night I asked Christ into my life."

His words, "I began to watch and listen and to try to argue it out" perfectly describe what we want our neighbours, young or old, to be able to do. Few will listen unless they are able to watch and see that the Christian faith makes a difference: this means spending time doing ordinary things together, and being ready to listen ourselves and to share in the process of 'trying to argue it out'. I certainly believe there is a place for explaining the Christian faith by definite teaching. Christianity is not simply common-sense: there is 'Good News' of what Christ can do for us, and many of our neighbours do not understand what it is. But it is often a long time before someone reaches the position where he sees any reason why he should want to understand any Good News. Leaders need to be around and approachable, so that when someone is keen to ask questions they can come and have someone to whom they can put them. Wendy was telling me that she had committed her life to Christ. I asked her when she had done this: she said, "It was some months ago after I had a talk with Miss Lodge Patch late one evening."

It is a maxim of ours that we cannot expect to talk to others about our faith in Christ unless we are prepared also to give them time and real friendship. It is also a maxim that, when someone has come to a clear faith in Christ, he should be given something to do in service for his Lord. Most of this group of young people are carrying definite responsibilities. For over two years some of them have been running a boys' club for under fourteens. Others run a mixed teenage club. While I was away in Australia, several new groups were started, and the leaders are our own young people who want to serve God in this way.

Christian work cannot be measured in numbers: our work can be gauged much better perhaps by listening in on a group of leaders as we sit round in George Burton's flat after the Sunday Group has gone home on a recent Sunday evening. Grace and I wrote down the names of those who had been prayed for as soon as we went downstairs to our flat. All are between the ages of 16 and 22.

First we pray for Doreen, leader of one of the groups; her parents are rowing with her over the time she comes in. Then we pray for Jill with whom I've had a good joke earlier in the evening. Peter's Dad is pressing him to give up the idea of being apprenticed: he wants him to earn more money as a labourer. Bill is going for a job tomorrow; he used never to stick in a job, and this is a great opportunity. Someone else prays for him and the girl he's starting to go out with.

Next there's a boy who used to be a very enthusiastic Christian; now he spends more time criticising. But he could be a fine leader. Another has been a Christian for some years; he's going out with a girl who may not help his faith. Eric and Rosie are mentioned; we're expecting them to announce their engagement in a month or two. Then Carol and Brian who are also engaged; they're not Christians, but they've been coming regularly for years, and erratically they seem quite interested. We pray for Alan and Rita who've just come home from their honeymoon, and have a flat a mile away from us. They have already invited a number of youngsters to their home including two boys who started coming to church after they had talked to them about Christian things. Then Jim and Janet are mentioned who have just announced their engagement; they are strong Christians, taking a lead in clubs and groups. Where will they find a home?

We pray for Sheila who's a bit 'down'. She's lonely, and needs a lot of encouragement. Then there's George who came and told us a week ago that he'd prayed during the service after much thinking, and had given his life to Christ. We pray for Bernie and Lois whom we know very well. They are not coming to us at all at the moment, but both have a personal faith. Her Granny is prayed for as well by George Burton who has visited her today. He mentions Frankie who's been made leader of another group. He goes on to pray for Micky and then Doreen and Rita, who have just been brought up with the Sunday Group. He finishes by going back to the other Doreen and her problem at home and Peter whose parents want him to take the labouring job.

These are only some. If we didn't believe in the Holy Spirit we could never think that we could hold them or help them. The following day Peter came and said that when he got home his Mum and Dad said they'd been talking. Not only could he become an apprentice, but they would give him the tools he needed for Christmas. He and Mr. Burton were standing in the corridor of the club: they had a short prayer together, and at the end the boy looked quietly up and said, "Thank you God."

We don't simply want to make them better citizens. And if we didn't believe in God we shouldn't have been involved in the work in the beginning. It's perhaps surprising that with my family background I wasn't more drawn to this sort of work before. But I wasn't, and it was only the challenge that my London neighbours presented to my Christian faith which drew me into it.

I remember having lunch with Sir Basil Henriques, a great Jew and a man with a great love for people, when I was wondering hard about my dreams of this sort of work. He was saying how difficult it is now to persuade young men to work among what he called 'the underprivileged'. "Where are the people from these missions?" he asked me. "I'm one of them," I said. As he saw my concern for the same sort of youngsters as he cared about, his interest in me seemed to grow. We talked about Oxford and Bermondsey where he had gone in the old days. 'The Doctor' had been in charge then, and Sir Basil said, "I saw there for the first time, and, I'm afraid to say, for the last time, a Christian faith which really worked."

'The Doctor' had become a hero to me some time before through Barclay Baron's book.* He was Dr. John Stansfeld and his driving force had always been an intensely down to earth trust in Jesus Christ. A young Scot named Alec Paterson came to join the Doctor in Bermondsey along with many other young men from Oxford: he had been brought up to think of Jesus only as a man. After some time he said of John Stansfeld, "You simply couldn't walk the streets of Bermondsey with the Doctor and not know that Jesus is divine." His new faith was

* *The Doctor* by Barclay Baron.

to lead Alec Paterson to a lifetime of service in prisons and Borstals.

When we had been at the Mayflower for some years an old friend of my father's came to stay with us. He was Charles Thompson, who had grown up in Bermondsey, and belonged to Oxford and Bermondsey as a boy. We talked about our purpose at the Mayflower; we are not simply there to keep people off the streets or to give them more interests. We believe that a youngster needs most of all someone to live for. I don't think Charles Thompson could have paid us a greater compliment when after an evening at the Centre he said to me, "You're trying to do what the Doctor and Alec Paterson tried to do. You're trying to bring people to Christ."

CHAPTER II

THE REVEREND RECALLED

OUR intention has always been to stay at the Mayflower for a
good many years. If we are to see a local church, in the real
sense of the word, built up on foundations of local Christian
leadership and Christian homes, we must be ready to stay a
long time. But there is the danger of going stale: a job like this
where our home is right on the spot could get on top of us.
My Council therefore have a policy that each member of the
staff should have a long leave of several months after some
years. Three other staff members had been away, and come
home much the better for the break, and my wife and I were
beginning to plan our long leave. A peaceful few months in the
country near Cambridge, with time to read and think, and to
live as an ordinary family with evenings to ourselves, was one
of our most attractive ideas. In the end it didn't turn out to be
such a peaceful break.

I had an unexpected visitor in January 1962, who started
my mind working on a different track. E. M. Wellings has often
written acid comments on my cricket in the *Evening News*. It
was quite a surprise when he asked if he could come and talk to
me for a few minutes, and proceeded to tell me that it was
desperately important for English cricket that I should go to
Australia the next winter as captain. When a story gets round
Fleet Street, no newspaper likes to be left out, and I soon had a
succession of visitors and telephone calls. Many whose opinion
I respected pressed me that I ought to make myself available.

Some years previously I had worked out that I would have
been ordained for seven years in September 1962, and that
M.C.C. was touring Australia that winter. But the thought
had been pushed into the back of my mind for some time. In
the previous four years I had played exactly nine matches for

Sussex, and in 1961 I had not played one. I told the Press that I was intending to take a long leave quite soon, and that it was a possibility that I might be available for Australia. I said, quite truthfully as far as I knew, that there had been no official approach to me.

In fact a message was waiting on my desk asking me to ring a Mr. Robins at a London number. For some reason my mind connected this message with a rather erratic man, who had wanted to talk at great length about something I could not help him with. That week was desperately busy, and I did not have time to ring. Our secretary was ill and away for a week. When she came back I said, "Who was that Mr. Robins who wanted me to ring back?" "I imagined it was Mr. Walter Robins," she said. It shows how far removed my mind was from cricket that I had not linked it with him at all. I rang Walter Robins, who was now chairman of the Selection Committee. He said, "If it's true that you are available for this tour, it's the best news I've heard for English cricket for a long time."

This was flattering but disturbing. Grace was expecting our first baby in March and, thinking of her earlier illness, I wanted to be sure that she could cope with my going away, and with travelling herself. If we were going to have a long leave, there must be some fun and change in it for her as well as for me. Going away from Mayflower for the best part of a year was also quite a step to take. Various other problems built it up to a decision I wanted to run away from. In the end it all went well for Grace and the baby and for the Mayflower, and I have never felt more sure of doing the right thing.

In May I said that I would play two months cricket for Sussex, and that I would be available for the tour of Australia in any capacity. The possibility of the captaincy had been mentioned to me, but I made no assumption in that direction. It produced a perfect subject for newspapers to debate— Dexter, Cowdrey or Sheppard for captain?—and debate it they did, day after day. I played a two-day match at Hornsey for M.C.C. against the Club Cricket Conference: newspaper and television reporters crowded there, and, when I made a hundred, they wrote about it as though it was made against the best bowlers in England, and as if my ticket to Australia was already booked. Then I played against Oundle School and made o, and a number of papers wondered if my form would be good enough.

When I started playing for Sussex, on June 20, there were a dozen or so reporters who came round every match to report every movement that I made. My first match was against Oxford University who had a very weak bowling side and I made 108 and 55. Again it was acclaimed as though I could now walk comfortably into a Test match, and do the same thing.

When I had played against Australia in 1956 it was only two or three years since I had been playing regularly. Now it was nine years since 1953 when I had last gone in first regularly. I might have dropped down the batting order to make it a little easier to find my form, but I reasoned that if I was going to be useful to England there was more need for an opening batsman than someone in the middle of the order. Going in first with the bowlers fresh and the seam on the ball hard and new demands much technical skill, and I needed to learn some batting lessons all over again. The English county game now belonged more than ever to the faster bowler. Green outfields and grassy pitches made the bowler able to keep the shine on the ball far longer. Of the first twenty batsmen in the first-class averages only five were going in first; ten years before, eleven out of the first twenty were openers. It seemed to have become more difficult to succeed in this job. In the end I was very glad that I did go back to going in first. My run of low scores meant that I was really 'getting down to it' again and tightened up my play in several ways.

I now came back (followed by my Press bloodhounds) to a series of matches in Sussex. The first was against Warwickshire at Hove: Mike Smith made a splendid, free-hitting, 163. But the headline of the paper I saw in its report of that day simply said SHEPPARD OUT FOR 0. It was the start of a hard month when cricket became a very difficult game again. o, 13, 8, 3, 37, 12 was the sort of run I had known before, but the Sussex crowds seemed to be willing me on to success, and their disappointment was the hardest part at this stage. I made 95 and 60 next match against Northamptonshire and began to feel that runs would flow again.

Then down at Cardiff I made one of those mistakes which can shake the confidence. Wheatley and Peter Walker made the ball swing all over the place in the heavy, thundery, atmosphere of the first evening when we had to bat after a day in the field. I was determined not to 'chase' a wide ball, and when I saw one from Walker start outside the off stump, I lifted my bat high in the air to let it go past. Unfortunately it swung in sharply and hit me on the pads right in front of the middle stump. I started to walk out before he shouted his appeal—certainly the only time that I have given myself out l.b.w.

So far I had not worried very much about my form with the bat. I was more anxious about sharpening up my fielding after so long away from it. I had had bad patches before and I felt sure that the runs would start coming again: but at Cardiff it dawned on me that I hadn't very much longer to show that I could score runs. I only had two more matches before the selectors made up their minds. One was against Surrey and the other was Gentlemen v. Players.

The Surrey match was an exciting game of cricket on a lively pitch which helped the seam bowlers all through. I never got beyond the stage of struggling for survival and neither did most of the batsmen. Only Stewart, Dexter, Barrington and May scored more than 40. Ted Dexter made a tremendous 94 in our second innings, having taken 7 for 38 in the Surrey first innings. But they seemed to be coasting easily to victory, needing 227 to win: Barrington and May took the score past 150 before the third wicket fell. May played as well as ever and made everyone feel what a pity it was that he was not available for Australia. May, Dexter, Barrington, Cowdrey would have provided a powerful 3, 4, 5, 6 for England. Surrey at one stage needed 30 to win with seven wickets standing. I then made my one useful contribution to the match by hitting the stumps with an underarm throw to run out Barrington. Surrey then collapsed and we scrambled home to win by 10 runs.

So Gentlemen v. Players was in many ways the last chance for me to make some runs. Trueman, Shackleton, Walker, Titmus and Gifford made sure that we worked hard for runs, but this time I began to take charge. What made all the difference for me was that Ted Dexter came in when we lost a wicket at 12, and immediately played all the bowling with the greatest authority. He ran down the wicket to Shackleton and drove him over the top: twice he drew back to the leg-side as Shackleton or Trueman was about to let the ball go, and hammered it through the covers for four. He was caught off Shackleton trying to hit him over mid-on for 55. It helped to put confidence in me at the other end and after a while I really began to play as well as I can. I doubt if I have ever been more satisfied with getting runs when I really needed to, and it was a great feeling when I reached 100 that day. Cricket seemed a different game after this and in spite of my bad start I reached 1,000 runs at 44 runs an innings.

We had the Players in dire trouble on the second day. Trevor Bailey bowled extremely well and six were out for 104 when Freddie Trueman, captaining the Players, joined Freddie Titmus. They added 90 by fine, vigorous hitting. Earlier in the day I caught Peter Parfitt at backward short leg off a hook. Captain Trueman was all sympathy when Parfitt went back in the dressing-room. "Bad luck, Peter lad," he said. "The Reverend has more chance than most of us when he puts his hands together." I provided some easy lines for Freddie's wit: when we flew anywhere on tour he would look round in the aeroplane to see if I had my clerical collar on, and would say, "We're all right lads. The Rev's got his working overalls on."

That evening we lost Craig's wicket early, and Prideaux and I batted out time. I went and had a bath and changed rather slowly, so that I was almost alone in the dressing-room when two newspapermen asked if they could come and talk to me. "What did I think of this appointment?" they asked with pencils poised. That morning they had all come out with banner headlines that I was certain to be made captain for Australia. "What appointment?" I asked, knowing nothing. "Ted Dexter has been invited to captain the side." "I hadn't heard," I said. "But I wish him all the very best. I admire him tremendously as a great cricketer."

We had both been put in some difficult positions that summer by the spotlight that was thrown on us. We were playing in the same side most of the time, and were getting to know one another, as we had rarely played together before. During that summer and the Australian tour Grace and I came to like Ted and his delightful wife Sue very much. Their Thomas was born just a week before our Jenny, and we kept a good deal of 'one-upmanship' going about this. For a long time Jenny was ahead in the matter of teeth, while Thomas was well in the lead when it came to crawling.

I batted a lot with Ted during the English and Australian seasons. Most of the time he was playing at a quite different level from almost any other batsman I have played with. The rest of us try to time and stroke the ball; he stands up and belts it with brutal force. I hardly remember an innings when I was at the other end in which he did not play a shot within three overs which I should not think of attempting until I had made 50 or more. I think the great freedom with which he starts off is part of the reason why he often makes a brilliant 60, 70 or 80, and then fails to make a very large score. When I have had days when everything has gone right, and I have reached 50 fluently and easily, there has been a great debate going on in my mind. "You don't often play as well as this," says the voice of caution. "Steady up, and make sure you don't do anything silly. You want to make a big score today." "Nonsense," replies the voice of confidence. "Everything's going your way today. Ride your luck, and keep going." Those fluent days are few and far between for me, and in a way I have found it easier to build up a large score when I have had to work hard at the start. Dexter's innings are inclined to start as though batting is a very easy matter, and I feel he has sometimes got out between 50 and 100 because of some such argument between caution and confidence as I have known.

But whether he makes huge scores or not, Ted Dexter is the most exciting and dominating English batsman since Denis Compton was at his best. He is a superb athlete: I once heard a sculptor say that he had the perfect figure for a man. A natural hitter of the ball, Ted would never accommodate himself to picking up runs slowly, when he first came into first-class cricket. They had to be made in the grand manner or not at all. Often in those early days it was not at all, and when we reached Australia in 1962 we met a number of cricketers, who had only seen him in his unsuccessful tour in 1958-9, who could not understand how we were all saying that he was a great player. They soon found out. He had gone on playing with all his natural freedom, but had tightened up his defence, and, when the situation demanded it, he was prepared to accumulate runs by hard graft. The steel had been hardened to meet the toughest of Tests.

The first half of the Australian season saw one powerful innings after another from him, and in the first two Tests he looked like dominating the whole series. But, like all attacking stroke-makers, he wants a fast wicket with the ball coming through to the bat. The Sydney pitch on which two of the remaining three Tests were played was sluggish and discouraging to anyone who wanted to drive. This cut him down to the size of an ordinary player who had to work hard for his runs, and his compelling stroke-play never quite returned on the tour.

I doubt if there are many, who have not taken part in modern Test cricket, who have any idea of how much strain is put upon a Test captain. A young man is expected to have the tact, the quickness of wit and the thickness of skin of a Prime Minister. (I had not then connected Ted Dexter with politics, but there could be no finer school for public life than captaining a Test team!) Every decision is put under the microscope, and every utterance printed and quoted back at him months later.

Dealing with the Press is not the least important part of a captain's job: the natural response of most cricketers is to avoid newspapermen's questions and to resent the persistence with which they probe behind the scenes. But the reporter has his editor constantly demanding a story: he has to write, whether the players tell him what he asks them or not. I have reasoned for years that he is more likely to write a fair account, if cricketers go to meet him and help him as far as they can. Dexter was always ready to meet the Press and to help them: sometimes a remark which he threw off casually as a joke would be taken up and would make headlines on the following day. But when he was let down by one paper or another, he was still ready to meet them and be forthcoming.

In one sense I feel he was too forthcoming: his opposite number Richie Benaud is extremely conscious of the importance of public relations, being himself a journalist. He started, and Ted Dexter followed suit, the habit of meeting the cricket reporters in the dressing-room at the end of every day's play. This is all right if it is simply a matter of clearing up some doubtful question of what actually happened on the field. But the captains would be asked what their hopes and tactics were for the next day. In the paper the following morning their answers were made to sound like America and Russia sparring for propaganda points in the cold war.

He was also cornered early in the tour on the subject of brighter cricket. This team scored as fast in the Tests as any England team in Australia since 1924–5. Yet we were accused of dull cricket, and the captain's remark, in answer to a series of questions, that he hoped we would score at 60 runs an hour was quoted back to prove how bad we were. In the famous series between Australia and the West Indies, the West Indies who scored the faster were averaging perhaps 50 runs an hour, and no Test team that I can think of has averaged over 60 runs an hour since the First World War.

As a captain on the field Ted gave a tremendous example of full-blooded effort as a fielder and as a bowler. He is in fact a more dangerous bowler than batsmen give him credit for.

His approach to captaincy was quite different from the Hutton tradition in which, for example, May, Cowdrey and I grew up. There were times when he made mistakes in field placing and tactical changes, which the more thoughtful, cautious school of captains would not have made. But I am convinced that he also made good decisions and changes on the strength of his intuition as a natural cricketer which others would not have made.

A good example was in the last Test of the tour at Christchurch. New Zealand had led us on the first innings and there was every reason why they should make a big score and beat us. Freddie Trueman had bowled them out first time, but we could not expect him to do it every time. At lunch Colin Cowdrey tried to persuade Ted that we should need Ray Illingworth, who was off the field with a slight ailment, to bowl some overs for us to get us through the day. "I don't agree," said Ted. "The fast bowlers will bowl them out." My mind was working the same way as Colin's, and I was wondering what we should do if, as seemed likely to me, the fast bowlers didn't bowl them out. So I tried a few minutes later, feeling it was important that Freddie Titmus should have the choice of which end to bowl; I said to Ted, "I think Freddie Titmus is going to be your most useful bowler." "I don't agree," he said. "I think the fast bowlers will bowl them out." There was a lot to be said for our point of view, but he was right and David Larter, who had bowled poorly in the first innings, 'came good' and the fast bowlers did break through.

I found Ted an interesting captain, different from others I have played under. Because he was more detached in his attitudes, he saw some of the great issues of the game very clearly. He is a full-blooded cricketer, occasionally a hot-blooded one. But his intention was always to play cricket the best way, and to meet the opposition as friends. It was to his credit and Benaud's that the teams continued to speak much to each other on and off the field in a way that for many years Test teams did not do. Bobby Simpson, Australia's opening batsman, said to me at the end of the Fifth Test, "This has been the friendliest series I have played in."

All the time I have been playing cricket there has been a similar chorus about England elevens. They can see how we are going to make some runs, but cannot imagine how we are ever going to get the other side out. This was the refrain again in 1962. As one of the batsmen I am always nervous about this sort of talk because my experience of Test cricket has been that it is much more often the batsmen who have failed than the bowlers. This time the selectors took something of a gamble in picking only seven batsmen in the party of seventeen. This left little insurance against the possibility of injury or loss of form: as so often we envied the Australians their string of all-rounders like Davidson, Mackay, Simpson and Benaud. I was the only batsman in the party who had been an opener by choice, as both Geoff Pullar and Colin Cowdrey had been conscripted into it after they started playing first-class cricket. But though there was a disastrous collapse which lost us the Third Test the batsmen did in fact do much better than had been the case in the three previous tours of Australia.

When we left England the punch in our bowling appeared to rest entirely with Trueman and Statham, and, if either of this famous 'old firm' failed, we found it difficult to see how we were going to get the Australians out. In English cricket no county captain bats on into the second day of a match, and a team rarely want to score more than 300, so that if the bowlers keep pegging away accurately, the batsmen get themselves out trying to score quickly in the later part of the innings, or else the captain declares. In Australia it is different. Unless you get them out, the batsmen will go on and on to a large total, and accurate medium-pace bowling will bring little reward, unless there are some other skills added to it. Dexter was given little room to manoeuvre, as apart from the fast or fast-medium right arm bowlers he had simply three right arm slow bowlers, all off-spinners. Allen, Illingworth and Titmus were the most successful slow bowlers in England in 1962 and it is no doubt better to take the best bowlers, regardless of their type, than, for example, to take a poor bowler simply because he is the only leg-spinner we have. But there must be some balance to the attack and Dexter was given a very difficult job to make this bowling side effective without turning to extremely defensive field placings.

Tony Lock had gone through a lean season in England, but he had bowled well in India the previous winter, and was probably a more effective bowler now on hard wickets overseas with his 'purged', slower method. The quick spinners he delivered from 1952-9 made him a great power on turning wickets in England, but they were not very effective overseas. He would not have taken a vast number of Test wickets, but Tony is a great competitor in big cricket and he would have brought some variety to the attack. Sir Donald Bradman was I think amusing himself by rubbing salt into English wounds, but was also stating his definite opinion when he told us that he thought Lock's bowling for Western Australia in one match was the finest piece of spin bowling he saw all the season.

Not many of our supporters gave us a chance of beating Australia when we flew off from London Airport to pick up the *Canberra* at Aden. We had no fancy ideas about this ourselves but it was a team which was prepared to work hard and pull together—and we very nearly pulled it off.

CHAPTER 12

AUSTRALIA REVISITED

ENGLISH cricketers all have a rather idyllic view of Perth. For those, like Ray Illingworth and me, who are bad sailors, it represents *terra firma* instead of a pitching liner which, even in these days of stabilisers, makes us wonder why we ever wanted to leave home. For all of us it means three weeks in the friendliest of cities, before the heat is turned on both with the pressure of big matches, and the literal heat of mid-summer.

They tell us that Perth can be horribly hot, with swarms of flies later on, but we played there in the spring, with a cool breeze to encourage us. Flies present a great problem in country matches inland in Australia, but for some reason they do not seem to infest the Test match grounds. It is just as well, for even when you have worked out a perfect technique of blowing upwards from the mouth (swatting is really no good when the bowler is about to let the ball go at you), there is no answer when a fly lands on the end of your nose just as the ball is approaching.

The differences between conditions in England and Australia soon make themselves felt. There is something about the brightness of a totally cloudless sky which seems to make the ball arrive much quicker than in England. Most touring teams drop a lot of catches in the first weeks of an Australian tour. I remembered a fielding practice at Perth in 1950. Trevor Bailey hit a skier straight up in the air until it seemed to shimmer and I wanted to take my eyes off it. I thought I was catching it until suddenly I was afraid that it was going to hit me on the head; I ducked and the ball fell three feet the other side of me. This memory made me keen for all the fielding practice I could get, and all of us spent a good many hours at it.

The harder Australian pitches give more bounce to the ball.

This is particularly true of the leg-spinners. Where in England it is safe to step on to the back foot and hammer the ball away, the extra bounce in Australia often means a catch to the wicket-keeper or to slip from a shot which might have counted four in England. But most Australian pitches allow the ball to come through more truly than the grassier wickets at home, and I believe that the batsman can play off the back foot with much more safety in Australia. A player like Neil Harvey would never have had the confidence to move in to drive a half-volley or a good length ball off the back foot as he does, had he first learned the game on 'green', seam-bowlers' wickets in England.

When Englishmen go overseas and play on these hard, true wickets, we often take too long to realise that we do not need to be so cautious as in England. We could go through with our strokes with much more confidence that the ball is going to come through evenly to the bat. But it is difficult to throw away the hard-learned discipline of years on English wickets.

Ken Barrington is one who flourishes overseas because he has adjusted his technique: liking to go on the back foot, he is a great cutter and hooker. He always looked very safe against the spinners. His great success on this tour, when he scored more runs in the Tests than any England batsman had done in Australia since Wally Hammond, was due most of all to tremendous determination and concentration. If the crowd got on to him at some moments when the scoring was slow, it only made him all the more determined to stay there. He cut out strokes which he felt might involve some risk, and went determinedly on with the run-making. Critics have been slow to call him a great player because he does not play the most exciting strokes, but on this tour he was a very tough and extremely successful Test match player. He was usually a quiet member of the team, with many flashes of humour, often at the expense of his room-mate 'Illie'—Ray Illingworth. And Ken is a great imitator, so that we were often treated to his favourite military band and drums in the dressing-room. For the last month of the tour the very realistic noise of a jet airliner taking off for England regularly came from his corner.

There was quite a romantic touch to the first match of the tour: we played at Kalgoorlie, the gold-mining town, and it was easy to imagine the fever of a gold rush in the early days of Australia. We were given the warmest of welcomes in the Town Hall, and the Mayor, who had been in office for twenty-five years, made the evening memorable at least for me, leaving a vivid picture of the rugged character of the men who came to the goldfields. Most receptions follow a settled routine and become one of the most difficult parts of a tour for players to be enthusiastic about. But the Duke of Norfolk, who was our manager, always rose to the occasion. He and Ted Dexter rarely repeated themselves and in brief speeches brought a touch of grace and humour to the occasion.

All Test cricketers suffer a certain amount from those who thrust their company upon them, because they want to be able to talk about what "My friend — said to me the other day." I realised on this tour that the Duke of Norfolk is badgered in this way all the time. He carries it off very easily. With his strong sense of duty and a gentle humour always in accompaniment, he added much to the party by his presence as manager. It was in some ways a very good thing to have someone at the top who was not too involved in the technicalities of cricket, because much more is involved in an M.C.C. tour than simply the play on the field. Alec Bedser was a model to me of what an assistant manager should be. He was efficient in the business side of the tour, approachable for every player, and full of the wisdom of the hard-working bowler.

When the first-class matches started, Ted Dexter quickly showed himself in form with 76 against Western Australia's lively set of fast bowlers, MacKenzie, Hoare and Bevan. Titmus (88) and Alan Smith (42) had a partnership, and Statham and Larter bowled Western Australia out twice. The wicket at Perth was the liveliest we met on the tour, and when we batted first against the Combined XI in the second match there, we lost 4 wickets for 14 to Hoare and McKenzie. Barry Knight and I had a bit of a stand but Tony Lock made a ball turn quite sharply just before lunch, and I was caught at slip for 43.

We were all out for 157 of which Knight made 65 not out. He looked full of natural ability as a cricketer; I don't remember seeing anyone hit the ball so hard with so little apparent effort, and he could 'murder' bowlers when they were a little tired. But there were few occasions like this first day at Perth when he looked as if he could handle the best fast bowlers. As a bowler he looked much more formidable in England when he could make the ball swing about than when he came on with the old ball on an Australian wicket.

Bobby Simpson, who had come over with Lawry and O'Neill to strengthen the Western Australian batting was into his stride straightaway. He made a century in this match, another for an Australian XI at Melbourne, and another for New South Wales against us. We regarded his as the most vital wicket to take all through the season. A neat little man, he is very quick and well-balanced in all his movements. He played Freddie Titmus best of anyone on the turning wickets at Sydney. Against the fast bowlers he seemed to me to break all the rules of batting. Yet he was the most successful opening batsman on either side. The only way of playing fast bowling I have ever known is to try to get well across, right behind the ball. Simpson often seemed well away from the line of the ball, but he was a good cutter, and his quickness of eye and his great determination got him out of a lot of trouble.

He was not bowling his leg-spinners very accurately at that stage of the season, but he could be dangerous, and he had a vital 5 for 57 against us in the Third Test. Add to his batting and bowling skill the fact that he is about the best slip fielder in the world, and you realise how useful to Australia he is.

We trailed a long way behind the Combined XI at Perth, and Colin Cowdrey was promptly out for his second o in the match. Ted Dexter and I then had a stand of 97, and we felt we were fighting back into the game. We were prevented from getting right on top by a typical piece of Australian bowling, supported by the keenest fielding. With the sun up, the shine and the hardness gone from the ball and two batsmen in control, there is not much that a fast bowler can hope for. But both Hoare and McKenzie came tearing in and let the ball go with all the speed they could muster, bowling a length to a defensive field.

Then came another typical Australian move. On came Norman O'Neill with leg-spinners and googlies. He is not always very accurate, and after the hard work against Hoare, McKenzie and Lock, we started thinking in terms of some quick runs. But he also spins the ball a lot, bowling a very good googly in particular. We made some quick runs in his first over. Then came another over when Dexter and Graveney were both out to him, and our chance of winning the match disappeared. Ken Barrington and I put on 103, but we were all out for 260 and the Combined XI won by ten wickets. I reached 93 before McKenzie had me caught at slip with the second new ball off a very good out-swinger.

Graham McKenzie is a tremendously strong man—'Garth' to his team-mates—and could keep his pace up for long spells. On a lively pitch he could be very hostile, with an occasional ball suddenly arriving much faster than the others. But to me he did not seem in the same class as Alan Davidson with the new ball. I opened the innings ten times against them in the Tests: McKenzie never got me out, but I was Davidson's 'rabbit' four times. McKenzie did not have the control of swing that Davidson had, and was inclined to pitch the ball shorter. This made him difficult to score off, but did not give the ball so much chance to swing. For England's sake I hope he does not learn too many more lessons about fast bowling, because he was only 20 when he first played for Australia in 1961, and he could be a power in the land for many years.

One Saturday morning while we were in Perth, Peter Parfitt and I went out to a cricket 'rally' for boys in one of the suburbs. It was the beginning of the cricket season and some sixty boys from about 8 to 14 years old turned up to be organised into teams for every Saturday morning. What impressed me most was the number of men who were prepared to turn up regularly to organise, umpire and provide transport. It was all voluntary and yet they were hoping to run six or eight teams every week.

Against South Australia and against an Australian XI at Melbourne we scored heavily and Barrington, Graveney, Titmus, Dexter, Knight and Barrington again all made big scores. The captain's hundred at Melbourne was a tremendous innings which whetted everyone's appetite for more. I was at the other end for the first hour of it when he sailed into Misson, Guest, Martin, Simpson and Veivers, and I remember the ball disappearing over the sight-screen off Veivers. Straight-driving of this kind made you feel in some danger when you were backing up at the other end, and as for the umpire, Paul Gibb remarked one day that umpiring when Ted was batting was just like looking down the barrel of a rifle. The Australian XI scored heavily, Simpson making his usual century, Ian McLachlan scoring 55 and 68, and Barry Shepherd making 144 and 91 not out after a very nervous start in the first innings.

There has long been a theory about the Australian XI match and the M.C.C. match against touring teams at Lord's, both of which are generally played before the Test matches start. The theory is that the home team is packed with Test batsmen, so that they can have a look at the touring team's bowlers, while the home Test bowlers are not on display. Both Australian and English selectors pick these sides on this basis. I felt that in 1962–3 at any rate, it worked in the opposite way. A series of five Tests of five days each is like a long-drawn-out military campaign. The two teams are made up of not unintelligent cricketers who watch the opposing batsmen very carefully.

After Lawry's great success in England in 1961, we spent a long time discussing how we should bowl to him, and how best to set a field to him. While Simpson was making all his runs against us before the first Test, several minds were ticking over, thinking how best to bowl him. When Brian Booth made an excellent hundred in the First Test, we sat down afterwards, and someone said, "We didn't bowl quite right to him," and a new plan was worked out. It's right to add that he made another hundred in the Second Test! But he was made to work much harder for it. Of course the Australian team did the same to us. After I made a hundred at Melbourne, I found that when I next batted, fielders were standing where I had been happily pushing the ball for runs. It is quite true that batsmen sometimes sort a bowler out so that he can hardly bowl to them: in modern Test cricket the sorting out seems to me to be done rather more by the bowlers.

While several of our batsmen were running into their best form Colin Cowdrey, our only player with regular success behind him in Tests in Australia, was having a very lean time of it. In fact at Perth and Adelaide he registered, 0, 0 and 0 in succession. He made a good score at Melbourne but it was not for another month or so that he really began to play well. Once he was really in his best form it was hard to say which out of Dexter, Barrington and Cowdrey was our greatest player. Colin is the most modest of men, and there are times when he does not seem to admit to himself just how great a player he is. He is very correct defensively, and has all the strokes I can think of at his command.

When I first saw him play it was the thumping shot off the back foot square on the off-side or past cover point which most took the eye. Later, as I played with him, I realised what a powerful on-side player he is. No off-spinner likes to have to bowl to him. Later again he had added his own brand of sweep off the leg-spinners which often sent the ball down to fine-leg for four. But better than any to watch is the easily flowing drive with all his weight behind it, which sends his ball racing through the covers. In case anyone thinks he has unfair advantage with more weight than anyone else, I can testify that this is not true. We both weighed ourselves on the *Canberra* on the way to Australia, and found we were both exactly 196 pounds—a mere fourteen stone.

Batting in Test cricket is not simply a matter of waiting for the right ball and then crashing it away with your favourite stroke. On many days the right ball is a long time in coming, and you have to keep the score-board clicking along by placing and pushing the ball for short singles. Whenever I have heard older friends speak of Hobbs and Sutcliffe batting together, they have talked about "those short singles they used to run".

Of all the players I have batted with Colin Cowdrey has been the best and safest runner I have known. He is always looking for the short single without being rash. He has also been a wonderfully good friend to me, whether visiting his sea-sick companion, or helping in hours of catching practice or meeting on the common ground of our Christian faith.

Colin's wife, Penny, came to Australia for part of the tour, but unfortunately she was not well much of the time. A visit to their home where their three children are growing up in the happiest of atmospheres makes me realise how hard it must often have been for Colin to agree to go on overseas tours. We expect a great deal of our top players if we ask them to be away for a six month tour in the winter as well as playing six days a week in the summer. Colin has been away for seven tours in the last ten winters.

He has been vice-captain of England in many Test matches, and there are those who undoubtedly think that his gentle charm and his natural caution do not equip him to be a strong Test captain. I am not sure that this has been proved: when he has captained the side he has generally felt that he was a caretaker only keeping things going for another to come back and take over. This feeling does not make it easy to take command in the way a captain needs to. He is perhaps more conscious than any cricketer of the value of cricket tours in fostering good will, and in Australia few English cricketers have been better known or better liked.

The Sydney cricket ground proved to be a bogey ground for us on this tour. We were beaten by an innings inside three days by New South Wales, and both batting and bowling came unstuck. We did quite well in the first innings when we scored 348 on a wicket which was a little damp. The usual pre-season talk had been full of rumours that Alan Davidson was overweight and unfit. He did not bowl very many overs in this match, but those he did were extremely sharp, and left me quite sure that we were going to face an opening bowler who was neither overweight nor unfit.

We survived his opening overs with two or three slices of

luck: on came Benaud and Johnny Martin who did most of the bowling between them as the ball turned a little all day. We had scored 101 runs off Johnny Martin in twelve overs in the previous match at Melbourne, and perhaps I was looking too much for quick runs off him. In his first over I went to force a short ball; it hurried through, and I was caught at the wicket. This sort of dismissal, getting out to a careless shot after I had already done the hard work of laying the foundations of an innings, has always made me more angry with myself than when a bowler beats me thoroughly with a good ball, for perhaps a smaller score. Ted Dexter played well, Colin Cowdrey made 50, but we lost wickets steadily, and it was 'Noddy' Pullar who held us together. He picks out the leg-spinners and the googlies very well, and he chugged along steadily to an invaluable 132. It was more like an engine pulling the heavy load of a vital goods train than a flying express, but it was a fine innings for his side. He had come into the runs at just the right time with the first Test a fortnight away.

Our bowling was very roughly handled by Simpson (110) and O'Neill (143), and this made our stock fall sharply for the Tests. Freddie Trueman bowled a tremendous first over in which it is no exaggeration to say that he beat Simpson and Thomas with six balls out of the eight. In his second over he knocked Thomas' middle stump out of the ground: but after five overs he went off the field with an injury. If he could not bowl, our spearhead was going to be greatly blunted. And even if he could play, at that stage it looked as though he might only be a wicket-taker when the shine was on the ball and he was able to make it swing.

Graham Thomas was very unlucky against us. Both for an Australian XI at Melbourne and for New South Wales he ran into Freddie's first three overs in which he was extremely fast, and when the ball swung a great deal. Neither time did he survive them to show what he could do against the easier bowling which followed. Norman O'Neill had often looked a very nervous starter, and at Perth David Allen had cramped him for a long time, and then dismissed him for 15. Now he strode to the wicket, and from the start showed the most dazzling strokes. He was very quick down the wicket, and murdered Allen and Illingworth. Simpson never looked like getting out and they put on over 200.

If our bowling looked weak when New South Wales batted, our batting looked worse when they bowled at us a second time. I left a ball alone from Davidson which I should have played, and received a most painful blow on the ankle which missed my pad. My ankle was swollen like a football, and I was very lucky not to miss a match because of it. Then I played a ball from Davidson which I should have left alone, and was caught behind the wicket. After this Richie Benaud took command: no one looked like staying in, and he had 7 for 18. We were beaten by an innings, and those critics who had thought we might give Australia some run for their money, even though they expected us to come in second, now abandoned us to our fate. "Englishmen can't play leg-spin", "M.C.C. have Benaud complex"—all of us needed either to go back to school or to a psychiatrist's couch before we could dare to tackle Australia.

The Queensland match at Brisbane did nothing to change the critics' ideas although we made 581 for 6 wickets and eventually came near to winning. I made 94, Parfitt 47, Dexter 80, Graveney 52, Knight 81 and Barrington 183 not out. Queensland made 433 including a dashing hundred from 'Slasher' Mackay.

I played against Wes Hall for the first time here: after the great West Indies tour of Australia Sobers, Kanhai and Hall went back to play for state teams. Peter Parfitt and I had to go in for thirty-five minutes on Saturday evening when we had been chasing the ball round the field all day. An opening batsman always has a certain dread of this, and facing the fastest bowler in the world in a fading light looked like making the problem of survival quite difficult. He was very fast— as quick as anyone I had met—with a long, fast run up and loose-limbed action. But we survived and went in feeling quite pleased with ourselves. In the dressing-room we were greeted by comments from those who had last played against him in the

Jenny was born in 1962 in the London Hospital within the sound of
Bow Bells.

Grace and Jenny get ready for Australia.

Another team picture. The Mayflower staff 1963. *Back row*: George Burton, Jean Lodge Patch, Dilys Gething, Joan de Torre. *Front row*: Margaret Fish, Hilary Harman, Grace Sheppard, David Sheppard.

West Indies: "Gosh he's slow!" "David, I'm not kidding you. He was three yards quicker in the West Indies."

One ball that evening was certainly quick enough. It lifted and hit me full on the hip bone: I skipped about, and rubbed the bone for some time, until I felt ready to start again. As I went back to the crease I realised that Wes was clutching his eye, surrounded by sympathisers. Wally Grout explained to me what had happened. Wes had a cross on a chain round his neck which jangled up and down on his long run up to the wicket. As he bowled the particular ball which struck me so painfully, the cross had jumped up and hit him in the eye. When play finished, I saw Wes and said, "It's dangerous hitting the Reverend! I promise you'll be quite safe if you bowl me half-volleys."

He bowled me a high full pitch on Monday morning. I ducked, and it pitched on a rough patch just in front of Wally Grout. It flew up from there and broke his jaw so that he missed the first three Tests. Later in our innings a bumper from Hall laid out Alan Smith our wicket-keeper. Since John Murray had been hit by a batsman in a country match less than a fortnight before, wicket-keeping seemed an especially hazardous business at that time.

The odds were heavily on Australia as we went into the Brisbane Test. Their batting seemed to stretch for ever, Lawry, Simpson, O'Neill, Harvey, Burge, Booth, Davidson, Mackay, Benaud, McKenzie, Jarman: and Benaud seemed to have established an ascendancy over us as a bowler. Most of our batting picked itself, but neither Graveney nor Parfitt had been making runs. The selectors were Dexter, Cowdrey, Bedser, Statham and myself, and we had an inspired choice at this point: as both were out of the runs, we decided that, in spite of Graveney's greater experience, we needed Parfitt's brilliance in the catching department. He proceeded to make 80, his highest score of the tour, in his first Test match. We all felt that Titmus was the best of our off-spinners, and that Alan Smith deserved a chance as wicket-keeper after some very good displays. We hoped Barry Knight would do some stock bowling

o

for us, and bring some aggression to the batting. But we knew that we relied tremendously on Trueman and Statham to get them out.

They very nearly did. At one stage on the first day we had 5 out for 140, three of them to Trueman. But the bowlers hadn't quite enough steam to drive home this advantage. Australia made an inspired choice too on the morning of the match. They picked Brian Booth though he had not made a good score that season, and he made a graceful and secure 112. After Davidson went at 194, 'Slasher' Mackay made an everlasting-looking 86 not out, adding 101 with Booth and 91 with Benaud (51). Richie batted confidently and aggressively as he often did during this series, after some lean batting years. From 140 for 5 they climbed to 404.

'Noddy' Pullar and I saw off the fast bowlers, and were going quite well when Benaud came into the attack. So far from having a 'Benaud complex', I had been inclined to say to myself, "I have never regarded him as a great bowler. He must prove this to me himself." Unlike most of the England batsmen I like to try to move up the wicket to slow bowlers, and I tried to do this straight away, before I had really had enough of a look at him. The result was that he got me into a rare tangle, and after a while I was hanging on desperately for survival. Eventually he got a ball to float in to me, and bounce a little, and McKenzie caught me at short leg. I have often heard commentators speak about Benaud's googly: he may bowl this to some players, but I don't think he has ever bowled one to me. This particular ball was one which dipped in to me in the air.

He bowled as well as I have ever seen him at Brisbane: the ball was floated up to a teasing length with an occasional quicker one. He did not spin the ball viciously, but some turned just enough from leg, while the top-spinners definitely drifted into the right-handers in the air. He certainly succeeded in winning my respect. Bruce Dooland used to spin the ball more than Benaud, and possessed all the tricks of spin, but if I had to have one of them in a Test match side, I would choose Benaud. He is so accurate that he can set himself to bowl on a good wicket to two or three runs an over, and when things go well for him there is no one who can more quickly exploit the atmosphere.

After a firm start Pullar and I were both gone with the score at 65. Cowdrey was still struggling and he was out for 21. But at the other end Dexter played supremely well, and with Cowdrey put on 80. Just towards the close with Dexter in command and Barrington looking very safe, we were 169 for 3. The game was going our way again. Then Dexter hit over a ball from Benaud, and was bowled for 70. So much depended on him that at once the game was swinging towards Australia. But next day Barrington played well, Alan Smith was an obstinate night-watchman, and Parfitt played very soundly. Slowly we were getting back on top when Barrington was out off Benaud for 78. Parfitt and Titmus carried on, but they were made to fight for every run. At 361 for 6 we were hoping for a reasonable lead, but a sudden collapse meant we were all out for 389. Benaud had 6 for 115 and had bowled extremely well. But our attitude was one of great determination to play him well. We felt that as we stayed in for a while, and became used to a type and class of bowling we do not meet in England, we should do better against him.

The first ball of Australia's innings Simpson played on to his stumps from Trueman, but the bails did not fall off. It was a long time before we looked like taking a wicket again. Simpson and Lawry ran very quickly between the wickets, and we had a lesson in stealing short singles. Simpson had 71 and Lawry was 98 when he pulled a ball from Titmus hard and straight at me. After this O'Neill, Harvey and Burge speeded things up, but Australia batted on to the close of play.

Before tea I had said to Colin Cowdrey, "Ask Ted if he wants to think of a change in the batting order. They're bound to declare and get us in tonight, and we must decide if we're going to try to chase the runs." But they didn't declare, and even on the last morning there was a long conference between Benaud and Harvey before a declaration was announced. We had to make 378 in six hours on the fifth day of this match.

By the time I was out there was only a very narrow strip left on a good length which the bowlers' footmarks had not roughed up. This gave the spin bowlers confidence, and made most batsmen hesitate before going through freely with a drive.

Ted Dexter had real ideas about winning the match in spite of the large target. But his orders were that we would try only if we had a firm start. This we succeeded in providing. Pullar made 56 and I got 53. To my delight, after playing Benaud so badly in the first innings, I began to judge the ball properly, and to play him with some comfort. Davidson came on to bowl a long defensive spell at medium pace, and it was he who got both of us out as we tried to accelerate. Dexter played so well that the impossible victory seemed for a while to be within reach. He and Cowdrey put on 56 together, Cowdrey making 9 of them. But the pace was too hot even for Dexter: after making 99 out of 143 he was bowled by McKenzie. We had a little collapse, but Titmus and Knight held firm and a fascinating game of ups and downs was drawn.

I felt that Richie Benaud let us escape at Brisbane. Had he declared on the fourth day and given us a smaller target, we were bound to have chased it all the way. I would think that the odds would have been 5 to 1 against us had we been set to make 330 and had to bat for half an hour overnight. He was later 'roasted' by the Press for not declaring in the Fourth Test: again the odds would have been strongly on the fielding side, as they always are, if the batsmen have to hustle to make the runs. In the Fourth Test Alan Davidson was unfit, and Benaud had good reason to feel that Australia would have a job to bowl us out. But at Brisbane this struck me as an ultra-cautious piece of captaincy.

Benaud suffered in 1962-3 from the romantic reputation which had been built up for him. Many journalists had written of him as the man who always did the daring thing whatever the situation was. For example in the famous Manchester Test in 1961 he came on to bowl his leg-spinners when Dexter was in full flow. This was presented by many writers as an act of high daring, when most captains would have been trying to shut the game up. What they did not say was that Mackay, his best defensive bowler, had been bowling for some time, but had been hit out of the firing line by Dexter, and Davidson and McKenzie were very expensive. Benaud himself was likely to be the most economical bowler and it was a good decision for him to bowl in any case.

Richie, who is a philosophical cricketer, did not write about that Manchester Test in the romantic terms which some of his followers used. He captained his side and bowled that afternoon at Manchester as shrewdly and as skilfully as he could. But he knew that he wasn't a magician, and that he needed the 'run of the ball' at the right moment. He wrote of the vital ball which dismissed Dexter, "If that ball had spun another quarter of an inch or even landed on the seam, it would have missed the edge of the bat, and England would have been lionised in the National Press next day, instead of being flayed." And of the attacks by the Press on the England team, "There, but for a sliver of willow about a sixteenth of an inch wide, could have gone I."

The picture of the dashing captain, always game for any risk, is not in my opinion a true one of Richie Benaud. He was put on a pedestal which was too high for anyone. But I think of him as the best Test match captain I have been on the field with. I have not played against West Indies when Frank Worrell was captain. Obviously in rating modern Test captains he must be put very near the top. But I cannot speak of him as a captain with first-hand experience.

Benaud was shrewd and knowledgeable. He was tremendously quick to press home an advantage once his opponents were struggling. He made mistakes because he is human; I think he made mistakes at Brisbane and at Adelaide, and I think he was wrong to talk so much to the Press about his tactics each day of a Test match—though this was better than the opposite mistake of trying to avoid the Press altogether. But he did the greatest thing which a captain can do. He got his team playing *for him*. Bradman and Hutton were respected by their teams for their vast experience and skill, but both were distant from their players, when compared with Benaud. There was no doubt in my mind that his team liked him, respected him, and would do anything for him.

When the Duke of Norfolk agreed to be manager of this M.C.C. Team he had made the condition that he must go home for some weeks in December and January to meet various commitments. As soon as he reached England the Australian newspapers all carried headlines that in England he had said that the Australians "were terrified of Dexter". This was at once followed by more quotes and counter-quotes.

It makes a good example of the mischief which can be done when a remark is removed from its context, and printed on its own. When the Duke reached London Airport he was asked if it was true that the English players had a 'Benaud complex'. He said that he didn't think it was so, and indeed that if it was true that the Englishmen were worried about Benaud, then it could be said that the Australians were terrified of Dexter.

It was the first time an England team had left Brisbane without being one down since 1936, and the First Test had increased our confidence in ourselves. The next two matches showed us something of the size of Australia: we flew off 700 miles north to play a two-day country match at Townsville. Then 700 miles back to Brisbane, 900 miles on to Melbourne, and a coach trip of another 80 miles took the team to Bendigo for another two-day match.

It was fascinating to me to have the chance of seeing so much of Australia. In Townsville I talked to a crowd of teenagers from the verandah of the Bishop of North Queensland's home one tropical evening. The warm air seemed to fold itself around us. I looked over their heads as they sat on the grass, and saw the dark shape of Magnetic Island and its lights reflected across the water, a hint of the Great Barrier Reef breaking the ocean forty miles further out. I had to refuse the great majority of invitations to speak here and there during the tour, as I was very conscious that I had been taken to Australia to play cricket. But I did preach at one time or another in the Cathedral of each of the main cities, and spoke occasionally at more informal gatherings. We had great crowds on many occasions, and I felt it was worth doing. On almost every occasion I used a talk which I had previously prepared and delivered at home as there was not time for lengthy preparation. I do not believe that a sermon must be entirely new for it to be useful. Part of the strain of speaking to the same people week after week in one place is that new material is essential. But when I am away from home, if I think and pray through my notes again to make ideas fresh and alive in my mind, it seems right to me to use the same talk again.

There were many arguments as to whether the country matches in Australia were a good idea. We played more than any English team for many years, perhaps since the days when they arrived in their horse-drawn coach to play Twenty-Two of this district or Eighteen of that back in the 1860's. The appearance of an international team in country districts was certainly likely to encourage the game. On the other hand these games add to the length of tours, and they do not really help a touring team to keep players in form who are not playing in the Tests. First-class cricket is needed for that. It seemed to us that a one-day match would do as well to let Test cricketers be seen in action.

I was surprised that Sheffield Shield matches were not taken away from the Test grounds on occasions. Many Shield matches have small crowds at Sydney and Melbourne, and it struck me that New South Wales v. Queensland at Newcastle or Victoria v. Western Australia at Geelong would 'fly the flag' of cricket and possibly be very profitable too.

From M.C.C.'s point of view, we must think of the length of time we ask our players to be away from home. A cricketer's family needs him at home more than he is normally there, and I believe that the constant demands of long winter tours has something to do with our best players retiring from cricket earlier nowadays than Hobbs, Rhodes, Hendren, Woolley and others did. Working out tours to Australia, New Zealand, West Indies, South Africa, India and Pakistan is like wrestling with a baffling jigsaw puzzle. We need to make use of air travel more, and explore the possibility of linking a tour of India and Pakistan with Australia this time, and with West Indies next time, so reducing the number of winters a player is away from home. The alternative seems to be to decide that no M.C.C. team should ever be away from home longer than four months. If players could have three months complete break from cricket, it would matter less if there was a tour every English winter.

My tour was made doubly enjoyable because Grace and our friend Hilary Harman joined us, together with our baby Jenny, in Adelaide just before Christmas. I believe that M.C.C. has never refused a player permission to take his wife on a tour, but it is expensive to think of doing so more than once, and when children are going to school every day it is much more difficult for both parents to be away. Sue Dexter and Penny Cowdrey were the only other wives to come out this time. Grace had a week at the hotel with us near Adelaide, a week with some friends in Melbourne over the Test match, and then went on to Sydney where we had rented a house. We felt that it was better not to wander round hotels with a baby, and she settled down in Sydney for six months.

Australian hospitality lived up to its great reputation as far as we were concerned. When I first reached Sydney for the New South Wales match I had to try to rent a house during a very hectic six days. It is certainly an ill wind which blows no one any good. The fact that New South Wales beat us in three days meant that I had a spare day in which to go house hunting. A friend of a friend of a friend—whom I had never previously met—had found more than a dozen possible houses at the right rent. We settled for a pleasant little house with a lovely garden in Killara on the North Shore of Sydney, whose owners were going to England for nine months.

On every Australian cricket ground Grace was made welcome in a way which, I'm afraid, puts to shame the hospitality we offer to visiting wives. And in Adelaide, Melbourne and Sydney, Jenny was able to come too. We claim a world record for her—having watched fourteen days of Test cricket before she was one year old. In Killara the genuine and continuing welcome of our neighbours was tremendous. Nothing was too much trouble, and we could see that this was how they normally helped one another.

If Australian hospitality did its stuff, the weather did not run quite so true to form. The day after Grace reached Adelaide the temperature was 100° in the shade for the South Australia–M.C.C. match, and she wondered if she would survive: but on the second day of the match the temperature dropped to 50°. It rarely stayed scorchingly hot for more than two or three days that summer. And when we stayed in Sydney for three months afterwards, it never seemed to stop raining at all. We were told that Sydney had more than its yearly rainfall (45 inches, or nearly twice England's rainfall) in five months. Here was no English drizzle, but almost in its intensity a tropical downpour. One day I looked out across our district just after the rain stopped and saw the steam going up as if it were an equatorial rain forest. But this made us realise how all the exotic, brightly-coloured shrubs and flowers grow. A thousand gardens in Sydney boast their frangipani, hibiscus, oleander, orange, lemon, grapefruit, banana trees. And when we left Sydney in its midwinter, the gardens were full of the red fingers of poinsettia and camelias and gardenias.

Newspaper critics are quick to look for reasons outside cricket to explain any poor form. So I was delighted that my first innings after Grace and Jenny arrived was my most fluent of the tour. Brooks, a good, hostile, fast bowler, opened for South Australia, and had me dropped early on. This gave me a chance to settle down, and I began to feel 'in good nick'. Sincock came on to bowl his left arm off-spinners and googlies. We had heard a great deal of him, and he had been hailed as Australia's new 'hope'. He had missed South Australia's first match against us, because he was studying for his dentistry exams. His first three overs to Colin Cowdrey and me were accurate, and he plainly spun the ball a lot. I then jumped up the wicket two balls running, and hit him for fours past mid-off. This made a great deal of difference to batsman and bowler alike. The next ball was short and I pulled it for four. Eventually he received a hammering. Colin showed all and sundry that he was no longer out of form and went on and on until he reached 307.

Those who had heralded Sincock as the wonder boy were inclined to forget him as quickly after his bad match against us. But few spin bowlers have reached the top before they were 30. No part of the game so needs the toughening of experience against good players as slow bowling. The Australians hit Laker out of sight in 1948, but they didn't find it quite so easy in 1956. Perhaps the M.C.C. tourists in 1970–1 may find Sincock a very formidable opponent.

I was bowled out for 81 by Garfield Sobers bowling his slow left arm 'chinamen'. He bowled me out in the second innings too: this time he was fastish left arm over the wicket after the manner of Davidson, and he was very good. In a heavy, thundery atmosphere he made his in-swingers move late and far, and put on one of the best pieces of swing bowling I have faced. I can understand how much he worried the England batsmen in 1963. He played a superb innings in this match, his drives and forcing back shots made like the crack of a whip. Of all the brilliant West Indians he stands out in my mind as the most talented. A tremendously exciting player, he can discipline himself to the needs of his side, though he always seems a little out of character in a hard-working, grafting innings. It made a great difference to the West Indies in 1963 to have the calm, determined Conrad Hunte making so many runs as well as the quick-silver—and quixotic—Kanhai, and the stroke-makers Sobers and Butcher.

South Australia benefited hugely from the presence of Sobers in their team. When there is a champion in the side, everyone plays up to him, and the whole team's level of performance is raised. But South Australia was full of talented young players: as well as Hawke and Jarman who played in Tests against us, McLachlan, Chappell, Cunningham, Brooks and Sincock might very well write their names into an Australian team.

CHAPTER 13

THE ASHES REMAIN

THE Melbourne cricket ground is an awe-inspiring thing to see
—and to hear—when a large crowd assembles. 70,000 came to
the first day of the Second Test, and the atmosphere of a big
day was set by a match played in costume, re-enacting Stephen-
son's XI playing their first match in Australia a hundred years
before. Spectators on foot and on horseback paraded on one
side of the ground, and we were able to combine looking at the
pitch we were to play on with joining in the atmosphere of
1863.

We felt we needed another front-line bowler and Coldwell,
who had bowled very well against Victoria, took Knight's
place. We hoped Len Coldwell might be rather like Alec
Bedser. It was an awful lot to hope, but in fact he did very well
on that first day having Simpson's and Harvey's wickets.
Australia reached 111 for 1 on a very humid, exhausting day,
and it seemed that they must rub in their advantage. But an
extraordinary crash saw the score go to 112 for 4. Coldwell
went off the field with heat exhaustion, but he came back
and somehow all the faster bowlers kept going.

Freddie Trueman stuck at it with great courage, though at
one point he seemed very near collapse and said to me, "Oh
David, I'm tired." But he went on, bowled a good length
and direction when he had no chance of breaking through, and
Australia never quite got off the hook. Freddie Titmus made
his first real impression on the series, bowling beautifully,
and picking up 4 for 43—two caught by Ken Barrington off the
sweep at deep square-leg. We had 6 out for 164 but Davidson,
Mackay and Benaud played well, and they pulled up to
316.

We went out to bat before lunch on the second day, but I

was 'l.b.w. b. Davidson o' in his first over. He made a ball swing in late to dismiss me, and he got one or two very good balls past Dexter in the same over. After lunch he bowled Pullar and we were 19 for 2. But we then saw what I regarded as the best batting of the series when captain and vice-captain put on 175. Ted was in his best form, only restricted at times by Benaud bowling very straight or at the leg stump to him, and so preventing his off-side strokes coming into full play. Colin was absolutely at ease, and for three hours they dictated terms to everyone. McKenzie came on and bowled a defensive spell of great speed and stamina which stopped them running away with it. Towards the end Benaud got Dexter out for 93, and this time it seemed as though sheer exhaustion had something to do with it.

The third day saw this game swing to and fro again. At 254 for 3 with Cowdrey's hundred applauded and Barrington going well we were only 62 behind. Then McKenzie had them both out, and when Graveney looked very much in command he was tragically run out. Davidson came into his own again and we finally scrambled a lead of only 15. This looked quite different when Australia were 69 for 4. Trueman bowled Simpson, and had O'Neill brilliantly caught by Cowdrey at slip. Then Harvey was run out going for a fourth run: this was one of four run-outs in the match, probably reflecting the tension and the difficulty of shaking off the grip which the bowlers held.

Lawry and Booth slowly pulled Australia up to 104 for 4. Just before the end as Trueman was about to bowl from the pavilion end, Ted Dexter said, "Come on. He's going to nick one to us." That very over Lawry edged one; I had to come forward with my left hand, got it into my hand, but dropped it. It was a catch I would have been proud to make, but accepting or missing half chances often makes the difference between success and failure. I had also dropped Benaud in the first innings. He whipped a ball from Statham hard round to backward short leg where I was standing rather too close, looking for the ball which is edged rather than played. Nine years before I like to think that I would have caught both these, but my reactions were not so quick after years away from the game. At this stage, having missed two catches, and made o, I said to my captain, "I'm going to get into this game some-time." And I was pretty determined to do so.

Missing Lawry looked as if it might be very costly; but after five hours or more for 57 he was bowled by a ball which shot straight along the ground. Dexter bowled the last over before lunch from round the wicket and this ball must have pitched in the bowler's footholes. Brian Booth completed an excellent 103, but there was no real recovery this time. Dexter very carefully held Trueman back so that he would be fresh when the time came for the new ball. The move worked splendidly as he tore into it, and dismissed Mackay, Benaud and McKenzie, finishing with 5 for 62.

We had two or three overs before the close, and Pullar was out to a full length diving catch on the leg-side by Jarman. This put the Australians in great heart: we had 234 to win and they remembered that they had bowled us out for 201 at Manchester the year before.

McKenzie bowled a tremendous over to Ted Dexter at the start of the last day, but apart from that we settled in. We managed to keep the score moving by running a lot of short singles. When Mackay came on, I set myself simply to try to place the ball for two singles every over. Against Queensland I had nearly driven myself frantic by trying to hit him through the field, and was eventually bowled playing a rash stroke. Now I found runs coming regularly in singles, plus an occasional four. In fact we scored 34 runs off 9 overs from him.

We naturally thought that Benaud was the key man, but I managed to get up the wicket to him this time, and we both scored quite freely from him. I thought of Manchester again when he went round the wicket to bowl into the footholes. But I also reasoned with myself that he would be unable to bowl his top-spinner which dipped in while he was bowling round the wicket. I felt that he might be less dangerous than bowling in his ordinary way. His first ball from round the wicket was a half-volley, and I hit it through the covers for four. Soon he returned to bowling over the wicket.

Our confidence was growing all the time and 96 for 1 at lunch had become 129 for 1 when I called Ted for a short single to cover. Benaud was running in as I played the ball, and he ran Ted out with a very quick return for 52. It was ironic that a short single should have got us into trouble as there is no doubt in my mind that it was running the singles which had first given us control. Alan Davidson bowled a long and very accurate spell at his medium pace, and it was some time before the score began to move easily again. Colin Cowdrey and I each gave a sharp chance in the slips, and if they had both been caught we should still have had a great struggle to win. But we gradually got started again: Colin played beautifully for 58 not out, and I reached 113, being run out rather stupidly when we thought we were running the winning run.

In one day the whole picture had changed. It was Australian heads which the newspapers demanded should roll from the guillotine. They forgot about our 'complexes' and failures, and spoke about the strength of the England team. We flew off to a successful week's cricket in Tasmania in beautiful surroundings.

There was an encouraging surprise waiting for me. A letter reached me in Melbourne asking if I remembered some brothers I had met in England six or seven years before. My mind went back to the day I first met their mother in a friend's home in London. She was dying from an incurable disease: the friend who had asked me to meet her told me that she was sure she would never talk about religion. But the first thing she said to me was, "We were watching you on the television the other day. When you finished, one of the boys turned to me and said, 'Mummy, how can you ask Jesus into your life?' "

We met several times after that and spoke about how Christ is real and powerful and how we can become sure of His forgiveness. Of course we talked and prayed about the future for her small boys. Then she had to go into hospital, and the vicar of the parish visited her most faithfully. The last time I saw her was not long before her death. I was warned that she was not often conscious. But when I arrived she was able to speak very clearly. The next step for the boys was settled. They were going to Australia with the Fairbridge Society, and she was satisfied that they would be well looked after. She spoke very decisively of her own faith. In the last few months she had committed herself to Christ, and was facing death with complete assurance that she was in His hands for ever.

I felt that I was seeing our prayers clearly answered when I spent a Sunday with the boys in their new home in Tasmania. The couple who were parents to them now had about a dozen youngsters in their home. I felt the sense of security and trust which stemmed from the couple to the children.

Cricket is not a game at which many of us can feel on top of the world for long. Though I went into the Third Test full of runs and confidence, I came out of it wondering how I was ever going to handle Davidson with the new ball. In the first innings I could not quite understand how I edged the ball to slip as I thought I was playing it easily: after the match Brian Johnston told me that he had watched this on film, and that I had played the ball in the middle of the bat, only to be caught at second slip.

Eventually I worked it out that I had gone back without noticing it to my 'pre-Hutton' days when I played my defensive shots out into the covers—'inside-out' as the theorists say. Davidson had so much life and bounce about him that a stroke, which would have played the ball safely down to third man off many bowlers, went instead as a catch to second slip. After the Third Test I produced an emergency answer to my problems by slipping my top hand round the back of the handle, as Hutton used to do. This meant that I produced a rigidly straight bat for a few overs until I felt that I was 'in'. At least Davidson did not get me out again.

It was a remarkable performance by Davidson to have made such an impression on the Sydney wicket, for it was brown and bare with only an occasional patch of grass. It was Benaud who had Dexter's wicket for the third time out of four dismissals by a bowler, and it was Bobby Simpson, who rarely looked dangerous as a leg-spinner that season who wrecked our innings. Pullar played stubbornly for 53 and we hoped he was going on to make a hundred as he had in the New South Wales match. But from the start driving was difficult because the ball did not come through to the bat, and making runs was always a struggle. The one exception to this was when Cowdrey was taking strike. He played one of the finest, and one of the least acclaimed, innings of the series: again and again he forced the ball off the back foot through the covers for a flowing 85. At one stage we were 201 for 3, Cowdrey and Barrington going well. Only a few minutes later we were 221 for 7: Simpson had two wickets and Davidson had two. Titmus and Trueman had a firm stand of 51 but we were all out for 279.

Lawry fell to a brilliant leg-side catch by John Murray off Coldwell. Murray, who had just come back into the side in place of Alan Smith, fell heavily on his shoulder in making the catch, and could not keep wicket again during the match. Neil Harvey struggled for a long time, seeming to have lost his touch altogether. Then he hit a gentle catch, straight at me at extra cover. I saw it all the way into my hands—and out of them. If ever I have wanted that secret trap door and underground route to the pavilion it was then. It is the kind of time when the fellowship of a good team helps you through. Brian Statham mouthed, "Bad luck" across the field. Everyone knows that no one drops a catch on purpose, but it is very difficult when so much turns on a chance. Freddie Titmus was the unlucky bowler, but he kept Neil Harvey on a tight string and eventually dismissed him for 64. He bowled Simpson for 91, an excellent innings, controlled, strong on the on-side.

Titmus called the tune to everyone except Simpson and Barry Shepherd, who came in to play a sturdy, fighting innings in his first Test match. Shepherd is a left-hander, very strong in his hooking and cutting: he played thoroughly well in this innings and Australia owed their first innings lead of 40 mostly to his 71 not out. All through the tour Titmus had looked the

Australian glee as I am l.b.w. to Davidson for 0 at Melbourne.

Straight drive off Benaud to reach 100 in the 2nd innings.

The ball that lost us the Third Test. Simpson catches Dexter off Davidson at Sydney.

Brian Booth on drives Titmus in the Adelaide Test 1963. Colin Cowdrey and Alan Smith follow the ball.

most capable of our off-spinners: for years he had played for Middlesex on wickets which had generally suited the faster bowlers. He had to play the supporting role and to pick up wickets when he received no help from the pitch. He learned his craft slowly in a hard school. But now he varied his pace from a high-flighted off-spinner, which had had me charging down the pitch at Lord's that July trying to hit it over the top of the pavilion, to a fast ball which would knock a stump out of the ground.

In the two Sydney Tests he had a wicket which gave him some turn all the time, but he never relied simply on his off-spinner. He was always liable to swing the ball away from the bat. His length and direction never seemed to falter: in the Fifth Test, Norman O'Neill hit him through the covers for four and I said, "Don't you think it might be worth having another man over in the covers?" "I shan't let him hit it there again," he said. And he didn't, so excellent was his direction. I have admired his bowling for a long time, and have generally provided him with a wicket or two every year.

Freddie was the ideal member of a touring team: nothing seemed to depress him. He always said, "I never get an ear-bashing." When someone was starting off on his pet theory or club story, Freddie somehow had the art of starting to talk determinedly about something else. Like a number of those who are slightly deaf he had brought to a fine art the ability only to hear what he wanted to hear. As a batsman he usually looked a nervous starter: he seemed so eager to play forward that it seemed he might fall flat on his face at times. But soon the Australians realised he was a cool customer with the bat, and it would not be long generally before he was busily accumulating runs here and there.

When our second innings started only 40 runs behind, we felt that a slight advantage rested with us, as Australia would have to bat last. But in another three-quarters of an hour the game had swung right away from us through as tremendous a spell of fast bowling as I have seen. Geoff Pullar played a short ball on to his stumps, and then Ted Dexter and I set ourselves

P

to see off the new ball. As I had got out three times to Davidson, Ted said he would take as much of the bowling from him
as he could. 'Davo' promptly bowled him as good an over as
you could imagine, beating him all ends up about four times.
I knew Ted wouldn't mind a gentle dig, so I went down the
wicket at the end of the over and said, "Thanks very much for
the protection."

Davidson's pace varied from day to day; that afternoon he
was letting it go with all the force he could possibly muster.
The whole body rocked back with the right shoulder pointing
at the batsman, and then swung through till the shoulder
seemed almost on the ground. One evening we talked late in
his room with Brian Booth, and I noticed the massive calves of
his legs and realised the strength which went into every
delivery. Like the other fast bowlers I rate highest, Lindwall,
Miller and Trueman, Davidson generally bowled within
himself and reserved his fiercest speed for key moments. Like
them also he had the ability to swing the ball. The angle across
the right-handed batsman from left-arm over the wicket
meant that a straight ball was almost as good as an out-
swinger: but his in-swinger, moving late into the batsman,
meant that you could not easily leave the ball alone. His pace
was always lively, and sometimes very fast: he used an occasional bumper to keep the batsman looking for trouble. Often,
as on this day at Sydney when the wicket seemed so bare, he
could get the ball to move off the seam as well as in the air.

Richie Benaud seemed always to get the best out of 'Davo'.
They like each other, and I'm sure there were times when he
was bowling for Richie. There was one day when he had been
bowling his heart out for a long spell on a very hot day. "Just
one more over, Al pal," said Richie. "Bowl him another like
that fourth one last over which moved in and then left him.
You're doing wonderfully." 'Davo' had his eyes shut: "Just
put the ball in my hand," he said, "and show me which way
to go."

After the tour was over I spoke at a Christian meeting in
Hurstville, Sydney, for sportsmen from the famous St. George

District. Alan Davidson came and introduced me, and I found myself telling one of my favourite stories about cricket. I sometimes have a fear that the best stories may turn out to be not quite true. Halfway through this one I realised that Alan was sitting behind me, and that he was concerned in the story.

It runs like this: Lindsay Hassett, Australia's captain in 1953 thinks that his batsmen ought to appeal against the light in the Nottingham Test. So he gives the order to Don Tallon (known as 'Deafie', being slightly hard of hearing), "Give the light a go Deafie when you get in." Deafie nods and a moment later he has to go in to bat as a wicket has fallen. As he goes to the door Hassett calls to him, "Don't forget to give it a go." Tallon reaches the wicket and goes straight up to Davidson who is batting at the other end and says, "Skipper says we've got to give it a go." So they do. They have a go at everything. After five minutes Tallon is caught off a huge skier, trying to hit the ball out of the ground. He goes back into the dressing-room, and walks straight up to Hassett. "Sorry, Skipper," he says, "I tried to give it a go, but I couldn't see anything. The light was terrible." It was nice to find from Alan Davidson that the story was absolutely true.

Dexter survived the great over from 'Davo' but a little later he was caught by Simpson at slip off a ball which went from leg. I was seeing the ball well, and felt that I must try to take command rather than let them bowl at us as they liked. I aimed an off-drive at a ball, but it was too good for that, and left me off the pitch. I too was caught by Simpson, and we were 25 for 3.

We never recovered from this terrible start, and for the only time in the series our whole batting side failed. Cowdrey received a very good leg-spinner from Benaud, and Simpson gobbled up another catch. Barrington was bowled by McKenzie after playing well, and though Peter Parfitt hung on, no one could stay with him. Peter had taken Tom Graveney's place as Tom was injured, and played a plucky innings of 28. John Murray stayed for a long time, using only one hand because of his shoulder injury. In fact heavy rain was not far away, but we should not have deserved to escape: nor would Australia have deserved to miss their victory which squared the series of matches to one-all. They had to score only 65 and they won by eight wickets.

Looking back I feel that we made two mistakes in selection during the series: these were the result of not believing our eyes when we looked at the wickets for the Third and Fourth Tests. At Sydney we picked Len Coldwell, who had done well at Melbourne, when we would have been glad to have another spinner. At Adelaide the wicket appeared to have more grass on it than we had ever seen there before. We could not believe that we should ever play on anything but an easy wicket at Adelaide. But it was a wicket on which the ball moved a little for the fast bowlers, and we should probably have done better to have another quick bowler instead of Illingworth there.

As it was Ray Illingworth made a very good start in the Fourth Test by bowling Lawry for 10 with Simpson already out for 0. Then came another call for that underground passage to the pavilion. Neil Harvey went to drive Illingworth and was dropped at slip: the very next ball he suddenly swung across it, and hit it very hard head high to me at square-leg. Down it went, and so did another catch to Cowdrey a little later. Harvey didn't need any more encouragement, and at last started to play at his best. Norman O'Neill played beautifully, and there was some magnificent stroke-play in their partnership of 194. Harvey made 154, O'Neill 100, and for almost the only time in this series they slipped from the tight rein of England's bowlers, and broke into a gallop.

It was good to watch, but not if you were thinking of the catch you might have caught. We did well in the end to have Australia all out for 393. I was stationed on the boundary at long on at the end of the innings: Graham McKenzie heaved a huge swing at Titmus, and the ball came soaring towards me. It went very high, and I managed to make the mental effort to look away from it, and then to look back again and watch it coming down. There was time for plenty of thoughts after four dropped catches, and time for some advice from the crowd too.

In the end I caught it easily, and was very glad to do so as you may imagine. The annoying thing about the catching was that I caught quite a number of catches on the tour, including some good ones, and the ones that I dropped were at such vital moments. By a great deal of hard work I had become a good 'catcher' close to the bat in 1953. But nearly ten years out of regular cricket meant that quickness of reaction and confidence were not what they had been. I was reminded of the luck that there is in catching during the last Test at Sydney. Both wicket-keepers made one very bad miss when they were standing back. Alan Smith dropped Peter Burge when he was 60, and he went on to 103 so that it mattered quite a lot. Wally Grout dropped Brian Statham who went on to score 17 not out, and hardly anyone noticed it.

Grout came back into the Australian team at Adelaide after his jaw injury at Brisbane. There seemed to be an aggressive presence lurking behind you when he was keeping wicket. It was almost as if it had been inherited from Don Tallon, his predecessor as Queensland's wicket-keeper. If ever a cricketer's surname was aptly descriptive it was Tallon's, for there was something of the bird of prey about him as a wicket-keeper. He did not keep wicket; he wanted to snatch it from you.

Pullar was bowled by McKenzie with our score at 17, and Barrington came in to make the most extraordinary start for such a solid player. His first ball from Davidson was very quick, and, aiming a firm defensive shot, Barrington sent the ball flying over the upstretched hands of the slips for four. Next ball was also very quick: he went to cut it, and this also flew high over the slips for four. The next was a wide half-volley: Barrington threw his bat at it, and this also went for four, square on the off-side. If the first three were fast, the fourth was extra fast and short: he went to hook and the ball flew off the edge over wicket-keeper and first slip. Four balls had brought sixteen runs without any of them being quite intentional.

Striving for extra pace was probably what caused Davidson to pull a hamstring muscle. But without him McKenzie,

Mackay and Benaud made us work very hard for runs. I struggled to break free, and was stumped a long way up the pitch off Benaud for 30. Barrington made 63, but we slumped gradually to 165 for 5. Ted Dexter came in number 6 this time and played well for 61, without quite lording it over the bowlers as he had in the first two Tests. Titmus (59 not out) and Trueman (38) had another valuable partnership, and we reached 331. McKenzie showed a wonderful feat of stamina, bowling 33 eight ball overs out of 85 bowled in the innings and taking 5 for 89.

Trueman and Statham put on what I thought was our most dangerous opening spell, and with a little bit of luck might have broken through. Australia were 37 for 2, but then Simpson (71) and Booth (77) batted extremely well. Dexter had them both out and Shepherd as well in a very good piece of bowling. At 228 for 7 we had just a chance to bowl them out quickly and win the match. But Benaud batted well, and decided not to risk anything in the absence of Davidson. I had watched most of their innings on the television as I was in bed with a very fierce bug in my throat. Ray Illingworth was also in bed suffering from a rather more violent cousin of my bug. I drove to the ground with hazy memories of Eddie Paynter batting heroically at Brisbane with tonsilitis. My innings was not so successful as Paynter's famous one. I scored one and then edged a swinger from Mackay to Benaud at second slip: he juggled with it two or three times, and then Grout dived across and caught it. Pullar was out for 3, but Barrington and Cowdrey looked very safe. Ken went on to make an excellent 132 not out and Graveney stayed with him at the end. They put on 101 without being separated.

So much had built up towards the climax of the series at Sydney. Not since 1937 had the Fifth Test started with the two teams level. If this match went well, everyone would feel that it had been a fine, keen series. But everything did not go right. It was obvious that it would not do so, when we looked down at the mud-brown strip in the middle of the lush green outfield of the Sydney cricket ground. There was even less grass on it than there had been in the Third Test.

Two days before the match the groundsman told me that he had had to cover it for twenty-five nights since Christmas. The covers were heavy plastic tarpaulins lying directly on the ground, and denying any air to help the grass grow. On our last Saturday in Sydney in June I sat on the 'Hill', and watched a Rugby League match between Parramatta and Balmain on a sea of mud which was the Sydney cricket ground. If the wickets are chewed up like this in the winter, it is essential that the grass be allowed to grow in the summer.

The wicket for the Fifth Test made driving a dangerous and profitless business for batsmen. Wally Grout told me that Colin Cowdrey hit a cover drive off Benaud right in the middle of the bat—and cover point had to run in to pick it up. A commentary on the Sydney wicket was the fact that Brian Booth, Australia's leading run-maker in the Tests, scored fewer than 70 runs at Sydney, his home ground, in all his matches there that season. His flowing stroke-play needed the ball to come on to the bat with some speed, and at Sydney it stopped and looked sullenly at him. When we went out to bat we found not only that the wicket was dead but that the outfield had not been cut because it had been raining all week: half of it still had not been cut on the second day of the match. This made it almost impossible to hit the ball for four. In the first two and a half hours of the Australian innings only three fours were hit.

The Fifth Test was a grim game, and it led many followers of the game to write off the 1962-3 series as a bad one. This was not quite right. There was much good cricket in the Tests, and had the Fifth Test proved the climax we hoped for, everyone would have acclaimed it an excellent series. As it was this game coloured the whole view which many had of the five matches. I would think that the majority of cricket followers thought that this was a very slow scoring series with the Englishmen mainly to blame. I did some personal research on the scoring rates in Australia to try to prove to myself whether

England teams have in fact been scoring slower and slower in recent years. From the beginning of the century the runs scored in the five Tests and the average of runs scored per hundred balls are these:

1903–4	2333 runs at	41.11 per hundred
1907–8	2584	45.72
1911–2	2833	47.96
1920–1	2779	49.13
1924–5	3067	41.50
1928–9	3757	38.33
1932–3	2726	37.67
1936–7	2416	38.36
1946–7	2866	37.72
1950–1	1865	37.35
1954–5	2176	35.80
1958–9	2113	33.23
1962–3	2761	38.33

Ted Dexter's side scored quicker than any post-war England team in Australia, and to find a team which scored significantly faster it is necessary to go back to 1924–5.

Cowdrey came in first with me at Sydney as Pullar was injured, and he was caught early off a lifting ball from Davidson. The fast bowlers soon realised that there was no pace to be had out of the wicket, and settled down to make scoring as difficult as they could. I found myself unable to get the ball away, and was understandably an easy target for the crowd. "Look out Reverend, your congregation will be leaving," came from the stand behind cover point. "Why don't you hit him out into the green pastures?" called someone from the 'Hill'. And, when I let a ball pass through to the wicket-keeper from a fast bowler, a big voice boomed from behind me, "And it came to pass." I felt I was just beginning to time the ball properly when Hawke made a good diving catch off his slower ball, and I was out for 19.

Dexter could not time the ball with any fluency but fought

on for some time before O'Neill had him out with a good ball
for 47. Barrington went on in his determined way, hooking and
cutting with great efficiency, and made 101: Illingworth,
Titmus and Trueman all battled it out and we finally reached
321. It was very slow and grim stuff, and I do not suggest that
we played as well as we might have. But some of the more
aggressive newspaper comments were very wide of the mark.
It was nonsense to suggest that we deliberately went slowly. As
batsmen we were as keen for the spectators to see good cricket
as anyone on the ground.

Yet cricket is a team game: when I reach the wicket and
find that the conditions have robbed me of most of the attractive
strokes, I know I could entertain the crowd with a few risky
shots, and then get out. But I was part of a team, who by a
tremendous, corporate effort had reached this last Test with a
chance of winning. We owed it to one another to produce as
many runs as we could: the other two occasions we had played
at Sydney had both seen us bowled out for just over 100, and
beaten. Hard grafting seemed to us the only way of producing
runs. In both the Sydney Tests it was the batsmen who were
prepared to work patiently for their runs who succeeded in
both teams, rather than the flowing stroke-makers. I do not
say we should not have done better, but I'm trying to show the
way a batsman's mind works.

There was a hard working stand of 109 between O'Neill (71)
and Peter Burge who was brought back into this Test and
scored an excellent 103. Australia inched their way past us at
a slightly faster scoring rate, and, thanks to an excellent 57
from Benaud, led by 28. Titmus and Allen bowled 90 eight-
ball overs between them. David Allen had seemed our most
likely off-spinner at the beginning in Perth. He was always a
cratsman in the art of subtle changes of flight and pace, but
often he would deceive a batsman, yet fail to get him out. He
went for months with hardly a wicket on this tour. But in the
last few games he seemed to have added a little extra 'bite', and
had rightly won back his place in the team.

I had a new partner in the second innings, Ray Illingworth

coming in first. He had been brought in to the side purely as a batsman: Pullar was not fit, Parfitt was only just recovered from an injury, and 'Illie' was batting really well in the other matches. We made 40 before he was caught off Benaud for 18. I went out in this innings determined to score fast, and prepared to hit Benaud back over his head if he pitched it up to me. His first over or two I said to myself, "I must have a look at him first." Then I said to myself, "I must see if he does pitch any up to hit." Having seen Ken Barrington almost caught off two skiers when he jumped up the wicket and drove him, I decided that he was too accurate and able to turn the ball too much on that wicket to make it a reasonable risk. Ted Dexter tried to do it as soon as he went in, and was quickly stumped off Benaud for 6.

I played about as well as I ever did that day, and, trying to score as fast as I could, reached 68 in three hours. We scored at four or five runs an over off McKenzie, Hawke, Simpson and Harvey. It was Benaud and Davidson who held us back, and they bowled most of the time. Barrington missed a third hundred in successive innings by only 6 runs and Cowdrey played very well for 53. We eventually declared at 268 for 8 and left Australia 241 runs to win in 240 minutes.

They could only win if two batsmen both went hard and went well. It seemed as if their plan was that Lawry should hold one end from the start, and that the other batsmen should try to do the scoring. It was too difficult a task if runs were only coming from one end. Harvey and O'Neill played very well. There was a flutter of excitement when Allen dismissed them, and then bowled Booth for o. But Burge held firm with Lawry, and the game died away sadly in a draw.

In T. S. Eliot's poem *The Hollow Men*, he wrote:

> *This is the way the world ends*
> *This is the way the world ends*
> *This is the way the world ends*
> *Not with a bang but a whimper.*

So this series of Test matches, which had promised so much, ended with a whimper. It made it easy to forget that there had been much good cricket, in very close-fought matches, played between two teams who were good friends on and off the field.

CHAPTER 14

HAPPY RETURN

ON Easter Day I preached in Long Bay Jail in the morning and in Sydney Cathedral in the evening: that day gives a picture in miniature of the scope of the work I did in two months in Sydney after I said goodbye to the team. The Archbishop of Sydney, the Most Rev. H. R. Gough, had been Bishop of Barking before he went to Australia. As such it was he who asked me to go to the Mayflower Family Centre as Warden, and he was our chairman for the first eighteen months of our existence. He was a very good friend to me. It was a great responsibility to mount a new Christian team on as large a scale as the Mayflower, and it meant a great deal to me to have readily available his level-headed advice, his strong vision of God's work, and his quiet faith.

When I was selected for the Australian tour, he pressed me to stay on for a while in Sydney, and I was very glad that I did. During the tour I was able to do a strictly limited amount of speaking—I mean speaking at meetings or services, not the constant discussion of the game and everything else in life, which no one would say was strictly limited among cricketers! Now that the tour was over a committee planned a very strenuous programme of meetings in and around Sydney.

There was a number of large meetings, for men, for the Mothers Union and their husbands, for teenagers (the largest of all), for sportsmen, for University students; there were also many crowded church services. As I thought about what to say to these crowds, I felt that the majority who would come to meetings like these would have some background of knowledge about Christianity: it seemed that I ought to bring them a challenge to 'get down off the fence'. It is so easy to have an

increasing knowledge about God, but never to commit ourselves to Him.

P. T. Forsyth wrote, "We have Churches of the nicest,
kindest people, who have nothing apostolic, or missionary,
who never know the soul's despair or its breathless gratitude."
Forsyth's faith, and mine, does not make religion respectable.
In fact our most respectable friends often find it hardest to
accept the religion of Jesus Christ. I set out in these meetings
to help the respectable to see themselves as God sees them—
urgently needing His forgiveness. I wanted them to see also
the completeness of the forgiveness which Jesus offers. When
we stand and say "I believe . . . in the forgiveness of sins",
we speak of an astonishing truth, that God is ready to forgive
completely the most undeserving when we turn and open our
lives to Him. And when at last this dawns on us, 'breathless
gratitude' ought to come with it. With the gratitude should
come a great intention to serve God with our lives.

I hope that my weeks in Sydney were useful in bringing the
right kind of challenge to many to give up half-hearted
allegiance to God and to commit themselves to Him. I know
that I saw much to encourage me. I've always enjoyed Psalm
48: "Walk about Zion; go round about her and tell the towers
thereof. Mark well her bulwarks, set up her houses, that ye
may tell them that come after. For this God is our God for ever
and ever. He will be our guide unto death." The psalmist was
thinking of the loyal Jew coming up from the country to see
Mount Zion which was part of Jerusalem, the City of God.
He rejoiced as he saw the strength of the city's towers and
bulwarks. The City of God today is made up not of bricks and
stones but of people serving Him in the fellowship of His
Church all over the world.

In Australia there was much healthy acceptance of responsibility by Christians. No ancient wealth and investment supports
the parishes there. This often seems to work out as an advantage
as each ordinary Christian sees that he must pull his weight
not only financially but in the whole life of the Church. I
met strong bodies of men, finding fellowship and purpose

together in the local Church family. There were well-organised and thoughtfully-planned Christian groups in schools, leading older teenagers on to definite Christian leadership; Christians were giving their time to new migrants to Australia, to overseas students brought there by the Colombo plan, and to aboriginals, the ancient people of Australia, who find it so hard to discern the good and bad parts of the modern world which has grown up beside them. And some of the 'towers' and 'bulwarks' of the Christian Church were those offering strong help to delinquents, unmarried mothers, to those in prison, to those who were near suicide, to the elderly, and to the incurable. I admired enormously those who were ready patiently to try to bring hope to some of those who had given up hope. This can only be done by long-continuing caring and love.

As anywhere in the world the whole picture I saw was not rosy. There were places where the Church seemed to have grown over-respectable, lazy and self-centred. There it appeared to be more taken up with improving its own buildings or arguing about its organisation than being deeply concerned for its unresponsive neighbours, blaming them for not coming rather than reaching out a hand of unjudging friendship to them.

I had insisted that part of my time in Sydney should be spent in industrial areas comparable with our own in London. This helped me to come back to earth. Here were no vast congregations waiting breathlessly for what I had to say. Few working people from these districts would come to religious meetings at all. They felt they belonged to their own family and their own group. They were fiercely loyal to their own mates, and suspicious of outsiders who came to put them under a microscope or to bring new ideas which Mum and Dad had never held with. Most of them, like most of my neighbours in London, have never had a room to themselves. They think, move and feel at ease in a group. From the age of one they had played in the street with a group. They had learned in a group at school. At fifteen they had gone to work in factories where again they had moved and thought in a group.

Often the challenge of the Church seemed to them that they must leave their friends and the whole world they could understand before they could grasp hold of the Christian message. Their neighbours who had imbibed new ideas had invariably moved out of the district to the suburbs and the North Shore. Those who stayed in Glebe, Erskineville, Waterloo, Paddington, Woollomoloo and Redfern had in some cases never been across the Harbour Bridge to see how the other half lived. There is a right Christian emphasis that each one of us must respond as an individual to God who cares about us as individuals. This is true and we must not lose sight of it, if we are to be true to Him. But Jesus seemed ready to meet people in a group before they were Christians, to handle them as a group as they came nearer to becoming His disciples, and to build them up in a group once they did belong to Him. We need to learn a lot more about this.

A long-standing belief became even stronger in me as I saw something of the Inner City districts and new housing areas of Sydney and Melbourne. If strong, 'indigenous', Churches with local leadership are to be established in such districts of our great cities, Christian families must be prepared to stay, and, if God calls, to move into these areas. Indignant voices sometimes break in when I say this: "Is it wrong to better yourself then?" "What about your children growing up there?"

Jesus said God's second command was "Love your neighbour as yourself." This implies that it is right to want the best for yourself; certainly to want the best for your children. But our family is not to be thought of in isolation. "Love your neighbour *as* yourself" means that when we think of bettering ourselves we must think at the same moment of bettering our neighbours. If Christians withdraw from whole areas and simply visit them with their good advice, they must not be surprised if no one believes that their Good News is something that works in the situation from which they have withdrawn.

On the way to Australia I had a long talk with John Groser who had worked for many years in the East End of London.

He said, "When I had been three or four years in Stepney, an intelligent docker said to me, 'I suppose you'll be off soon, like all the rest'. Along with other things this was part of God's word to me that we must stay and bring up our children there." When Jenny was born, several neighbours said to Grace, "You won't bring her up here, will you?" Of course this raises all sorts of questions. We haven't any theory of what is the best way to bring up a child in an industrial area. But we believe that God has called us as a family to serve Him, and that as one problem of upbringing after another crops up, He will show us the right way through. We have already come to see that there is a difference between wanting a child to "have the best", and wanting him to "be the best".

A week or two is far too short to do anything very significant in industrial areas: the visitor can only 'ride in on the backs' of those who in a long-term way are praying, caring and offering genuine friendship to their neighbours. Ken Child with whom I teamed up in Redfern, had lived in the Inner City Area all his life and has been a Rector there for twelve years. My visiting factories, and trying to meet working men, helped a little in showing that the Church cared about ordinary men and about ordinary life, and in backing up the work which Ken and others were doing. Cricket proved a bridge in some places—even in its most melancholy moments like those dropped catches. I went into the railway locomotive workshops at Everleigh where some had been nervous that we might have a very cold reception. The first man I saw as I walked into the workshops at once went through the motions of dropping a catch: I laughed and he laughed, and at once there was a certain bond between us. That day two hundred men came and stood around in the sunshine during their dinner break, eating their sandwiches and listening, while Clive Way sang and I spoke about Christ and us in the middle of working life.

There were many situations in which cricket was of no value in building the bridges of friendship. A genuine interest in people and their homes, jobs and relationships with others is the only human weapon I know which will break down the suspicion with which any outsider and particularly a parson is viewed.

I spent some evenings in Barney's Club in Broadway where the Rev. Bernard Gook has a very lively club for teenagers who would normally go nowhere near a church. I spent most of the first evening in a billiard room with a dozen older boys. No one noticed me or spoke to me for the first quarter of an hour— the treatment which I know is given to our helpers when they first go into a club at the Mayflower. Loyalty to the group seems to involve refusing to be impressed by or interested in anyone from outside the group. The event which helped me to be accepted might be thought of as a stroke of luck, or a rather unorthodox way for God to organise circumstances.

There was a good deal of coming and going in and out of the billiard room. Accompanied by much laughter a bag of apples and some bottles of a new brand of fizzy soft drink were brought in. The bottles were shaken up and squirted out of the window across the street. The apples were handed round and I had one. A few minutes later the warning came. "The coppers are coming!" and at much the same moment someone said that both bottles and apples had been stolen off a lorry that had been left open down the road. I was holding the core of my apple, and said to the others, "I suppose you'll go bail for me," when the boy sitting next to me said, "Here, give it to me, I'll stick it up my jumper." The police came in, recovered a number of bottles, delivered a stern warning to the young men responsible and left. But the next evening that I came into the club the story of how the Reverend had been protected from the police had gone round everyone, and I was accepted in a small way as part of the club.

So we came home to the Mayflower after almost a year away. It was exciting to sense that many of our friends and neighbours felt that we were coming *home* as much as we did. It was exciting too to feel that the little local Church had grown in taking on leadership and responsibility as well as having grown in numbers.

Q

Colin and Mary, whom I had married a week or two before I set off for Australia, had made friends with a sixteen-year-old girl, Janet, who lived across the street. After a while she started to come to the Sunday evening service, and joined one of the groups for teenagers meeting in the flat belonging to one of our staff members. When she had prayed in Colin and Mary's home and committed her life to Christ, it must have been like a seal on a decision they had made. It was very much for Christian reasons that they had changed their minds about their ambition to move out into the suburbs. They wanted their home to be an influence for Christ in their own district. It was good too to find Vic and Barb established in their home nearby. They had travelled across London to help us two or three times a week for three years, and when they were married they found a flat near us so that they could be more deeply involved with those they met through the Mayflower.

We met another couple for the first time. Their boys had been coming for some years to us: leaders in Scouts and Cubs had visited their home, and, as two of the boys moved up into the groups, staff members had visited them as well. We met them at an Open Family Day we had on August Bank Holiday; they told us that they were going to come to church that Sunday within half an hour of one of our congregation going off for a few minutes to ask God specifically in prayer that they would start coming to church. When I visited the home a little later, Dad told me, "It would have put us off if anyone had tried to push us into coming to church. We've got to come back at our own pace."

While we were in Australia we heard that our little chapel was being redecorated: many of our congregation were involved in washing down the walls and painting it. The floor had been sanded and sealed and polished. My mother was called in to take charge of making new curtains, and she had a legion of helpers. One of the congregation is a skilled carpenter, and he added wooden pelmets and a new entrance.

Ted, one of our young men, started a series of oil paintings which now hang on the walls of the chapel. Just before we had gone away he had told me that, after years of being rather hostile to Christianity, he had committed his life to Christ. The first two of these paintings were done before this as a present for his youth leader. They were of Jesus hanging on the cross. After the Christian faith had become a personal thing in his own life he said, "I don't want to paint Him as a dead man any more because I know Him as a living Person in my life." So there is one of a conversation with James after He has risen. Another shows Christ undoing the chains of an old man in prison, while light shines in on them; "I painted that after I heard a hymn on the wireless about Jesus taking off our chains." A third illustrates His promise, "Knock, and the door will be opened"—Christ is opening the door and inviting us to enter a room which is full of light.

On many Sunday evenings now we are very crowded in our small chapel, and George Burton, 'for a holiday task' he said, set a crowd of young people to work, painting our large chapel which is still waiting for a new heating system to be installed. Some of the youngsters who worked most eagerly at this were those who had smashed some of the windows not long before. In two weeks many willing hands had made light work of a large task.

The walls were ready in time for an important wedding in our Mayflower Family life. Alan and Rita were the first from the Sunday Group of young people to be married. They have a flat not far from the Centre and hope to invite others into it. Like many of the Sunday Group they have been involved for two years or more in leading clubs or groups of youngsters. They have shown a skill and 'stickability' in this which many older helpers have not been able to match.

Also while I was away the Sunday Group had their first week-end away together in which the Bible was the central theme. We have felt that to hammer the discipline of daily reading of the Bible at those who have not been in the habit of reading for pleasure can have two very bad effects. First it can lead to despair which says, "I can't keep this up. I don't find it interesting. These Christians must be different from me. It's all right for them, but I must give the whole thing up." Secondly it can lead to a wrong understanding of the very nature of Christianity. If the central teaching to young people is about the absolute necessity of a discipline of reading the Bible and praying and going to church, they will easily think of Christianity as a set of rules and habits to keep.

But the central thing is that Christ accepts sinners as His friends, and goes on accepting us though we never deserve it. In gratitude we need to come to know His will better and to do it in His strength. Our youngsters have come to know Him through the fellowship at the Mayflower. They have gradually come to see that reading the Bible can be interesting and very helpful. Moving at their own pace, several have definitely begun to read it regularly for themselves.

One of the hardest problems in many churches is the way old and young get on together, and we are not without this. But I'm thankful that many of the adults rejoice in what they see happening among the teenagers, while many of *them* pray for the older members of the congregation and see their point of view. Mrs. Olley who has been coming here for many years, told me how delighted she was to see a young man whom she had known as a difficult and destructive youngster, now a strong Christian leader. He and some of his friends thanked God when they were praying together for the way she understood the young people and their approach.

This book cannot tell a completed story of the Mayflower. The work is only six years old. In any case it is never possible to speak of success in Christian work as you might of a Test tour, when you have won the series. The yardstick by which success and failure is measured is quite different. The numbers who come to our church and our clubs and groups cannot be a safe guide. Only after many years will it be possible to see if a strong Christian work has been planted with its roots firmly embedded in local leadership.

Just before I finished the book we were present at a meeting of some forty of our young leaders. The new winter's plans were being put in front of them. New groups were starting;

some were moving up to membership of the Sunday Group; almost all were being given leadership in one way or another. Those who were not given it were faced with the challenge that they had not shown willing in the past. The problems of jealousy and unreliability were brought out into the open. We were reminded that in doing youth work we should not receive many thanks: and we were reminded also of the motive behind all that we try to do in Christian service—gratitude to Christ for all that He has done for us.

The Mayflower has brought us a job which fills our horizons. Sometimes I have been told "You must miss cricket very much". But this is not really true. If I play a little, then I will admit that I want to go on playing because cricket is deeply in my blood. But our life stretches us and absorbs us so much that there is no time to regret what else we might be doing. As with so many things in the Christian life, it has not so much been a case of 'giving it up', as of 'taking up' something else which is infinitely worthwhile.

INDEX